Towards an Urban Nation

German Historical Perspectives Series
General Editors:
Gerhard A. Ritter and Anthony J. Nicholls

Volume I
Population, Labour and Migration in 19th- and 20th-Century Germany
Edited by Klaus J. Bade

Volume II
Wealth and Taxation in Central Europe: The History and Sociology of Public Finance
Edited by Peter-Christian Witt

Volume III
Nation-Building in Central Europe
Edited by Hagen Schulze

Volume IV
Elections, Parties and Political Traditions: Social Foundations of German Parties and Party Systems
Edited by Karl Rohe

Volume V
Economic Crisis and Political Collapse: The Weimar Republic, 1924–1933
Edited by Jürgen Baron von Kruedener

Volume VI
Escape into War: The Foreign Policy of Imperial Germany
Edited by Gregor Schöllgen

Volume VII
German Unification: The Unexpected Challenge
Edited by Dieter Grosser

Volume VIII
Germany's New Position in Europe: Problems and Perspectives
Edited by Arnulf Baring

Volume IX
Western Europe and Germany: The Beginnings of European Integration 1945–1960
Edited by Clemens Wurm

Volume X
The Military in Politics and Society in France and Germany in the Twentieth Century
Edited by Klaus-Jürgen Müller

Volume XI
Culture in the Federal Republic of Germany, 1945–1995
Edited by Reiner Pommerin

Volume XII
The Problem of Revolution in Germany, 1789–1989
Edited by Reinhard Rürup

Volume XIII
Science in the Third Reich
Edited by Margit Szöllösi-Janze

Volume XIV
The Third Reich Between Vision and Reality
Edited by Hans Mommsen

Volume XV
The Divided Past: Rewriting Post-war German History
Edited by Christoph Kleßmann

German Historical Perspectives/XVI

Towards an Urban Nation

Germany since 1780

Edited by
FRIEDRICH LENGER

Oxford • New York

First published in 2002 by
Berg
Editorial offices:
150 Cowley Road, Oxford, OX4 1JJ, UK
838 Broadway, Third Floor, New York, NY 10003-4812, USA

Berg is the imprint of Oxford International Publishers Ltd.

Library of Congress Cataloging-in-Publication Data

A catalogue record for this book is available from the Library of Congress.

British Library Cataloguing-in-Publication Data

A catalogue record for this book is available from the British Library

ISBN 1 85973 586 X (Cloth)

Typeset by JS Typesetting, Wellingborough, Northants.
Printed and bound in Great Britain by Antony Rowe Ltd., Chippenham, Wiltshire

Contents

Editorial Preface
Gerhard A. Ritter and *Anthony J. Nicholls*   vii

Acknowledgements   ix

Introduction: Urban History and the History of Urbanization in
Germany
Friedrich Lenger   1

Urbanization and the Spread of an Urban Culture in Germany in
the Nineteenth and Twentieth Centuries
Klaus Tenfelde   13

Burgher Cities on the Road to a Civil Society: Germany 1780 to
1870
Gisela Mettele   43

Burghers and other Townspeople – Social Inequality, Civic Welfare
and Municipal Tasks during Nineteenth-Century Urbanization
Sylvia Schraut   69

Building and Perceiving the City: Germany around 1900
Friedrich Lenger   87

Normal Pollution: Industrialization, Emissions and the Concept of
Zoning in Germany, 1800–1970
Franz-Josef Brüggemeier   107

Urban Society and Urban Politics in Germany between the Wars
Hans-Ulrich Thamer   127

Urban Reconstruction and Urban Development in Germany after
1945
Axel Schildt   141

Three Cities, Three City Models – Urban Development: Perspectives
for the Twenty-first Century
Stefan Zappe   163

Notes on Contributors   185

Editorial Preface

The purpose of this series of books is to present the results of research by German historians and social scientists to readers in English-speaking countries. Each of the volumes has a particular theme that will be handled from different points of view by specialists. The series is not limited to the problems of Germany but will also involve publications dealing with the history of other countries, with the general problems of political, economic, social and intellectual history as well as international relations and studies in comparative history.

We hope the series will help to overcome the language barrier that experience has shown obstructs the rapid appreciation of German research in English-speaking countries.

The publication of the series is closely associated with the German Visiting Fellowship at St Antony's College, Oxford, which has existed since 1965, having been originally funded by the Volkswagen Stiftung, later by the British Leverhulme Trust, by the Ministry of Education and Science in the Federal Republic of Germany, and starting in 1990, by the Stifterverband für die Deutsche Wissenschaft with special funding from C. & A. Mode Düsseldorf. Each volume is based on a series of seminars held in Oxford, which has been conceived and directed by the Visiting Fellow and organized in collaboration with St Antony's College.

The editors wish to thank the Stifterverband für die Deutsche Wissenschaft for meeting the expenses of the original lecture series and for generous assistance with the publication. They hope that this enterprise will help to overcome national introspection and to further international academic discourse and co-operation.

Gerhard A. Ritter   Anthony J. Nicholls

Acknowledgements

The present volume originated in a series of lectures organized at the European Studies Centre of St Antony's College in Oxford in Hilary Term 1998. I am most grateful to the Warden and Fellows of St Antony's and to the Stifterverband für die Deutsche Wissenschaft who enabled me to spend the academic year 1997/8 as a visiting fellow in Oxford and thus provided the opportunity for organizing a seminar on German urbanization. Amongst the many people who were responsible for my friendly reception at St Antony's and for a highly stimulating intellectual environment I would like to single out Anthony J. Nicholls, Director of the European Studies Centre, whose cordial support was crucial.

Here in Giessen Renate Lange, Justin Salisbury and above all Dr Rainer Liedtke took over a considerable part of the editorial work. I owe thanks to them as well as to Melanie Aspey (London) who assisted with the language correction of the English texts. I should like to express my gratitude to the Justus-Liebig-Universität Giessen for funding her work.

Friedrich Lenger
Giessen

FRIEDRICH LENGER

Introduction: Urban History and the History of Urbanization in Germany

I

While there has always been a strong interest in late medieval and early modern towns in Germany, the nineteenth and twentieth centuries as the period when more and more people actually lived in cities have much less attention.[1] So historical research on the urbanization of Germany hardly began before the end of the Second World War and a brief survey therefore can be limited largely to the post-war period. There had been, of course, the groundbreaking attempts of economists and early sociologists like Karl Bücher, Werner Sombart and Georg Simmel to come to terms with the rapid urban development of their times but these attempts were largely ignored by contemporary historians.[2] Even after the Second World War urban problems were conceived of by historians mainly as problems of politics and administration rather than as core aspects of social change. Thus the most impressive example of this type of work – Heinrich Heffter's history of self-administration in nineteenth-century Germany – tried in the second half of the 1940s to recapture a liberal tradition of self-administration on which a new and democratic Germany could build.[3] As the subtitle to this voluminous work documented, this was a history of ideas and institutions. But by the early 1960s authors like Helmuth Croon and Wolfgang Hofmann broadened the picture considerably by researching the social and political composition of municipal councils, thus linking the realm of urban government and administration to the conflicts of urban society.[4]

While the interest in urban administration remained quite strong, urban history since the 1960s became increasingly a sub-discipline of the newly emerging social history. There had been earlier attempts to replace the older state-centred variants of German historiography by 'Volksgeschichte' – not adequately translated either as people's history or as folk history – but this older tradition had located the 'Volk' almost exclusively in rural surroundings.[5] After 1945 some of the proponents of 'Volksgeschichte', many of whom had been involved in the planning and organization of murderous settlement schemes in East Central Europe under the Nazi dictatorship, now reluctantly accepted the inevitability of an industrial and urban society and redirected their research towards it.[6] As early as 1960 Wolfgang Köllmann's study on the social history of the city of Barmen in the nineteenth century demonstrated the fruitfulness of combining approaches from demography, economics and sociology.[7] Since then Köllmann, who had been a student of Werner Conze and Gunther Ipsen – two leading proponents of the earlier 'Volksgeschichte' – concentrated largely on the demographic preconditions of urban growth. Although his general approach, viewing the peasantry in an idealized way, still mirrored the anti-urban prejudices of his teacher Ipsen, Köllmann's numerous articles nevertheless made an important contribution to the understanding of population growth, migration and urban growth.[8]

Despite such important efforts it took the wider reception of French and Anglo-Saxon research to establish a broader basis for social history in Germany.[9] It was hardly a coincidence that the first issue of the new journal *Geschichte und Gesellschaft* (1975), which tried to define history as historical social science, contained articles by one French and three American social historians. Three of them dealt with single cities while the fourth presented a report on the new social history in the United States that demonstrated quite clearly that the new social and the new urban history were almost identical. With the rise of social history cities became a convenient unit of analysis for studies concerned with different aspects of social change. While social and geographical mobility first occupied centre stage the thematic scope was soon broadened to include housing conditions or working-class culture.[10] The changing understanding of the role of migration gives a good example of a more general trend in urban studies since the mid-1970s. While Wolfgang Köllmann was still interested almost exclusively in the net population gains made by the cities owing to migration, Dieter Langewiesche soon made it clear that those net gains formed but a fraction of all migratory movements and that therefore migration was by no means to be understood as a one-way road from the country to the city.[11] Mobility – amounting to as many as 300 migrations per 1,000 inhabitants each year – thus was not only the prerequisite for urban growth but centrally affected the stability of urban communities and thus created a whole range of urban problems. Following Langewiesche's lead local studies soon revealed that most migratory moves were made by young unmarried men and women who often left the towns after only a few days of looking for a job or after working for a few weeks in a particular, sometimes seasonal, position.[12] They coexisted with a rather more stable population of families who moved frequently within the city but seldom left it. And again a detailed look at those internal movements revealed that an enormous mobility – 400 moves per 1,000 inhabitants each year – was quite compatible with rather stable social relationships because the vast majority of all moves took place within the same neighbourhood.[13]

A similar move from the attempt to ascertain the quantitative dimension of a problem to a differentiated analysis of its structure and finally to a microscopic approach that allows for small spatial units to integrate the individual experience of city dwellers can be observed if one looks at the numerous studies dealing with urban housing problems. Although there had been considerable contemporary concern over the 'housing question' around the turn of the century Lutz Niethammer's and Franz Brüggemeier's attempt to answer the question 'how are workers housed in Imperial Germany?' set a new standard in the mid-1970s.[14] The housing conditions in German cities were controversially debated during the following years, a debate that gave rise to more quantitative precision in the discussion of housing problems.[15] At the same time there was a certain uneasiness about reducing some of the more complicated problems involved to mere numerical indicators. Particularly when the relationship between social structures and geographical space was analysed the qualitative dimension of what it meant to live in a certain quarter proved indispensable.[16] But only recently has the question of the individual appropriation of the immediate housing environment been integrated in broader syntheses. Making good use of autobiographical material Adelheid von Saldern has convincingly demonstrated how different social groups in nineteenth-century Germany shaped their different housing conditions.[17]

The examples indicate that as urban history became social history it largely followed the development of this larger subdiscipline. Social history also shared with urban history a rather one-sided concentration on the nineteenth century. Although the divide of the First World War is occasionally bridged, the bulk of more recent studies deal with the nineteenth century, a tendency that may have been strengthened by the prominence of architects and urban planners among those who do address more recent problems and do so in a way that is not always congenial to the concerns of urban historians. An additional reason for the preoccupation with the nineteenth century is certainly the close link between the new urban and the new labour history of the 1970s and 1980s. The above mentioned analysis of housing problems by Niethammer and Brüggemeier, for example, interpreted the widespread presence of lodgers within working-class households as an indicator of a semi-open family structure fostering class solidarity. In similar ways most of the numerous case studies that analysed the social dimension of working class formation were contributions to urban as well as to labour history.[18]

Despite this close link to the new labour history, urban history does not seem to share the decline of labour history that resulted from – among other things – the political changes of 1989/90. On the one hand the shift of interest away from the working class and towards the middle classes – well under way not only in Germany during the 1980s – did not harm urban history. Not only were the research strategies successfully employed in the analysis of working-class formation easily adjusted to the middle classes, but very soon it turned out that the city had been at the centre of middle-class concerns culturally as well as politically.[19] On the other hand the interest in the middle-class rule of the cities of the nineteenth century also attributed a renewed importance to urban administration. Who really governed the towns: increasingly professional administrators or – owing to suffrage regulations – mostly very wealthy members of the municipal council? And why did they engage in the costly modernization of the urban infrastructure while blocking the democratization of the urban political system until the First World War?[20] Questions like these have fuelled some rather technical investigations of tram systems or canal development as well as of other sectors of urban administration.[21]

But in a more interesting way some recent research on urban administration has also addressed general conceptions of health and hygiene that informed the various reform concepts underlying many of the administrative activities.[22] It is therefore closely linked to questions of how the city was perceived. Here it is not so much the older concern over a presumably specifically German anti-urbanism that motivates new work.[23] Rather Simmel's theme – how the metropolis changes the whole personality and its psychological functioning – is being taken up again. The social anthropologist Gottfried Korff speaks of 'inner urbanization', and there have been attempts to analyse this 'inner urbanization' for specific areas like the consumption of the metropolitan press.[24] Thus there is clearly a trend towards cultural approaches within recent urban history. Occasionally it overlaps with the varied impulses from gender history when, for example, the representations of sexual murder as a specifically urban crime are being analysed.[25] To sum up very briefly one can say that since the mid-1970s urban history in Germany has increasingly become part of social history and has shared the movements of this broader subdiscipline ever since. This includes the growing openness towards the concerns of gender history as well as the most recent turn towards a cultural history informed by anthropology. The latter trend is – among other things – likely to direct attention towards specific discourses but it will hardly weaken the strong interest in microhistorical approaches from which urban history has benefited so strongly in the past and will continue to do so in the future.[26] At the same time as urban history mirrors the shift from social to cultural history the field also reflects the renewed interest in political and comparative history. And it is this interest in comparative politics, witnessed by studies such as *Capital Cities at War* or on extremist political movements in inter-war Paris and Berlin, that promises that more attention will be paid to twentieth-century urban developments in the future.[27]

II

Over the last twenty-five years urban history has become an increasingly lively discipline in Germany without reaching the level of institutional anchorage that it has in Britain or the United States. Some of the more recent research has already found its way into textbooks devoted to German urban history over the last two hundred years.[28] These are, however, already somewhat dated on the one hand and not available in English on the other. Given this situation the present volume pursues three aims. It tries to present to the English-speaking public an account of key problems of German urban history since the late eighteenth century. In doing so it offers a selection of articles that represent a broad variety of recent approaches including perspectives from environmental and gender history as well as the present discussions of architects and urban planners. Finally, by combining a chronological and a thematic organization of the material, the volume aims at a balanced treatment of both the nineteenth and the twentieth century.

This is already witnessed by the opening contribution by Klaus Tenfelde. He seeks to determine the importance of urbanization as one of the central aspects of social change in Germany over the last two hundred years. He uses the distinction – provided only by the German language – between *Verstädterung* as the numerical increase of the percentage of the population living in towns and *Urbanisierung*, a term that has come to subsume the qualitative and cultural aspects of urbanization within the German discussion. The prominence of this distinction is not only a result of the intricacies of 'the awful German language' but it has also played a central role in the analysis of urbanization in areas shaped by the rapid growth of heavy industry. Thus the Ruhr area in particular has been considered as one of 'deficient' urbanization, i.e. one where the development of an urban culture and infrastructure has not kept pace with the enormous growth of the urban population.[29] But, of course, the conception of a specifically urban lifestyle and mentality that informs the distinction between *Verstädterung* and *Urbanisierung* is by no means limited to urban agglomerations of the type of the Ruhr area but goes back to the classics of urban sociology. This conception is an especially fruitful one if one deals with the twentieth century, which for longer periods has not experienced any urban growth at all.

Following this far-reaching overview the first part of this volume offers three articles focusing on the nineteenth century. First Gisela Mettele introduces the Frankfurt research project on the importance of the older – legally defined – burghers for the constitution of the urban middle class and the modernization of society at large.[30] While Mettele draws mostly on material from the late eighteenth and from the first half of the nineteenth century, Sylvia Schraut covers chiefly the period from the 1840s to the 1880s. Different as their perspectives on urban society are, both Mettele and Schraut deal mainly with elite groups within it; in the first case because the legal definition of a burgher, the prerequisite for political participation and cultural

activity, excluded important and varying parts of the urban population, in the second because the numerous urban poor only come into
view via the (women's) organizations that were trying to support
them.[31] Something similar could be said about my own contribution
on problems of urban development and urban perception around
1900. The concentration on the views and activities of what I call
'urban practitioners', i.e. medical doctors, architects and urban
administrators, etc., is not meant, however, as the continuation of
the 'mayor's perspective' so prominent in much of what has been
written on urban administration. These groups seem interesting
rather because they occupy something like a middle ground between,
on the one hand, those artists, sociologists and critics who comment
upon the urban scene from a considerable distance and, on the other,
the mass of the urban population that has left precious few documents
about its view of city life.

Among the many problems the rapidly growing cities of the
nineteenth and twentieth centuries encountered the environmental
consequences of an Industrial Revolution dominated by coal mining
and the iron and steel industry feature prominently. Franz-Josef
Brüggemeier deals with them in a contribution that owing to its
regional focus on the Ruhr area is able to analyse developments from
the mid-nineteenth century to the present. In the long run the
attitude towards environmental problems also mirrored changing
degrees of state interventionism. Already during the First World War
the activities of urban administrations had been subordinated to and
dependent upon the decisions of the organizers of the war effort.[32]
The economic and financial crisis of the Weimar Republic did not
provide an environment in which the cities had a chance to regain
their earlier autonomy and whatever was left of that was eroded under
the Nazi dictatorship. This general process is clearly mirrored in the
area of social policy, which occupies centre stage in Hans-Ulrich
Thamer's contribution. On the other hand, as Axel Schildt points out,
even before the end of the Second World War architects and urban
planners were rejoicing at the opportunities that were being created
by the widespread destruction of German cities owing to air raids.
Fortunately not all of their planning ambitions became reality after
1945. That is true of both East and West Germany but otherwise
urban development soon showed a marked divergence that is still
visible today.

A decade after the reunification of Germany many problems – and
not only urban ones – crystallize around Berlin as the old and new

German capital. Today's heated discussions are at the centre of the last contribution to this volume, one focusing exclusively on the architectural dimension. As an architect working in Berlin Stefan Zappe cannot but present his personal concept of a possible centre of (and for) Berlin. That such concepts stand at the end of the book does not, of course, imply that the discussions about Berlin's architectural form and the symbolic dimension surrounding it mean that the end of Germany's path 'towards an urban nation' has been reached. It is to be hoped, however, that the reunified Germany may become a more *urban* nation than its Bismarckian predecessor in the sense of a common encyclopaedia definition of *urban* as 'town-like, fine, educated', which appeared in the same year as Karl Bücher first coined the term *Urbanisierung*.[33] And it is also to be hoped that this volume captures some of the more important dimensions of German urbanization over the last two centuries.

Notes

The notes to this brief survey are by no means intended to offer anything resembling a comprehensive bibliography; they rather give some works representing general and especially most recent trends in the field. Cf. for a more extensive review of recent trends Friedrich Lenger, 'La recherche allemande sur l'histoire de la ville et de l'urbanisation depuis la Seconde Guerre mondiale', in *La recherche sur la ville en Allemagne, Actes des journées Franco-Allemandes du PIR Villes*, Paris 1996, 141–57.

1. The results of the extensive research on medieval and early modern towns are easily accessible via Eberhard Isenmann, *Die deutsche Stadt im Spätmittelalter, 1250–1500. Stadtgestalt, Recht, Stadtregiment, Kirche, Gesellschaft, Wirtschaft*, Stuttgart 1988; Evamaria Engel, *Die deutsche Stadt des Mittelalters*, München 1993; Klaus Gerteis, *Die deutsche Stadt in der Frühen Neuzeit. Zur Vorgeschichte der 'bürgerlichen Welt'*, Darmstadt 1986 and Heinz Schilling, *Die Stadt in der frühen Neuzeit*, Munich 1993.
2. Cf. Karl Bücher, 'Großstadttypen aus fünf Jahrtausenden', in id., *Die Entstehung der Volkswirtschaft. Vorträge und Aufsätze. Erste Sammlung*, Tübingen 1919, 365–92 (first publ. 1893); Werner Sombart, 'Der Begriff der Stadt und das Wesen der Städtebildung', *Archiv für Sozialwissenschaft und Sozialpolitik* XXV (1907); Georg Simmel, *Die Großstädte und das Geistesleben*, reprinted in *Georg Simmel Gesamtausgabe*, vol. 7: *Aufsätze und Abhandlungen 1901–1908*, vol. 1, Frankfurt 1995, 116–31 (first ed. 1903).

3. Heinrich Heffter, *Die deutsche Selbstverwaltung im 19. Jahrhundert. Geschichte der Ideen und Institutionen*, Stuttgart 1969 (1st edn 1950).

4. Cf. e.g. Helmuth Croon, *Die gesellschaftlichen Auswirkungen des Gemeindewahlrechts in den Gemeinden und Kreisen des Rheinlands und Westfalens im 19. Jahrhundert*, Cologne 1960; id., 'Das Vordringen der politischen Parteien im Bereich kommunaler Selbstverwaltung', in id., Wolfgang Hofmann and Georg Christoph von Unruh (eds.), *Kommunale Selbstverwaltung im Zeitalter der Industrialisierung*, Stuttgart 1971; and Wolfgang Hofmann, *Die Bielefelder Stadtverordneten: Ein Beitrag zu bürgerlicher Selbstverwaltung und sozialem Wandel*, Lübeck 1964.

5. Cf. on this tradition Winfried Schulze, *Deutsche Geschichtswissenschaft nach 1945*, Munich 1989; Willi Oberkrome, *Volksgeschichte. Methodische Innovation und völkische Ideologisierung in der deutschen Geschichtswissenschaft 1919–1945*, Göttingen 1993, Hartmut Lehmann and James van Horn Melton (eds.), *Paths of Continuity: Central European Historiography from the 1930s to the 1950s*, Cambridge 1994; and most recently Winfried Schulze/ Otto Gerhard Oexle (eds.), *Deutsche Historiker im Nationalsozialismus*, Frankfurt 1999.

6. Cf. as an excellent example of such a changing perspective Gunther Ipsen, 'Bevölkerung I', in Carl Petersen et al. (eds.), *Handwörterbuch des Grenz- und Auslanddeutschtums*, vol 1, Breslau 1933, 425–63 and id., 'Stadt (IV) Neuzeit', Handwörterbuch der Sozialwissenschaften, vol IX, Stuttgart 1956, 786–800.

7. Cf. Wolfgang Köllmann, *Sozialgeschichte der Stadt Barmen im 19. Jahrhundert*, Tübingen 1960.

8. Cf. e.g. Wolfgang Köllmann, *Bevölkerung in der industriellen Revolution. Studien zur Bevölkerungsgeschichte Deutschlands*, Göttingen 1974.

9. One may include here the reception of modernization theory, which is most obvious in the groundbreaking work of Horst Matzerath, *Urbanisierung in Preussen 1815–1914*, Stuttgart 1985.

10. Cf. e.g. David Crew, *Town in the Ruhr. A Social History of Bochum, 1860–1941*, New York, 1979.

11. Cf. Dieter Langewiesche, 'Wanderungsbewegungen in der Hochindustrialisierungsphase. Regionale, interstädtische und innerstädtische Mobilität in Deutschland, 1880–1914', *Vierteljahrsschrift für Sozial- und Wirtschaftsgeschichte* LXIV (1977), 1–40.

12. Cf. e.g. Friedrich Lenger, *Zwischen Kleinbürgertum und Proletariat. Studien zur Sozialgeschichte Düsseldorfer Handwerker 1816–1878*, Göttingen 1986, and Stephan Bleek, 'Mobilität und Seßhaftigkeit in deutschen Großstädten während der Urbanisierung', *Geschichte und Gesellschaft* XV (1989), 5–33.

13. Cf. e.g. Stephan Bleek, 'Das Stadtviertel als Sozialraum', in Wolfgang Hardtwig and Klaus Tenfelde (eds.), *Soziale Räume in der Urbanisierung. Studien zur Geschichte Münchens im Vergleich 1850–1933*, Munich 1990, 217–34.

14. Lutz Niethammer/Franz-Josef Brüggemeier, 'Wie wohnten Arbeiter im Kaiserreich?', *Archiv für Sozialgeschichte* XVI (1976), 61–134; cf. also Lutz Niethammer (ed.), *Wohnen im Wandel. Beiträge zur Geschichte des Alltags in der bürgerlichen Gesellschaft*, Wuppertal 1979.

15. Cf. e.g. Clemens Wischermann, *Wohnen in Hamburg vor dem Ersten Weltkrieg*, Münster 1983 and Hans-Jürgen Teuteberg (ed.), *Homo habitans. Zur Sozialgeschichte des Wohnens in der Neuzeit*, Münster 1985.

16. Cf. e.g. Heinz Reif, *Die verspätete Stadt. Industrialisierung, städtischer Raum und Politik in Oberhausen, 1846–1929*, Cologne 1993.

17. Adelheid von Saldern, 'Im Hause, zu Hause. Wohnen im Spannungsfeld von Gegebenheiten und Aneignungen', in Jürgen Reulecke (ed.), *Geschichte des Wohnens*, vol. 3: *1800–1918: Das bürgerliche Jahrhundert*, Stuttgart 1997, 145–332.

18. Cf. e.g. Hartmut Zwahr, *Zur Konstituierung des Proletariats als Klasse. Strukturuntersuchungen über das Leipziger Proletariat während der industriellen Revolution*, Berlin 1978.

19. This is most obvious in a huge research project directed by Lothar Gall; cf. id. (ed.), *Stadt und Bürgertum im 19. Jahrhundert*, Munich 1990; id. (ed.), *Vom alten zum neuen Bürgertum. Die mitteleuropäische Stadt im Umbruch*, Munich 1991; id. (ed.), *Stadt und Bürgertum im Übergang von der traditionellen zur modernen Gesellschaft*, Munich 1993, as well as the numerous monographs written in connection with this project.

20. Cf. e.g. the important case study by Richard J. Evans, *Death in Hamburg. Society and Politics in the Cholera Years 1830–1910*, Oxford 1987.

21. Cf. e.g. Hans Heinrich Blotevogel (ed.), *Kommunale Leistungsverwaltung und Stadtentwicklung vom Vormärz bis zur Weimarer Republik*, Cologne 1990.

22. Cf. e.g. Jürgen Reulecke/Adelheid Gräfin zu Castell-Rüdenhausen (eds.), *Stadt und Gesundheit. Zum Wandel von 'Volksgesundheit' und kommunaler Gesundheitspolitik im 19. und 20. Jahrhundert*, Stuttgart 1991; Clemens Zimmermann, *Von der Wohnungsfrage zur Wohnungspolitik. Die Reformbewegung in Deutschland 1845–1914*, Göttingen 1991; Beate Witzler, *Großstadt und Hygiene. Kommunale Gesundheitspolitik in der Epoche der Urbanisierung*, Stuttgart 1995.

23. Cf. e.g. Klaus Bergmann, *Agrarromantik und Großstadtfeindschaft*, Meisenheim 1970, or Andrew Lees, *Cities Perceived. Urban Society in European and American Thought, 1820–1940*, Manchester 1985.

24. Cf. Gottfried Korff, 'Mentalität und Kommunikation in der Großstadt. Berliner Notizen zur "inneren" Urbanisierung', in Theodor Kohlmann and Hermann Bausinger (eds.), *Großstadt. Aspekte empirischer Kulturforschung*, Berlin 1985, 343–361 and Peter Fritzsche, *Reading Berlin 1900*, Cambridge, Mass. 1996.

25. Maria Tatar, *Lustmord. Sexual Murder in Weimar Germany*, Princeton, N.J. 1995.

26. An interesting attempt to combine the focus on one particular city with discourse analysis is provided by Martin H. Geyer, *Verkehrte Welt. Revolution, Inflation und Moderne: München 1914–1924*, Göttingen 1998.

27. Some recent works demonstrating this trend are discussed in Friedrich Lenger, 'Berlin, Berlin . . .', *Bulletin of the German Historical Institute London* XXII (2000), 7–17.

28. Cf. Jürgen Reulecke, *Geschichte der Urbanisierung in Deutschland*, Frankfurt a.M. 1985 and – more narrowly on the legal, political and administrative aspects – Wolfgang R. Krabbe, *Die deutsche Stadt im 19. und 20. Jahrhundert*, Göttingen 1989.

29. Cf. e.g. Lutz Niethammer, *Umständliche Erläuterung der seelischen Störung eines Communalbaumeisters in Preußens größtem Industriedorf oder: die Unfähigkeit zur Stadtentwicklung*, Frankfurt a.M. 1979.

30. For my own views on this project cf. Friedrich Lenger, 'Bürgertum, Stadt und Gemeinde zwischen Frühneuzeit und Moderne', *Neue Politische Literatur* XL (1995), 14–29.

31. Since it was not possible to include an additional article on the urban working class I can only refer the reader to the above-mentioned case studies by Köllmann (note 8), Lenger (note 13) and Zwahr (note 19).

32. This is not sufficiently reflected in the conception of Jay Winter and Jean-Louis Robert (eds.), *Capital Cities at War. Paris, London, Berlin 1914–1919*, Cambridge 1997.

33. *Meyers Konversations-Lexikon*, 5th edn, vol. 17, Leipzig 1897, 116; cf. on Bücher's coinage of the term Hans Jürgen Teuteberg, 'Historische Aspekte der Urbanisierung: Forschungsstand und Probleme', in id. (ed.) *Urbanisierung im 19. und 20. Jahrhundert. Historische und geographische Aspekte*, Cologne 1983, 2–34, esp. 3.

KLAUS TENFELDE

Urbanization and the Spread of an Urban Culture in Germany in the Nineteenth and Twentieth Centuries

Clearly, it is too ambitious a task to present a comprehensive overview of the fascinating process of urbanization within the scope of one essay, even when referring to just one, albeit comparatively large, country like Germany. All the more ambitious against the background of an amazing amount and quality of research that has been devoted to urbanization in Britain, much of it in a comparative perspective, so that for a time, for a student of urbanization in Germany, it seemed advisable to study at a selection of places in Britain where a solid knowledge of German urbanization had also been acquired.

This is not just a *captatio benevolentiae* on British scholarship. There is no doubt that British studies on comparative demographic features of urbanization, on types of cities, on the urban space, or on the history of urban planning and urban utopias in a comparative perspective have opened up many avenues, and have been extended to Germany and other European countries, strongly influencing a growing number of recent German case studies. In addition, it is well known that a profound British interest in German urbanization,[1] or rather, in the mode by which German urban planners and city administrators managed to cope with the many problems caused by industrialization and urbanization, dates back to the turn of the twentieth century. Also, the legal conditions and procedures, and the consequences of German communal self-administration, would have been studied. The books published in the course of that interest generally display a certain curiosity about such legal grounds and procedures, and about the achievements of urban planning and social welfare in the big German cities until then. In general, recent research from the German academic community apparently confirmed that under the leadership and decisive influence of the German middle classes – the *Bürgertum*, which in fact had been privileged by franchise to govern virtually all towns and large cities – city governments fundamentally modernized during an age of the most rapid urban growth, at least until 1914.[2] Unfortunately, as is the case with most social history in Germany, knowledge of long-term social developments in the twentieth century, and that includes fundamental urban developments, has developed far less. Thus for instance, the important book by Matzerath on urbanization in Prussia[3] has been limited to the period of emergence and growth, whereas recent introductions to German urbanization presented by Reulecke and Krabbe to a large extent focus on the period before 1914.[4] To a degree, this is understandable in the light of a well-founded dominance of political history which felt compelled to devote itself to the origins of National Socialism, and to the other fundamental events which shaped German and European history so much in the twentieth century. It seems that from German perspectives, even in social (and urban) history, the caesura of 1933 is insurmountable. Of course in urban history this may also be understandable because of the natural interest of historians in emergence rather than in stagnation and decay. Yet it remains true that knowledge of the development of the urban landscape in Germany in the twentieth century, and especially in the post-war period, is deplorably poor. There is, for example, scant knowledge about the social historical meaning of the rupture of the Second World War, when the core of the urban world had been brought to ruin almost everywhere, and of the time periods, the means and the aims of reconstruction.[5]

In a short essay, there is little opportunity to improve on faulty research conditions, though I do want to shift the interest to rather more general developments of the German urban landscape in the twentieth century. Any attempt to grasp only the most important features of that phase would of course look like squaring a circle. Thus it seems wise to limit the scope to three strands of argument: the first, resulting from a general survey of the phases of urban growth; the second, from an attempt at differentiation of functional types of city growth; and the third, from a certain perception of urban culture, and a rather rough analysis of the major components of what may be called 'urban culture'. As we shall see, the sections will connect easily, with the first section also serving as an introduction to the main features of German urban development in general.

I

The percentages of urban population as part of the whole population easily display the phases of German urbanization in the nineteenth and twentieth centuries, though of course they do not tell so much about the very nature of that process.

Certain problems with the figures presented in Table 1 (p. 16)[6] are caused by the changing size of territory. In general, we refer to the German Federation for 1830; to the Kaiserreich including Alsace–Lorraine from 1871 to 1910; to the territory of the German Reich for 1925 and 1939, (for the latter year, the territory of 1937 is used); to both Germanies from 1950 to 1980. It may be unsound to combine the two German states since urban development in the GDR apparently took a different shape. However, knowledge on this is poor, and I shall not concern myself with that problem. The fact that different territories are covered does not influence the numbers too much. Rather, it is important to direct the reader's attention to another problem with these figures, that is, community incorporation and the so-called communal reform of the 1970s. In four different waves – that is, in the 1890s, during the first decade of the twentieth century, again in the 1920s, and finally in the 1970s in the FRG – the county and community territories underwent dramatic changes of boundaries and population size whereby the nearby settlements and suburbs that had developed until then were incorporated. During the 1920s, for instance, the large city territories of greater Berlin, and also of the big industrial cities such as Dortmund and Essen, attained their final size.

Dortmund is taken here as an example to explain some of the demographic consequences (see map on p. 17).[7] In the centre, the white area is encircled by the walls of old medieval Dortmund, which was a privileged Free Imperial City (*Freie Reichsstadt*) of the Holy Roman Empire of the German Nation until 1803. The shadowed area around the centre had belonged to that town, and had been populated for centuries, but especially during the first half of the nineteenth century when Dortmund grew from some 4,000 to some 10,000 inhabitants. In the same area, a core urban population of about 170,000 had settled around 1900, while quite a few villages surrounding Dortmund, such as Hörde in the South, had been growing rapidly as well. Some of these suburbs in the Ruhr area – Hamborn in the west of the Ruhr region is a well-known example – exceeded city size, i.e., 100,000 according to German statistical standards, without being granted the legal privilege of self-administration. The Prussian authorities were fearful of socialist infiltration of the big cities, and would delay the granting of a minimum communal autonomy to the newly created cities of the so-called 'Wild West'. In the region that was to become Greater Dortmund in the 1920s, Hörde for some decades even formed a county in its own right.

Everywhere, the enlargement of city territories led to a massive population increase so that any attempt to measure urbanization in terms of urban population growth would be misleading. In fact, population density in Dortmund in the period covered by Figure 1, decreased from 5,700 to some 2,000 inhabitants per square kilometre. Everywhere, city incorporation to some degree completed former and facilitated further city development; this included, in particular, the creation of new space for urban planning. A final communal reform, taking place to different degrees in the *Länder* of the Federal Republic in the 1970s, and clearly reflected in Table 1, apparently changed the size of city and county territories once and for all, and resulted in a reduction of the sheer number of urban settlements from some

Table 1   Germany: Population by Size of Settlements (percentages)

	Below 2000	Below 20.000	20.000– 100.000	Above 100.000	Population (Mio.)[1]
1830		95.4[2]	3.2	1.3	29.4
1871	63.9	87.5	7.7	4.8	41.1
1890	53.0	78.1	9.8	12.1	49.4
1910	40.0	65.3	13.4	21.3	64.9
1925	35.6	59.5	13.7	26.8	62.4
1939	30.1	54.7	13.6	31.6	69.3
1950[3]	27.7	57.2	15.4	27.5	68.6
1970	20.3	50.2	19.5	30.2	77.7
1980	9.9	43.3	25.3	32.3	78.3

[1] Population (absolute numbers): German Federation (1830, without Schleswig), German Reich (1871–1910, including Alsace-Lorraine etc.), German Reich (1925, 1939: territory of 1937), Federal Republic of Germany (1950–1980, GDR included)
[2] I.e. below 25.000 and 25.000–100.000, respectively
[3] GDR: 1955; FRG: 1950

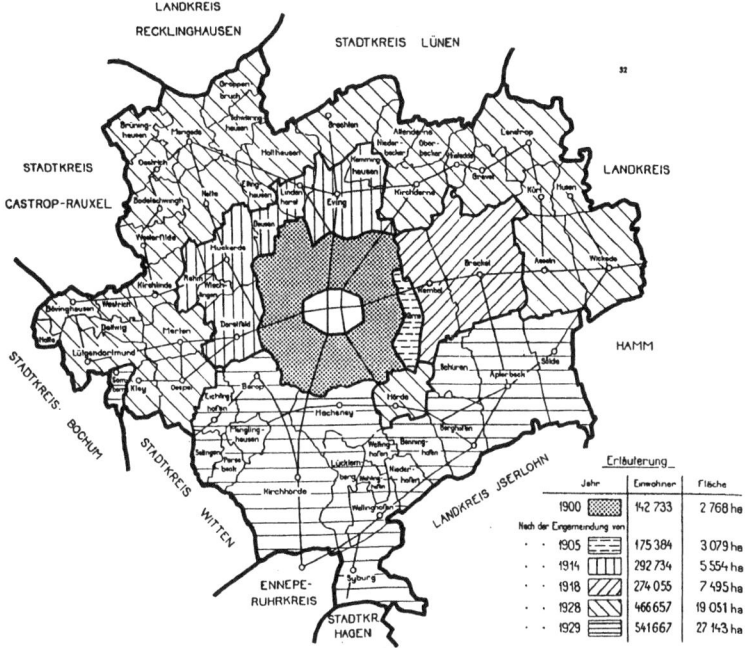

Figure 1   The Spacial Development of Dortmund 1900–1929

22,500 to no more than 8,500 in the FRG. Also in the GDR, a clear but much less fundamental adjustment occurred. Therefore the figures given for 1980, especially in Table 1, require careful use. On the other hand, to a certain degree the communal reform of the 1970s may be taken as an indication of the different dimension urbanization had acquired since the peak of urban growth had been reached. It is clear that even during a time of very rapid urban growth, that is, from about 1890 to 1910, two-thirds of the German people still lived in what Mack Walcker once labelled 'German home towns', that is, in small towns with less than 20,000 inhabitants. We may safely assume that settlements of a size of 2,000 and below, and even up to 20,000, at least until 1914 did not develop strong urban administrations, but retained a rather rural character, with a large proportion of house owners, and strong family structures, but few centre functions. The growth of these settlements during the time of rapid urbanization must not be underestimated, but little change occurred in fact.[9] Rather, in the light of recent research on rural Germany in the twentieth century,[10] a different type of urbanization should be considered: the urbanization of the countryside, which overlapped with the urbanization of the big cities. This started in the 1930s at the latest, when the availability of electricity spread, and has been completed since the 1960s, when modern communications reached the villages, and individual mobility became a part of farmers' lives.

At any rate, an impressive growth of the share of the big cities in the total population started with the foundation of the Reich, and lasted well into the 1930s when, in spite of the economic depression and some verbal but unnecessary enmity to cities on the part of the National Socialists, a peak was reached. However, for the 1920s in particular, the figures are misleading because city incorporation made up for most of the urban population growth, whereas since about the turn of the century, urban fertility rates – except for heavy industrial cities – fell dramatically, and from 1914 migration to the big cities dried up.[11] During the Second World War and the immediate postwar period, and with the exception of a handful of cities of minor importance, the vast majority of the big cities above 200,000 suffered from severe population losses in both German states. Recovery occurred in the 1950s when strong city growth again took place in the West, while the population share of the big cities of this size in the GDR even until 1980, with only one exception (Halle), did not make up for the losses suffered during the war, and in the post-war period. In the West, the 1950s were a period of renewed city growth, which generally reflected major post-war population shifts in the period of reconstruction, the so-called 'economic miracle', and in particular the temporary revival of old industries such as coal and steel in the Ruhr area. Urban population growth stagnated in the 1960s, though, as has been indicated before, urbanization in the form of development of urban lifestyles, administrative standards and a particular kind of local political participation continued to spread in the countryside.

Thus it is safe to conclude that in terms of rapid urban population growth, urbanization in Germany mainly shaped the five decades or so of the Kaiserreich. The process witnessed phases of stagnation and even of temporary de-urbanization during the economic crisis, but regained impetus as part of the economic recovery from about 1936. In general, the speed of urbanization has diminished since the First World War. During the 1950s, cities made up for the losses in the West, while in the East, the big cities caught up much more slowly. At this point, a comparison may be useful.

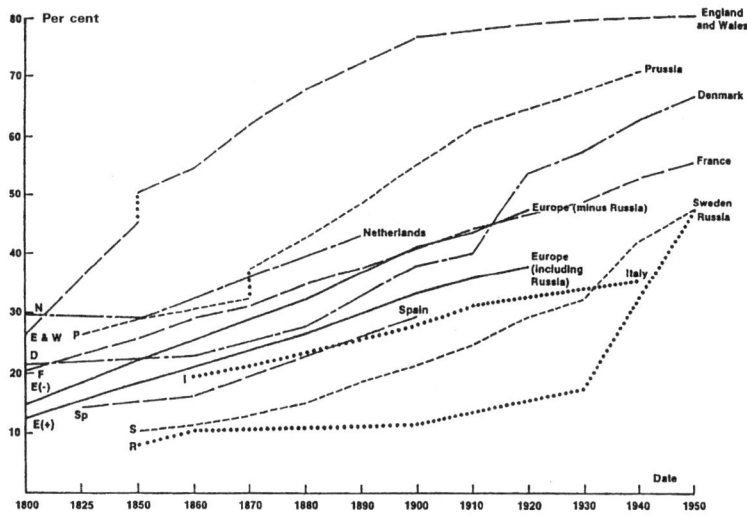

Source: Paul H. Hohenberg; Lynn Hollen Lees, *The Making of Urban Europe 1000–1950*, Cambridge, MA: Harvard University Press, 1985, p. 219.

Figure 2　Percentages of Urban Population in European Countries, 1800–1950[12]

We now turn to a definition of the urban population that includes settlements above 2,000 inhabitants, and for our purposes, we take Prussia as a synonym for Germany. The picture displayed in Figure 2 is well known: England and Wales leading urbanization for centuries, but slowing down in the 1890s; Prussia/Germany near the bottom until about 1870, but growing rapidly from then; Russia speeding up with Stalin's industrialization; France with a slow development, which in fact was heavily dominated by Paris and a handful of big cities. Among the smaller countries, Switzerland, Belgium, the Netherlands and Denmark as well as Sweden all deserve interest. I shall stop here because to follow this path for the post-war period would need further investigation. Suffice it to say that among the European nations, an extraordinary high growth rate of the urban population occurred in Prussia/Germany, and lasted for a comparatively long period of time, but slowed down or turned into stagnation from the 1920s. In spite of this, in what follows, I shall argue that urbanization, if we were to understand it as a cultural process, would display a different time structure, and would reach its peak in our times rather than, say, before

1914. Before I shift the argument towards urban culture, I want briefly to direct the reader's attention towards the components of urban growth by city type, and to some of the demographic features of such growth.

II

Recent research, especially by urban geographers such as Blotevogel,[13] clearly distinguishes the growth features of different types of cities in Germany. From among a variety of such types, I mention particularly the industrially diversified city, the heavy industrial city, port cities, and the large functional centres such as Berlin and a number of state capitals with a long tradition of court rule. We call the latter 'residence cities' (*Residenzstädte*, a German and Austrian peculiarity). Among such types, many characteristics of course overlap, and the features mentioned would refer to dominant structures only. For instance, long before 1914, Berlin as one former residence city among many others, had become a major service centre, and a most important economic centre as well, characterized by highly diversified industrial structures. To a degree, the same is true for Munich or Dresden. Looking at the components of urban population growth as represented by the city types mentioned, we can discover quite different developments.

In general, and with the exception of capitals as service centres, such as Berlin, and highly diversified cities, such as Cologne or Düsseldorf, it should be noted that migration to the big cities, and in general to the west, had ceased to a degree by 1914 or, at the latest, in the early 1920s. The decade from the outbreak of the First World War is difficult to assess because of: first of all a lack of figures; secondly, mobilization and demobilization; thirdly, structural change of industries; fourthly, certain influences of the inflationary boom until about 1922, and finally, because of the consequences of the Versailles arrangements and the Ruhr occupation which reduced the numbers of the Ruhr Poles who had been Prussian citizens before, to a third or so of the Polish population in the industrial district in 1914. Also, though most studies on this phenomenon have been carried through to 1914 only, it seems safe to assume that a degree of internal migration, the so-called fluctuation within the city walls, vanished during the 1920s, a development that apparently was fostered by the stabilization crisis of 1924 and by a high degree of basic unemployment from then on, not to mention the economic crisis from 1930 onwards.

Apparently, the urban population of the lower and lower-middle classes stabilized. This is especially true for the heavily industrialized cities of Upper Silesia as far as they still belonged to the German Reich; of the Saar (though there we must take account of special living conditions); and predominantly of the Ruhr. In the Ruhr, a strong and almost continuous influx of a rural, predominantly male population had occurred since the 1850s. During a first phase, the nearby regions were drained of young men aged 20 to 35, and from the 1880s onwards, that famous flood of migration from the east to the west crowded the industrial sites north of the Ruhr, and made for a new type of heavy industrial city. This was characterized by a one-sided employment structure in coal and steel only; by a disproportionately low middle-class presence; and by a large degree of company housing, which almost completely ceased by 1914, only to be revived by the National Socialists, albeit on different grounds. Other characteristics include chaotic urban planning until well into the 1890s; defective and delayed infrastructures and hygiene; an overburdened elementary school system; and with regard to the income structures of city budgets, a comparatively low tax yield so that, for want of regional and national compensation of such deficiency, infrastructure problems tended to accumulate.

We have become used to account for an incomplete, 'deficient urbanization' in these regions, which by 1914 may have numbered a total population of some 6 to 7 million people, that is, at least 10 per cent of the whole German population.[14] In order to understand why it took such cities well into the 1960s to cope with their problems, and why they could master them only with the assistance of a change of population structure, by the retreat of heavy industries, and not least by constitutional pressure for compensation introduced in 1949, we must briefly turn to the process of family building.[15]

Wherever heavy industries demanded a large labour force, be it in the Ruhr, or in British coal and steel districts where the Irish moved in – who in many respects compare with the migrant Poles – unskilled and predominantly Catholic workers of rural origins tended to carry their customary attitudes towards fertility into the industrial cities. Prevented from creating their own families within their original backgrounds, these people almost immediately turned to marriage despite a lack of young women in their new environments. After the turn of the twentieth century, the marriage rate among miners and steel workers reached over 90 per cent. In addition, their fertility rate was the highest of their respective professional structure, ahead even of Catholic farmers' families, and remained so for at least two generations, dominating fertility in the Ruhr, at least in the northern parts of that region, well into the 1960s. A part of that story concerns gender relations. Heavy industries were male industries, and heavy industrial regions rarely offered jobs to women, so that traditions transferred into the regions and the conditions of labour markets worked together to press workers to form families with numerous children where paternalist gender relations prevailed. As one might expect, such families served to perpetuate and foster a conservative mode of family building. In contrast, a skilled, settled and 'urbanized' printer's family tended to produce smaller family units as early as the 1850s. At the same time the printers became reluctant to form families – as were other professional groups, and especially white-collar and civil service workers, who settled at an average family size of four well before 1914. These were the ones who tended to settle in cities as service centres, in the capitals, in industrially diversified urban structures, and who had become 'urban' by the second gener-ation. On the other hand, the children of migrants to the heavy industrial cities, who remained less educated, and who, because of a one-sided labour market, had to stick to the jobs and living conditions of their parents' generation, and furthermore suffered from a chronic lack of infrastructure, prolonged the mode of reproduction that had become typical for them. From 1945 this mode was again nurtured by a new and strong influx of workers, especially from the formerly German territories of the East – migrants who were badly needed because of the huge demand for energy and raw materials during the period of reconstruction.

All this means that since the middle of the nineteenth century, the gap had widened between most of the capital and functional centre types of city, and the heavy industrial cities, which in some cases were founded on green belt sites and grew most rapidly before 1914, being enlarged additionally by administrative incorporation, which ended in the 1920s or 1930s, as mentioned before. Of course in other cities that experienced industrialization, such as Berlin, though for different reasons, the mode of family formation and repro-duction described above was important as well, but did not dominate because labour demand was already focused on services and skilled people. To some extent, the newly founded settlements of the chemical industry such as Ludwigshafen or Leverkusen are comparable to the Ruhr. There, strong growth caused by fertility rather than migration continued throughout the 1920s and 1930s. In contrast, working-class fertility within the old large cities sharply decreased to the extent that the population actually fell, to be compensated for by skilled migration notably during periods of economic prosperity.

Among the severe consequences of peculiar labour market and family structures in heavy industrial districts, the low tax yield available for communal budgets must be mentioned. Contrary to what one might expect, because of high fertility, low degrees of female occupation and low life expectancy, and despite a rapid influx of young unmarried men prior to 1914, in such 'regions of work' the proportion of actively working people ranged much below the average. In addition, there was a lack of well-to-do and wealthy middle-class people, whereas the really rich people, who made their money in coal and steel, tended to settle outside a region blighted by dust, smoke, and dirt. Also, because of the restricted needs of an overwhelmingly working-class population, services were less developed, so that tax revenues remained low well into the post-war period. During the world economic crisis of the early 1930s, some Ruhr cities were on the brink of bankruptcy.[16] Thus, there was a sheer necessity for large companies to provide housing, and also, albeit reluctantly, to shoulder some responsibility for making good infrastructure deficiencies wherever this seemed advisable. In a region that was badly in need of schools, money to construct them was extremely scarce.

To a large degree, rapid urbanization in Germany was dominated by the new type of heavy industrial cities well into the 1930s and, for slightly different reasons, also in the 1950s. From then on, conditions in the Ruhr normalized, owing to the gradual but severe decrease of employment in mining and steel industries. Within the space of just one generation, family structure and modes of reproduction fundamentally changed, fostered by diversification of employment structures and a sort of revolution of the educational system.[17] As everywhere else, family size went down to normal, that is, one to two children at most. If families were formed at all, a new bottom layer of urban population is being created by a fresh migration of foreigners from Turkey or even from the African nations, and from Eastern European and Russian people of German origin, from asylum seekers, and from illegal immigrants. Taken together, these groups account for some 10 to 15 per cent of the urban population, but the Ruhr to date does not differ any more from Hamburg, Cologne or Berlin. These immigrants are responsible for the numerical stability of the urban populations everywhere, whereas urban Germans seem to be strictly controlling their fertility. As a particular indicator of urbanity, the demographic conditions fundamentally changed, whereby the Ruhr also has achieved urbanity and kept up with structural conditions that usually dominate the European and North American type of urbanization.

III

At this point it would seem advisable to turn briefly to the use of terminology in this article. There are not so many advantages to the German language, but among the few, we enjoy the ability to distinguish between *Verstädterung* and *Urbanisierung*.[18] *Verstädterung* might be taken to mean the relative increase of growth of city populations in general, and of the populations of big cities in particular; the emergence of clusters of cities within increasingly densely populated regions; the increase of the number of legally or statistically defined places of settlement; the increase of the number of people accommodated therein, and of their share of the total population. So far, central European history can be seen to have experienced two important phases of (quantitative) *Verstädterung*, namely, in the Middle Ages from the twelfth century to about 1350, and during industrialization, mainly from 1850 to 1950. *Urbanisierung* as a process would refer to those fundamental changes of urban life styles that are usually but – as the example of heavy industrial cities has shown – not necessarily associated with strong or rapid urban population growth. Such *Urbanisierung* would therefore comprise changes of structures and institutions, social entities and administrations, human relations and communications in a rather qualitative sense, as opposed to *Verstädterung*, an aiming for 'urbanity',[19] *Urbanität*, or urban culture. From now on, I shall use the notion of urbanization in this sense. It should be added that by 'culture' I tend to understand a set of distinguished and identifiable values associated with distinguishable and identifiable structures and life styles, a set that has become common because of meanings shared by the people who repeatedly understand reality in a specified way.

Now, what might be meant by urban culture, and *Urbanität*, in the German case? Among the many points coming to mind so far, the ten points that follow may cover at least some of the most important developments:

1.   The components of *demographic development* fundamentally changed during urbanization. This has been touched upon before in some

detail. In fact 'demographic transition' as it has been labelled by demographers occurred with regard to urban rather than industrial conditions.[20] From a fragile balance of births and deaths in pre-modern times, regulated by food supply and extraordinary circumstances such as wars, epidemics, and hunger, the mode of reproduction under urban circumstances after a long period of transition reached another fragile balance of births and deaths on a much lower level. The decrease of the birth rate is to a degree compensated for by an increase of life expectancy, and further population losses are counter-balanced by immigration, which nowadays, in countries that reached a general urbanity of life style, usually originates abroad. As has been shown before, with the example of heavy industrial cities, time lags occurred that connected to the schedule of city growth and immigration, and the respective type of industrialization, i.e., the role of leading sectors such as mining or services, and also to the degree of centrality peculiar to each city. Apart from mentioning this, it seems important to realize that fundamental value changes are more or less directly related to the *urbanization of reproduction*. Childhood and youth become separated and identified positively. Generations are distinguished from each other. Death and lingering illness vanish behind real life and joy. Natural uncertainties of life explained away by religion were minimized, and the life cycle became subject to personal efficiency and rational market chance rather than fate and some hidden divine scheme.

2.   The demographic explosion so common in most European countries during the decades of transition, from the *ancien régime* to modern societies, apparently continued during an initial phase of city growth, but found an end, stagnated or even reversed, when urban value components spread. At the core of all this, it is the urban family that counts for the most decisive developments. Basically, the emergence of urbanity is characterized by an essential *de-familialization of social networks*.

Figures that prove this process are easily available, and need not be repeated here.[21] At first glance, such evidence seems to be contradictory. During heavy waves of migration into the cities, as has been indicated before, young unmarried men of rural origins in particular successfully established their own families, and their sometimes apparently unlimited fertility increasingly contributed to *Verstädterung*, as city hygiene improved and infant mortality declined, a process that was clearly underway in German cities since the late

nineteenth century. The second generation of migrant family descend-
ants, 'urbanized' as they were, rather consciously started to limit
fertility at around the time when interior migration into the cities
ceased, that is, in the 1920s, but with the exception of heavy industrial
regions. The decline of the birth rate originated in the cities, and spread
to the countryside in the 1960s. As a secular process, it was inter-
rupted only by post-war social conditions, including vigorous migration.

De-familiarization of urban life has many different meanings. It
has meant, first of all, de-functionalization of the family in the light
of progressive urban division of labour. Work separated from the
family setting, and basic domestic tasks, such as those relating to
consumption and waste, became organized increasingly by an urban
service society. Networks formerly constituted by family relations
became replaced by rather anonymous supra-familial voluntary
organizations, which to a degree, and during further development,
were absorbed by city intervention especially in the realm of social
policy. Thereby, the family was divested of emotional concern. Leisure
activities developed and were themselves taken out of the domestic
setting, only to be commercialized elsewhere. Increasingly, family
existence as a common and highly esteemed lifestyle fades away in
modern urban societies. Reproduction no longer constituted a major
concern. The family was reduced to a one-generation phenomenon
to regulate sexual relations rather than care for reproduction. Thus
some sort of partnership not formally legalized, and therefore easy
to change, might suffice. Also, the welfare state compensated for
inter-generational care, which had been fundamental to the survival
of rural families. Daily, weekly and annual rhythms of life became
directed by work and community life, and the influence of church
parishes vanished. Within the life cycle, those periods during which
families perform the most fundamental functions for society as a
whole, were shortened to a rather transitory time phase of some three
to five years covering birth and the raising of infants. Thus, for the
first time in social history, women found new roles. Increasingly,
competitive value orientations have overshadowed the value systems
so closely connected to the normality and self-evidence of family
experience, which had been so much akin, though limited in scope,
to pre-urban structural conditions and had been strengthened during
a first phase of urban growth.

3.   Urbanity, furthermore, is characterized by an utmost degree of
structural differentiation in terms of work division, including of course

the separation of the family from the work place, but leading towards a highly differentiated urban professional structure, which ends up servicing rather than producing. In Germany at least early *Verstädterung* was primarily a result of the move of industries from the countryside into the cities, and until recently, industries have been the most important impetus for urbanization, though not so many towns were founded because of industrial settlement. Things changed only recently when individual mobility and the degree of infrastructure development of sites outside the cities allowed for different locations. Thus, structural differentiation to a large extent followed the needs of industry via the labour and consumption markets. Moreover, service systems such as trade and banking were closely connected to industry.

So far, it is easy to understand that the city has been the real job generator, and not only in modern times. Job differentiation also meant status differentiation as a dynamic process. Since a new phase of city growth started in Germany at the end of the eighteenth century, gaining unprecedented speed in the 1890s, urban social structure has been reshaped several times, to the point where in the end a certain type of structure is no longer discernible. In a first phase, during which the old town elites managed to survive thanks to electoral privilege, the work place and the new kinds of market organization tended to dominate social structure and urban space,[22] so that social segregation became the norm. Yet urban planning,[23] the origins of which in Germany date back to the 1870s, from the beginning carried a sense of social regulation that aimed to avoid one-sided spatial structures, and took different forms in various cities. Thus it may well be that segregation of living quarters according to status in Germany did not reach the extent of, say, US cities, despite the fact that urban home ownership among the lower classes was much less widespread in Germany than in England or the United States. Impoverishment of city quarters resulted rather from medieval architectural structures in need of renewal since the last quarter of the nineteenth century, thereby forming a major responsibility for urban planners, but apparently only rarely followed social segregation.[24] Also, the process of city building, which encompasses the functional standardization of commercial city centres, may have been less sweeping than in other countries.

As to social stratification,[25] two major processes were concentrated in the cities, varied only according to functional city types. First, the working classes spread, their numbers reaching a peak some time in the 1920s. From then on, the 'new middle classes' displayed higher growth rates. Secondly, the composition of the middle classes changed several times. During the first half of the nineteenth century, the emergence of industrial entrepreneurship added to the conventional burgher elites composed of merchants and the educated class, sometimes making the town a battleground in the struggle for supremacy.[26] The importance of self-employed artisans and small traders has been on the decline in Germany throughout urbanization, though their professional composition changed, whereas white-collar work within industries since the 1880s, and within services mostly during post-war times, has seen a considerable rise in importance.[27] As a result, white-collar urban work, even in formerly heavy industrial cities such as the industrial centres of the Ruhr, nowadays outnumbers the size of the working class. In addition, even there, the 'free professions' such as lawyers and medical doctors count for an increasing proportion of employment; since the 1960s, the educated classes have gained in numbers. There is reason to assume that the 'homogeneous middle-class society' (*nivellierte Mittelstandsgesellschaft*, H. Schelsky) portrayed already in the 1950s, and as a thesis strongly debated in those days,[28] now more adequately describes social reality in the cities than ever before.

To an important degree this situation is the result of status differentiation by consumption and lifestyles rather than by professional position. In the self-perception of urban people, the importance of work of whatever kind has declined to function as a means of social distinction, or even stigmatization. While for a long period extending well into the post-war years, the classes who were subject to the labour market really dominated the stage, it is apparent now that a mixture of old and new criteria of distinction has repressed good old urban class society. Among modern sociologists, milieu theory has been revived. Modern lifestyles, which by origin and meaning are urban, are considered to shape new but no less decisive class lines. This has created a new urban poverty, and a two-thirds-majority of highly individualized existences distinguished by non-economic, or not primarily economic, interests such as preferences, tastes, and customs that have been developed by education.

4.   Among the various factors that made for an urban society qualitatively different from pre-urban town societies, the rise of *modern city bureaucracies* has played a decisive role.[29] The need to organize a local life so much threatened by immigration and growth, soon broke the limits of traditional city bureaucracies, which in fact may have

developed in Germany earlier than elsewhere. After an initial phase of private investment, services such as water and energy supply, food markets, waste disposal, and in particular city traffic systems, were provided by public authorities, and surprisingly early, even conservatives deliberated about municipal socialism. The field has been reconquered by capitalism only recently, and even then to a small degree. From the 1890s, public services became a major concern of city administrations, which rapidly expanded also because of urban planning, construction control, and social policies, which themselves became increasingly diverse. At its core, urban society is a service society which is also destined to serve the hinterland. In German research, these functions have been termed 'the emergence of an efficient communal services administration' (*Aufstieg der kommunalen Leistungsverwaltung*),[30] a phrase that may be misleading because of its positive connotations, exaggerating the actual state of affairs. Yet the pride of German city administrators in their achievements up to 1914 was widespread and such achievements were admired abroad.[31]

5.   Family breakdown and the devaluation of traditional institutions during urbanization everywhere corresponded to the emergence of *non-government and supra-familial organizations,* which to an important extent characterized urban culture. Yet, the political culture given in the various German territories greatly shaped such developments because of legal restrictions and government repression, and the meaning of voluntary associationism in place of *sociabilité* (M. Agulhon) has been changing only recently. In fact, at least in the German case, the time period between, say, 1850 and 1950 may safely be called 'the century of associations'.[32] Associations of all forms and for all purposes clearly originated from towns of all sizes, and only hesitatingly spread into rural Germany, where they gained a foothold in the twentieth century. The tendency towards non-government and non-familial organizations somewhat diminished in the face of the emergence of the new, strongly individualizing techniques of communications since the 1960s. Also, in present-day German cities, voluntary associations for leisure, sports and culture, support and philanthropy and many more civic concerns, play an important role. It is not too far-fetched to envisage an urban theory of associationism which would maintain, as a sort of vacuum theory, that associations have emerged from the widespread need to compensate for the loss of the old world, that is, the functions of the family, and the closely knit clan, village and parish networks of pre-urban rural Germany.

The consequences that this development had for the emergence of an urban culture, in the sense that new social relations and institutions created a new perception of each other, and a different realization of the material world, are quite obvious, but cannot be treated in detail here. Suffice it to say that civic participation via associations changed the nature of urban politics. In a first phase of urbanization, associationism initiated by the middle classes, and soon imitated and re-created by the workers, to a very large extent filled the gap between the family and community rule, and organized the processes of urban opinion-forming and decision-making. It is the city from which the modern modes of representative and parliamentary politics derive, especially in Germany.[33] The modern party system was generated to a considerable degree through municipal politics. Also, municipal politics as a subset of national politics were formed by a loose organization of cities within their respective territories as well as nationally.[34] Not least, associational experiences and the vision of municipal socialism made German Social Democracy a factual parliamentary rather than a hypothetical revolutionary party. The middle-class franchise privilege, which universally, but in different modes, upheld an unjust system of proportional representation on the city councils for many decades until 1918, did not hinder civic concern in the working class. It may have facilitated problem-solving because of the homogeneous structure of municipal rule it tended to provide.

6.   So far, the points made have been of a more structural nature. I am turning now to a few points that may be considered to be rather more 'cultural' in nature. Among them the *perception of the urban space and time* deserves special attention. It is hard to find sufficient research on the symbolic meanings of urban streets and places because of a natural lack of sources capable of elucidation.[35] It is with the built environment that urban life achieves regularity in terms of experience, mobility and movement, and human relationships. Of course, as mentioned before, urban historians and sociologists long ago discovered the main features, such as social and spatial segregation, suburbanism and city building, de- and re-functionalization of quarters, favourable and unfavourable space. After all, in terms of the built environment, the urban landscape in Germany has displayed a remarkable stability, in spite of the influences of industrialization, the growth differentiation during *Verstädterung*, and the destruction wrought by war. On the other hand, the new image of the big city significantly changed the enduring image of the German town during

urbanization, owing to the new architectural structures, traffic systems, and spatial requirements of industries and modern tech-niques in general. To a decisive degree, modern urban space and time perceptions have been shaped by electricity, which was introduced into Germany from the 1890s, and spread into all realms of social life in the inter-war period. The big city never sleeps.[36] In the city, the daily rule of the clock, of shift work, of routines governed by timetables almost completely replaced the natural time rhythms such as seasons, and culturally imposed time rhythms such as the church calendar.

7. *Communications, social control and conflict,* obviously in the urban world are different from the village and small town. It seems clear that urban culture to a large extent rests on intra- and supra-personal communication systems, organized anonymously, serving ubiquitous purposes, and as such, no longer urban by nature as they are not limited to the urban space. The techniques of communication available at different times defined the number of messages to be exchanged, the individuals and groups involved, and to a degree, even the contents of the messages. These techniques are not urban by origin, but display effectiveness under urban conditions, and decisively form perceptions and expectations. In our day, relations and communications, which formerly had been shaped by formal organizations and institutions, are on the decline, and this would count for the partial retreat of associationism mentioned before. The messages available to every-body are anonymous, manifold, abundant and uncontrollable, and increasingly they are made use of, and are structuring time schedules, future plans, expectations. After all, the availability of such techniques seems to foster a tendency towards hyper-individualization, which in fact has encroached upon the core of urban life. Having become used to urban mass transport and communication systems during the twentieth century, we might have to face a new phase of de-urbanization: technically and principally, mass communication is now available everywhere. At the same time, new vacua of social control are opened, while new means of social control have become available, and are already widely used. The crime rate, youth criminality as an urban phenomenon, and suicide rates will continue to shape one important side of urban culture. In the course of the twentieth century, urban conflict has increasingly become characterized by variety instead of one-sidedness: class conflicts in the shape of strikes, which for a time seemed to dominate the urban conflict scene, have become regulated outside or above the urban world. Instead, multiple tensions occur

between ethnic groups, migrants and residents, between generations, tenants and landlords, interest groups, or neighbourhood gangs, to mention just a few.

8.   Urban culture, urbanity, of course includes what may be labelled *high urban culture* (*Hochkultur*). For a long time, and in accordance with the hegemony of the middle classes within urban life and rule, such high culture was understood to characterize urbanity primarily. In the German mind, city culture is strongly associated with such *Hochkultur*, taken to comprise theatre, opera and concert houses, museums, institutions of higher learning and education in general, literature and the arts. As a legacy of pre-modern territorial dissipation, former residence cities in particular have invested their cultural pride in support of the arts and education until the present day. Nurtured by the middle classes with great devotion in the nineteenth century, the willingness of city councils to subsidize such activities never ceased, not even during the last war, and spread again to a degree that after all probably does not compare to most foreign cities. In fact, looking at 'Ruhr city', nowadays a dense landscape of a dozen major urban settlements with some 5 million inhabitants, it is easy to find a dozen or so opera houses and public orchestras, dozens of public and a hundred or so private theatres, hundreds of museums of all kinds, public libraries everywhere, and five large universities, and a cultural mindset somewhat distinguished from what one would expect in, for example, Munich, but as such an indication of plurality rather than uniqueness. Thus the shape of urban high culture is coloured by local tradition, city size and community budgets. Increasingly, private sponsorship is emerging, traditionally underdeveloped in Germany. The middle classes lost their unique access defined by education and money, but in fact remain core consumers.

9.   The development of the *rural–urban difference* in lifestyles and minds unfortunately has not come to the attention of urban historians very much, but has been a concern of sociologists for many years.[37] Historical research shifted its attention to the mutual images of urban and rural life rather than to the material bases of such differences. Thus, there is a thorough knowledge of the development of anti-urban sentiments within the German mind in general as they were expressed from the middle of the nineteenth century, at the onset of *Verstädterung*.[38] Also, the many legal differences forming urban life in pre-modern times are well known, and must be understood to have

contributed to the emergence of anti-urban sentiments in the nine-teenth century. Apparently, a strong anti-urbanism frequently assoc-iated with anti-Semitism evolved parallel to the rise of cities, and gained a foothold among conservative, mostly agrarian elites as well as the educated classes, and to a degree, within the *petite bourgeoisie*, forming parts of the traditions within which National Socialism emerged. Quite obviously such sentiments, rather than theoretical approaches, reached peaks during years of agrarian price crises, e. g. during the early 1890s, and under different conditions, during the Great Inflation of the early 1920s[39] when the rural–urban conflict became violent. It is not so easy to interpret the development of 'real', that is to say measurable, differences of lifestyles such as education, living conditions, property, religiosity, or crime rates, to mention just a few. Though knowledge here is poor, in general it seems that the differences as well as the sentiments have been fading away during the post-war decades. The share of self-employed farmers in Germany decreased from some 25 to 30 per cent in the immediate post-war years to less than 5 per cent nowadays. Concerning sentiments, the experience of the Third Reich may have been influential, but in reality it seems that the second type of urbanization briefly mentioned above, that is, the extension of urbanity to the countryside, levelled the differences quite forcefully, making one of the features of 'German thought' disappear. Rather moderately, modern critics of urban life and culture would devote themselves to mental deficiencies or architectural failures.[40]

10.   Finally, it seems appropriate to raise some thoughts on the relation between urban lifestyles and the *value orientation of urban life*, and recent developments of it. It is quite clear that religious belief no longer provides a dominant attitude to be shared by the vast majority. Belief, confession and the organization of religion have become, first, individualized, secondly, placed at random in urban life, and thirdly, they seem to be limited to confessional milieux that at the same time eroded for different reasons. At this final stage of urbanization, and fostered by the unification of the two German states in 1990, even the manifold colours and divisions of the German confessional landscape which governed the country by war and dispute for centuries have been overcome. But this statement may give rise to controversy. In my opinion, urban culture accounts decisively for these changes. Instead, we find nowadays constantly redefined notions of individuality within the big cities, to the extent that, thanks to modern

techniques of communication, people have become unable and unwilling to socialize within family groups. At the same time, the urban world is in a constant flow of re-modelling according to need and interest. In this, it seems that there is nothing especially urban any more.

IV

A few concluding remarks may be appropriate to sum-marize German urban history. As a result of market development, economies of scale and service, and the media society, there is no countryside any more. There is substantial evidence to maintain that during this final phase of urbanization, the spread of urban culture has reached everywhere, even to places and regions where there are no towns and cities at all. Urbanity as a mode of life and value orientation is universalizing. Even those movements which, at the turn of the century, tended to oppose urbanization by organized retreat to the countryside, faded away; such retreat has become an individual concern and may be organized on sectarian grounds, but would in no way be realized as a manageable alternative. Also, within the German – and to a large degree European – experience, industrial cities as a functional type, exemplified especially in the shape of the heavy industrial cities, have disappeared from the stage. Instead, the functionally diversified big cities, heavily and even increasingly loaded with service functions, dominate the picture.

Thus, the distinction between *Verstädterung* und *Urbanisierung* helps us to understand that cultural developments may follow different paths, apart from demography, allocation of economic resources, factual centrality and growth analysis in general. Though cities of the German and the (north, west and south) European landscape have ceased to grow, urbanity is spreading, even into the *Mezzogiorno*. In stating this, it must be kept in mind that elsewhere, the experience of urbanization has exceeded the European scope. The Brazilian, Indian or Chinese megalopolis certainly transcended the European experience of 'mature urbanity'.

Within the European experience, certain German experiences are worth mentioning. They would have to be related to the rich and multiple experiences of the pre-modern legal construction of the town, which were so consciously revived in the nineteenth century, to foster middle-class pride, and to legitimize liberal city govern-ment.[41] Within such perceptions, for instance, the tradition of the residence city has remained powerful in terms of architecture and culture, and to a degree, spread into city representation and self-consciousness. Yet, other traditions are still easy to realize, such as Hanseatic pride, or long-lasting university influence. There is no doubt also that the constitutional reform leading to partial but far-reaching self-determination within an appropriate tradition, introduced in Prussia and the other German territories from the beginning of the nineteenth century, made the cities remarkably capable of managing an unforeseeable growth. The sort of social distribution and realization of political power that the German city witnessed in the nineteenth century as part of the rise of liberalism may also have been a consequence of the constitutional and political frameworks up to the end of the Kaiserreich, but as a general feature, can be found in France, England and elsewhere within their respective frameworks. So far, the existence of a well-educated bureaucracy that readily spread to the cities when demand for effective town planning and social technology sprang up, decisively helped the 'burghertown' to manage the challenges during the most rapid phase of urbanization, that is, from about 1890 to 1914.

Notes

1. As a more recent example, see Jay Winter and Jean-Louis Robert (eds.), *Capital Cities at War: Paris, London, Berlin, 1914–1919*, Cambridge 1997. Other attempts to reach at comparative grounds include, e.g., Robert Dickinson, *The West European City. A Geographical Interpretation*, London 1991; Richard Rodger (ed.), *European Urban History. Prospect and Retrospect*, Leicester and London 1993 (on Germany: Clemens Zimmermann, pp. 151–69); Theo Barker and Anthony Sutcliffe (eds.), *Megapolis: The Giant City in History*, London 1993 (on Berlin: Gerhard Brunn, pp. 96–115); Ad van der Woude, Akira Hayami and Jan de Vries (eds.), *Urbanization in History. A Process of Dynamic Interactions*, Oxford 1990 (almost exclusively: early modern and nineteenth century).

2. Several research projects, more or less large in scope, have been devoted to the history of the middle classes in Germany. Among them, Lothar Gall and his collaborators clearly focused on the history of the urban *Bürgertum* at the onset of industrialization, see e.g. id. (ed.), *Vom alten zum neuen Bürgertum. Die mitteleuropäische Stadt im Umbruch 1780–1820,*

Munich 1991; id. (ed.), *Stadt und Bürgertum im Übergang von der traditionalen zur modernen Gesellschaft*, Munich 1993; Ralf Zerback, *München und sein Stadtbürgertum. Eine Residenzstadt als Bürgergemeinde 1780–1870*, Munich 1997; Karin Schambach, *Stadtbürgertum und industrieller Umbruch in Dortmund 1780–1870*, Munich 1996. As an attempt at comparison, see Brigitte Meier and Helga Schultz (eds.), *Die Wiederkehr des Stadtbürgers. Städtereformen im europäischen Vergleich 1750 bis 1850*, Berlin 1994.

The Bielefeld Research Project undertook a long-term investigation of the middle classes, not necessarily bound to the history of the urban landscape, but guided by the debate on the German *Sonderweg*; among the many publications, see most recently Michael Schäfer, '*Bürgertum* in der Krise. Städtische Mittelklassen in Edinburgh und Leipzig zwischen Jahrhundertwende und 1920er Jahren', unpublished *Habilitationsschrift* Bielefeld 2000, and Klaus Tenfelde and Hans-Ulrich Wehler (eds.), *Wege zur Geschichte des Bürgertums*, Göttingen 1994 (includes K. T., 'Stadt und Bürgertum im 20. Jahrhundert', pp. 317–53).

Many publications have been produced by a 'special research project' located at the University of Münster in the 1970s and 1980s, and are devoted to comparative urban history, see *Sonderforschungsbereich 161. Vergleichende geschichtliche Städteforschung. Annotierte Gesamtbibliographie 1976–1988*, Münster 1989.

3. Horst Matzerath, *Urbanisierung in Preußen 1815–1914*, Stuttgart 1985; see id. (ed.), *Städtewachstum und innerstädtische Strukturveränderungen. Probleme des Urbanisierungsprozesses im 19. und 20. Jahrhundert*, Stuttgart 1985; id., 'The Influence of Industrialization on Urban Growth in Prussia (1815–1914)', in H. Schmal (ed.), *Patterns of European Urbanization since 1500*, London 1981, 143–79.

4. Jürgen Reulecke, *Geschichte der Urbanisierung in Deutschland*, Frankfurt 1985; Wolfgang R. Krabbe, *Die deutsche Stadt im 19. und 20. Jahrhundert*, Göttingen 1989. See also Clemens Zimmermann, *Die Zeit der Metropolen. Urbanisierung und Großstadtentwicklung*, Frankfurt 1996 (comparing Manchester, St Petersburg, Munich and Barcelona). For a decade or so, Jürgen Reulecke (ed.), *Die deutsche Stadt im Industriezeitalter. Beiträge zur modernen deutschen Stadtgeschichte*, Wuppertal 1978, served as a textbook on German urbanization. To mention just the more widespread volumes of conference papers covering the field: Hans-Jürgen Teuteberg (ed.), *Urbanisierung im 19. und 20. Jahrhundert. Historische und geographische Aspekte*, Cologne and Vienna 1983; id. (ed.), *Städtewachstum, Industrialisierung, Sozialer Wandel. Beiträge zur Erforschung der Urbanisierung im 19. und 20. Jahrhundert*, Berlin 1986; Hans Jäger (ed.), *Probleme des Städtewesens im industriellen Zeitalter*, Cologne and Vienna 1978; Matzerath (ed.), *Städtewachstum* (see fn. 3).

A comparative analysis of research developments may be found in Christian Engeli and Horst Matzerath (eds.), *Moderne Stadtgeschichtsforschung in Europa, USA und Japan. Ein Handbuch*, Stuttgart etc. 1989; as a huge bibliography, the *Bibliographie zur deutschen historischen Städte-forschung*, ed. Heinz Stoob et al., Cologne and Weimar, Parts 1 and 2: 1986, 1996 (with an additional index volume), part 3 in preparation, must be mentioned. Apart from the well-known *Journal of Urban History*, information on the progress of German writing on urban history may be obtained from several journals, such as: *Die alte Stadt. Zeitschrift für Stadtgeschichte, Stadtsoziologie und Denkmalpflege*, 1974—., and especially: *Informationen zur modernen Stadtgeschichte*, 1970—.

5. A few examples, dealing with post-war urban history, are Klaus von Beyme, *Der Wiederaufbau. Architektur und Städtebaupolitik in beiden deutschen Staaten*, Munich and Zurich 1987; Hermann Glaser et al. (eds.), *So viel Anfang war nie. Deutsche Städte 1945–1949*, Berlin 1989 (a richly illustrated volume, including a number of short essays on a selection of German cities during the time of reconstruction); Marlene P. Hiller et al. (eds.), *Städte im Zweiten Weltkrieg. Ein internationaler Vergleich*, Essen 1991 (only two articles on Germany: Hamburg and Dresden). Rather, the field has been covered by sociologists, urban geographers and city planners; see among the many examples, Jürgen Friedrichs, *Die Städte in den 90er Jahren. Demographische, ökonomische und soziale Stadtentwicklungen*, Opladen 1997; as a – rather outdated – introduction to the state of sociological affairs concerning the city, see id. (ed.), *Soziologische Stadtforschung*, Opladen 1988. Peter Saunders's *Social Theory and the Urban Question* (1981) has been translated: *Soziologie der Stadt*, Frankfurt and New York 1987. An interesting attempt at comparison is Hans-Joachim Kadatz, *Städtebauliche Entwicklungslinien in Mittel- und Osteuropa. DDR, Tschechoslowakei und Ungarn nach dem Zweiten Weltkrieg*, Erkner b. Berlin 1997.

6. Figures have been taken, and newly composed, from Wolfram Fischer et al., *Sozialgeschichtliches Arbeitsbuch I. Materialien zur Statistik des Deutschen Bundes 1815–1870*, Munich 1982; Gerhard Hohorst et al., *Sozialgeschicht-liches Arbeitsbuch II. Materialien zur Statistik des Kaiserreichs 1870–1914*, Munich 1975; Dietmar Petzina et al., *Sozialgeschichtliches Arbeitsbuch III. Materialien zur Statistik des Deutschen Reiches 1914–1945*, Munich 1978; Ralf Rytlewski and Manfred Opp de Hipt, *Die Bundesrepublik Deutschland in Zahlen 1945/49–1980*, Munich 1987; id., *Die Deutsche Demokratische Republik in Zahlen 1945/49–1980*, Munich 1987.

7. Taken from Luise von Winterfeld, *Geschichte der freien Reichs- und Hansestadt Dortmund*, 6th ed. Dortmund 1977, appendix. By incorporation, the territory and the population of Dortmund grew by a percentage of 11 and 16 (1.4.1905), 80 and 15 (10.6.1914), 35 and 4 (1.4.1918), 154 and 41 (1.4.1928), 42 and 15 (1.8.1929); same source. See Wolfgang R. Krabbe, 'Eingemeindungsprobleme vor dem Ersten Weltkrieg: Motive, Wider-stände und Verfahrensweise', *Die Alte Stadt* 7 (1980), 368–87.

8. Cf. Hein Hoebink, *Mehr Raum – mehr Macht. Preußische Kommunalpolitik und Raumplanung im rheinisch-westfälischen Industriegebiet 1900–1933*, Essen 1990.

9. See Mack Walcker, *German Home Towns. Community, State, and General Estate 1648–1871*, Ithaca and London 1971. More recently, in particular, Josef Mooser has shifted attention to this basic fact which tends to be neglected by urban historians; see: 'Kleinstadt und Land im Industrialisierungsprozeß 1850 bis 1930. Das Beispiel Ostwestfalen', in Manfred Hettling and Claudia Huerkamp (eds.), *Was ist Gesellschaftsgeschichte?*, Munich 1991, 124–34; also: Wilfried Reininghaus, 'Idylle oder Realität? Kleinstädtische Strukturen am Ende des Alten Reiches', *Westfälische Forschungen* 43 (1993), 514–29 and *Informationen zur modernen Stadtgeschichte*, ed. Deutsches Institut für Urbanistik, Berlin, no. 2/1999: 'Kleine Städte'.

10. See Peter Exner, *Ländliche Gesellschaft und Landwirtschaft in Westfalen 1919– 1969*, Paderborn 1997, and Thomas Fliege, *Bauernfamilien zwischen Tradition und Moderne. Eine Ethnographie bäuerlicher Lebensstile*, Frankfurt 1998.

11. On demography, see below, n. 20.

12. Taken from Paul H. Hohenberg and Lynn Hollen Lees, *The Making of Urban Europe 1000–1950*, Cambridge, MA 1985, 219.

13. Hans Heinrich Blotevogel, 'Methodische Probleme der Erfassung städtischer Funktionen und funktionaler Städtetypen anhand quantitativer Analysen der Berufstatistik 1907', in Wilfried Ehbrecht (ed.), *Voraussetzungen und Methoden geschichtlicher Städteforschung*, Cologne and Vienna 1979, 217–69. Among urban geographers, Christaller's 'theory of central places' remains influential; see Walter Christaller, *Die zentralen Orte in Süddeutschland. Eine ökonomisch-geographische Untersuchung über die Gesetzmäßigkeit der Verbreitung und Entwicklung der Siedlungen mit städtischen Funktionen*, Jena 1933, reprint Darmstadt 1968.

14. There is a fine case study on urban growth in the heavy industrial Ruhr region: Heinz Reif, *Die verspätete Stadt. Industrialisierung, städtischer Raum und Politik in Oberhausen 1846–1929*, 2 vols, Cologne and Bonn 1993. Furthermore, see Cäcilia Schmidt, *Bergbau und Verstädterung im Ruhrgebiet. Die Rolle der Bergwerksunternehmen in der Industrialisierung am Beispiel Gelsenkirchen*, Bochum 1987, and especially Detlev Vonde, *Revier der großen Dörfer. Industrialisierung und Stadtentwicklung im Ruhrgebiet*, Essen 1989, where the assumption of a 'deficient urbanization' in the Ruhr area is elaborated.

15. See Klaus Tenfelde, 'Arbeiterfamilie und Geschlechterbeziehungen im Deutschen Kaiserreich', *Geschichte und Gesellschaft* 18 (1992), 179–203.

16. The two most recent elucidations of such budget problems of industrial cities are Lothar Weiß, *Rheinische Großstädte während der Weltwirtschaftskrise (1929–1933). Kommunale Finanz- und Sozialpolitik im Vergleich*, Cologne and Weimar 1999, and Burkhard Zeppenfeld, *Handlungsspielräume städtischer Finanzpolitik. Staatliche Vorgaben und kommunales Interesse in Bochum 1913– 1935*, Essen 1999; an example of a long-term analysis is Hans-Joachim Bohnsack, *Die Finanzverwaltung der Stadt Hamburg. Ihre Geschichte von den*

Anfängen bis zum Ersten Weltkrieg, Hamburg 1992. Generally on city investments see Karl Heinrich Kaufhold, *Investitionen der Städte im 19. und 20. Jahrhundert*, Cologne etc. 1997; on budgets: Jürgen Bolenz, *Wachstum und Strukturwandlungen der kommunalen Ausgaben in Deutschland 1849 bis 1913*, Diss. Freiburg 1965.

17.   Among others, see Klaus Tenfelde, 'Gesellschaft im Wohlfahrtsstaat – Schichten, Klassen und Konflikte', in Karl Teppe and Hans-Ulrich Thamer (eds.), *50 Jahre Nordrhein-Westfalen – Land im Wandel*, Münster 1997, 23–42.

18.   See esp. Reulecke, *Urbanisierung*, Introduction.

19.   On urbanity as a sociological term, see especially Georg Simmel, *Die Großstädte und das Geistesleben*, 1903, reprinted in id., *Brücke und Tür. Essays des Philosophen zur Geschichte, Religion, Kunst und Gesellschaft*, ed. Michael Landmann and Margarethe Suschan, Stuttgart 1957; Louis Wirth, *Urbanism as a Way of Life*, 1938, reprint: id., *On Cities and Social Life. Selected Papers*, Chicago 1964; there are several German translations, see Ulfert Herlyn (ed.), *Stadt und Sozialstruktur*, Munich 1974, 99. 42–66.

20.   See Peter Marschalck, *Bevölkerungsgeschichte Deutschlands im 19. und 20. Jahrhundert*, Frankfurt 1984, 41ff.; Heinz-Gerhard Haupt and Peter Marschalck (eds.), *Städtische Bevölkerungsentwicklung in Deutschland im 19. Jahrhundert. Soziale und demographische Aspekte der Urbanisierung im internationalen Vergleich*, St. Katharinen 1994.

21.   As an example, see Rüdiger Peuckert, *Familienformen im sozialen Wandel*, Opladen 1991. A Munich *Habilitationsschrift* by Merith Niehuss on the development of post-war families in Germany will be published (Göttingen 2002).

22.   See Wolfgang Hardtwig and Klaus Tenfelde (eds.), *Soziale Räume in der Urbanisierung. Studien zur Geschichte Münchens im Vergleich 1850–1933*, Munich 1990.

23.   On urban planning, see Ludwig Grote (ed.), *Die deutsche Stadt im 19. Jahrhundert. Stadtplanung und Stadtgestaltung im industriellen Zeitalter*, Munich 1974, and Juan Rodriguez-Lores and Gerhard Fehl (eds.), *Städtebaureform 1865–1900. Von Licht, Luft und Ordnung in der Stadt der Gründerzeit. Bauordnungen, Zonenplanung und Enteignung*, 2 vols. Hamburg 1985. The field was widened by Anthony Sutcliffe, *Towards the Planned City: Germany, Britain, the United States and France, 1780–1914*, Oxford 1981; the most important case study has been provided by Stefan Fisch, *Stadtplanung im 19. Jahrhundert. Das Beispiel München bis zur Ära Theodor Fischer*, Munich 1988.

24.   There have been only a few studies on city quarters up to now; see especially Stephan Bleek, *Quartierbildung in der Urbanisierung. Das Münchner Westend 189–1933*, Munich 1991. Unfortunately, Volker Wagner's recent book, *Die Doretheenstadt im neunzehnten Jahrhundert. Vom vorstädtischen Wohnviertel barocker Prägung zu einem Teil der modernen Berliner*

City, Berlin 1998, is concerned with architecture rather than social space.

25. Concerning stratification, German studies on the history of single cities mostly follow the example of Wolfgang Köllmann, *Sozialgeschichte der Stadt Barmen im 19. Jahrhundert*, Tübingen 1960.

26. See, e.g., many of the articles collected in the volumes edited by Gall (n. 2); for the end of the century, see also Philipp Sarasin, *Die Stadt der Bürger. Struktureller Wandel und bürgerliche Lebenswelt. Basel 1870–1900*, Basle and Frankfurt 1990.

27. Friedrich Lenger, *Sozialgeschichte der deutschen Handwerker seit 1800*, Frankfurt 1988, 203ff., and Günther Schulz, *Die Angestellten seit dem 19. Jahrhundert*, Munich 2000.

28. See Paul Nolte, *Die Ordnung der deutschen Gesellschaft. Selbstentwurf und Selbstbeschreibung im 20. Jahrhundert*, Munich 2000, 318ff.

29. Although much research has been devoted to the 'constitutional' history of German cities, usually praising the achievements of 'communal self-administration' and linking administrative efficiency to Freiherr vom Stein, I deliberately do not cover this field here. See Henning Gröttrup, *Die kommunale Selbstverwaltung. Grundlagen der gemeindlichen Daseinsvorsorge*, Stuttgart etc. 1973; Bernhard Kirchgässner and Jörg Schadt (eds.), *Kommunale Selbstverwaltung – Idee und Wirklichkeit*, Sigmaringen 1983; as a source book: Christian Engeli and Wolfgang Haus (eds.), *Quellen zum modernen Gemeinverfassungsrecht in Deutschland*, Stuttgart 1975. As a social history of communal elites, still to be mentioned: Wolfgang Hofmann, *Die Bielefelder Stadtverordneten. Ein Beitrag zur bürgerlichen Selbstverwaltung und zum sozialen Wandel 1850–1914*, Lübeck 1964.

30. This field has been of major interest recently: Wolfgang Krabbe, *Kommunalpolitik und Industrialisierung. Die Entfaltung der städtischen Leistungsverwaltung im 19. und 20. Jahrhundert. Fallstudien zu Dortmund und Münster*, Stuttgart etc. 1985; as an introduction: id., 'Die Entfaltung der kommunalen Leistungsverwaltung in deutschen Städten des 19. Jahrhunderts', in Teuteberg (ed.), *Urbanisierung*, 373–91. On health and social policies ('the welfare city'): Jürgen Reulecke (ed.), *Die Stadt als Dienstleistungszentrum. Beiträge zur Geschichte der 'Sozialstadt' in Deutschland im 19. und frühen 20. Jahrhundert*, St. Katharinen 1995; id. (ed.), *Stadtgeschichte als Zivilisationsgeschichte. Beiträge zum Wandel städtischer Wirtschafts-, Lebens- und Wahrnehmungsweisen*, Essen 1990; id. and Adelheid Gräfin zu Castell-Rüdenhausen (eds.), *Stadt und Gesundheit. Zum Wandel von 'Volksgesundheit' und kommunaler Gesundheitspolitik im 19. und frühen 20. Jahrhundert*, Stuttgart 1991; Beate Witzler, *Großstadt und Hygiene. Kommunale Gesundheitspolitik in der Epoche der Urbanisierung*, Stuttgart 1995 (compares six major cities); Ralf Stremmel, *'Gesundheit – unser einziger Reichtum'? Kommunale Gesundheitspolitik 1800–1945 am Beispiel Solingen*, Solingen 1993; Ingo Tamm, *Die Entwicklung des öffentlichen Gesundheitswesens an Beispielen aus Hannover und Linden (1850–1914). Ein Beitrag zur*

Urbanisierungsforschung, Tecklenburg 1992; Hedwig Brüchert-Schunk, *Städtische Sozialpolitik vom Wilhelminischen Reich bis zur Weltwirtschaftskrise. Eine sozial- und kommunalhistorische Untersuchung am Beispiel der Stadt Mainz 1890–1930*, Stuttgart 1994; Martin Weyer-von Schoultz, *Stadt und Gesundheit im Ruhrgebiet. Verstädterung und kommunale Gesundheitspolitik dargestellt am Beispiel der jungen Industriestadt Gelsenkirchen*, Essen 1994; important, though voluminous: Wilfried Rudloff, *Die Wohlfahrtsstadt. Kommunale Ernährungs-, Fürsorge- und Wohnungspolitik am Beispiel Münchens 1910–1933*, 2 vols. Göttingen 1998. Increasingly, the field is covered by environmental historians: Jürgen Büschefeld, *Deutsche Flüsse oder deutsche Kloaken? Städtehygiene und Gewässerschutz in Preußen (1870–1918) zwischen Wasserversorgung und Abwasserbeseitigung*, Diss. Bielefeld 1994; on water supply and sewage also: Peter Münch, *Stadthygiene im 19. und 20. Jahrhundert. Die Wasserversorgung, Abwasser- und Abfallbeseitigung unter besonderer Berücksichtigung Münchens*, Göttingen 1993. Generally on economic activities of cities: Hans Pohl (ed.), *Kommunale Unternehmen. Geschichte und Gegenwart*, Stuttgart 1987; as an example: Hans-Dieter Brunkhorst, *Kommunalisierung im 19. Jahrhundert, dargestellt am Beispiel der Gaswirtschaft*, Munich 1978. On food markets, Hans-Jürgen Teuteberg (ed.), *Durchbruch zum modernen Massenkonsum. Lebensmittelmärkte im Städtewachstum des Industriezeitalters*, Münster 1981. On energies recently: Dieter Schott (ed.), *Energie und Stadt in Europa. Von der vorindustriellen 'Holznot' bis zur Ölkrise der 1970er Jahre*, Stuttgart 1997. On urban traffic, no major recent work has come to my knowledge, but see Karl Heinrich Kaufhold, 'Straßenbahnen im Deutschen Reich vor 1914. Wachstum, Verkehrsleistung, wirtschaftliche Verhältnisse', in Dietmar Petzina and Jürgen Reulecke (eds.), *Bevölkerung, Wirtschaft, Gesellschaft seit der Industrialisierung*, Dortmund 1990, 219–38, and generally: John P. McKay, *Tramways and Trolleys. The Rise of Urban Mass Transport in Europe*, Princeton 1976.

31. See, e.g., the remarks of Brian Ladd, *Urban Planning and Civic Order in Germany, 1860–1914*, Cambridge/Mass. and London 1990, 9 and *passim*.

32. See Otto Dann (ed.), *Vereinswesen und bürgerliche Gesellschaft*, Munich 1984; Klaus Tenfelde, 'Civil Society and the Middle Classes in Nineteenth-Century Germany', in Philipp Nord and Nancy Bermeo (eds.), *Civil Society before Democracy. Lessons from Nineteenth-century Europe*, Lanham 2000, 83–108.

33. See, for instance, James Sheehan, 'Liberalism and the City in Nineteenth-Century Germany', in *Past & Present* 51 (1971), 116–37; the story varies according to the territory: see the examples analysed in Friedrich Lenger, 'Bürgertum und Stadtverwaltung in rheinischen Großstädten des 19. Jahrhunderts. Zu einem vernachlässigten Aspekt bürgerlicher Herrschaft', in Gall (ed.), *Stadt und Bürgertum*, 97–169; Paul Nolte, 'Bürgerideal, Gemeinde und Republik. "Klassischer Republikanismus" im frühen deutschen Liberalismus', *Historische Zeitschrift* 254 (1992), 609–56.

34. See Hermann Beckstein, *Städtische Interessenpolitik. Organisation und Politik der Städtetage in Bayern, Preußen und dem Deutschen Reich 1896–1923*, Düsseldorf 1991.

35. Important: Manfred Smuda (ed.), *Die Großstadt als 'Text'*, Munich 1992.

36. See Peter Jelavich, *Berlin Cabaret*, Cambridge/Mass. 1993; Joachim Schlör, *Nachts in der großen Stadt*, Munich 1991.

37. See Pitrim Sorokin and Carle C. Zimmermann, *Principles of Rural-Urban Sociology*, New York 1929, 56f. and *passim*, which comprises of many tables and comparisons, but does not deal with urban–rural conflicts. Cf. two more recent articles: Christoph Nonn, 'Arbeiter, Bürger und "Agrarier": Stadt–Land-Gegensatz und Klassenkonflikt im Wilhelmin-ischen Deutschland am Beispiel des Königreichs Sachsen', in Helga Grebing et al. (eds.), *Demokratie und Emanzipation zwischen Saale und Elbe*, Essen 1993, 101–13; Klaus Tenfelde, 'Stadt und Land in Krisenzeiten. München und das Münchner Umland zwischen Revolution und Inflation 1918 bis 1923', in Hardtwig and Tenfelde (eds.), *Soziale Räume*, 37–57.

38. See Klaus Bergmann, *Agarromantik und Großstadtfeindschaft*, Meisenheim, 1970, and Andrew Lees, *Cities Perceived: Urban Society in European and American Thought 1820–1940*, New York 1985; Dirk Schubert, 'Großstadt-feindschaft und Stadtplanung. Neue Anmerkungen zu einer alten Diskussion', in Die Alte Stadt 13 (1986), 22–41; Wolfgang Sofsky, 'Schreckbild Stadt. Stationen der modernen Stadtkritik', ibid. 1–21. It is interesting to follow up how the city has been mirrored in literature and poetry. See Oskar Hübner and Johannes Moegelin (eds.), *'Im steinernen Meer'. Großstadtgedichte*, Berlin 1910 (preface provided by Theodor Heuss, in 1949 the first President of the Federal Republic of Germany); Waltraud Wende (ed.), *Großstadtlyrik*, Stuttgart 1999.

39. See Gerald D. Feldman, *The Great Disorder. Politics, Economics, and Society in the German Inflation, 1914–1924*, New York and Oxford 1997, 188ff. and *passim*; a terrific case study has been provided by Martin H. Geyer, *Verkehrte Welt. Revolution, Inflation und Moderne: München 1914–1924*, Göttingen 1998.

40. Influential: Alexander Mitscherlich, *Die Unwirtlichkeit unserer Städte. Anstiftungen zum Unfrieden*, 1961, 16th ed. Frankfurt 1982; more recently: Wolf Jobst Siedler, *Stadtgedanken*, Munich 1990; other critics such as Henry Lefèbvre and Richard Sennett have been translated into German.

41. See Klaus Schreiner, 'Die Stadt des Mittelalters als Faktor bürgerlicher Identitätsbildung – Zur Gegenwärtigkeit des mittelalterlichen Stadt-bürgertums im historisch-politischen Bewußtsein des 18., 19. und beginnenden 20. Jahrhunderts', in C. Meckseper (ed.), *Stadt im Wandel*, vol. 4, Stuttgart 1985, 517–41.

GISELA METTELE

Burgher Cities on the Road to a Civil Society: Germany 1780 to 1870

The Research Project 'Stadt und Bürgertum im 19. Jahr-hundert', which will be described below, was initiated by Lothar Gall at the University of Frankfurt am Main in 1988 and ran until 1996. It was an extensive comparative study of the historical origins and milieus of the German *Bürgertum*[1] as the key to an understanding of the nineteenth-century political, socio-economic and cultural make-up that brought about the transition from the corporate world to the modern age of the *Bürgertum*. The project's central hypothesis was that the *Bürgertum* was created and defined by processes of social communication and interaction in the cities. Consequently, the aim was to uncover the social networks which established the cohesion of the *Bürgertum* and which also made it possible for individual citizens to experience it. The single-minded concentration on individual component groups of the *Bürgertum*, such as entrepreneurs, members of the educated classes or artisans, or on single aspects, as for example economic trends, cultural activities or education, which until then was common in studies of the German *Bürgertum*, was abandoned in favour of a larger perspective. Thus it was possible to explore the progress of the constitution of modern civil society in connection with economic, political as well as cultural factors and their interplay. Amongst the various factors that characterized the *Bürgertum* in the nineteenth century the focus was placed on the following:

1. The *Bürgerrecht* ('burgher-right') as the central constituent factor of middle-class society in the traditional sense and its continuing significance (different in the various cities) in the nineteenth century.

2. Voluntary associations as the most important medium of social interaction and communication for the *Bürgertum* in the nineteenth century.
3. The economic position and
4. the assumption of political representation in the local self-governing body.[2]

The computer-based analysis of different quantitative sources, such as directories, tax lists, lists of inhabitants with political rights, lists of elected representatives on local councils or assemblies, lists of members of different voluntary associations, chambers of commerce, trade associations, etc. was an important part of the methodology. These data were compiled in machine-readable form (where possible) and linked on the basis of individual persons. In many cases this alone produced an astonishingly vivid picture of a person, his or her public activities, career and social standing. Furthermore, it was thus possible to paint a very detailed picture of the personal composition of the social networks of a city. The diversity of sources made it possible to study the processes of social interaction in which the *Bürgertum* was formed and defined from different angles. By linking the data, connections between the different areas could be discovered. This linking of information takes into account the fact that the protagonists interacted in a variety of institutions and their lives touched on various scenes.

In addition to the quantitative sources, qualitative analysis of very different sources such as petitions, association reports, newspapers, biographical literature and material from family archives was undertaken. In every case the history of the individual city with its specific conflicts, as well as the economic and institutional conditions and prospects, of influence were, of course, taken into account.

Another change from previous historical studies was the team-based approach: fifteen historians each carried out detailed research on one city based on the same set of questions.[3] From the outset through the entire project the methods of analysis were agreed upon in detail in order to ensure comparability of the results.

The selection of the cities was based on the consideration that they belong to specific types, all of which had to be represented. The construction of the different types was based on the dominating political, economic and social structural characteristics that largely determined the development of the individual city: the principal economic areas, the political constitution, the size, denominational structure, location, transport links, etc. Thus it was possible to distinguish between merchant cities, capital cities (Residenzstädte), administrative cities, university cities, early industrial commercial cities and industrial cities. These types, however, were not regarded as static, but as progressive. They had to accommodate the dominance of a certain structure for a certain period of time as well as the transformation process. The assumption was that these structural characteristics exerted a decisive influence on the social make-up of the *Bürgertum*, its ways of living, mentalities and relations to other social groups in the city. Any generalizations drawn prematurely would blur the individual characteristics. Thus with the creation of structural types we attempted to find a happy medium between abstract generalizations, which appear inadequate for historical research on the one hand, and an individualizing perspective on the other, which would result in writing merely the biography of a city.

What did the *Bürgertum* of very differently structured city societies have in common? Here, I would like to elaborate a few points although many particulars and details have to be omitted in an attempt to assess the overall developments on the basis of fifteen individual studies.[4]

Perhaps the most important result of the survey was the discovery of the German *Bürger*[5] as a political animal in contrast to the standard image of the member of the middle class of this period, who is usually thought of as a very apolitical person with essentially domestic interests. During the nineteenth century the *Bürgertum* was for the most part not involved in governmental decision-making processes, but it did not withdraw into a Biedermeier-like idyll. It was in the domain of the city that the *Bürgertum* was seen to take its affairs into its own hands. The essay will give a picture of some elements of self-organization that existed in the nineteenth century in the German cities. It will focus on communal self-government, the communal welfare system and the different voluntary associations that emerged in the period and in particular it will attempt to show the ways in which women contributed to the 'male' theatre of middle-class public life and politics.

I

In the traditional city society the *Bürgertum* was clearly defined by communal law as the group who held the *Bürgerrecht*, a right which identified them as an economically and politically privileged class in contrast to the other inhabitants. Only those endowed with the *Bürgerrecht* were allowed to participate in political decisions, that is, to vote in local elections, to be elected to the local council or to hold an office in the local administration. In order to be able to acquire the legal status of burgher one had to be a 'resident' householder in the community, economically 'independent' and married. In all cities the nucleus of the community of *Bürger* consisted of merchants and craftsmen, who were organized in guilds.[6] A woman was a *Bürger* by sharing her husband's status; she herself had no political rights, but was represented by her husband as the patriarchal head of the household. In the early modern age, there was also an individual *Bürgerrecht* for unmarried women, yet this granted them only certain economic privileges. Political rights, however, were not extended to women in any city.[7]

The *Bürgerrecht* established the male *Bürger* as a mature individual and a responsible political subject. The *Bürgertum*'s understanding of politics was marked by a 'co-operative' (*genossenschaftlich*) spirit, i.e. it was based on the self-government and self-regulation of the political community of the *Bürgertum*, which was regarded as a community of householders with equal rights. This obviously was a somewhat idealistic self-perception, but it nevertheless represented a powerful mental concept. By the end of the eighteenth century, the degree of actual self-government varied in the different types of cities, but the demand for the principle existed everywhere.

For the German *Bürgertum* the ability to govern their own affairs was a constituent part of their status, and it was something they laid claim to in the nineteenth century. During the period from 1815 to the March Revolution of 1848 (*Vormärz*) the city took on increasing significance as the 'co-operatively-based (*genossenschaftlich*) middle-class counterpoise to the state'.[8] This dualism of society and state was not, as Hegel understood it, a dualism between opposing private interests in society ('system of needs') and a state which embodied the 'reality of the moral idea', but rather a dualism between self-confident citizens who felt competent to participate in the construction of the entire social order and a state which did not intend to allow them this influence.

In the *Vormärz* period, '*Gemeindefreiheit*', the independence of the local bodies of self-government from the central state, became one of the essential demands of the liberal reform movement that was supported by almost all levels of society in the cities.[9] In contrast to the eighteenth century, however, the citizens no longer limited their political demands to the issue of local autonomy; now the idea of local self-administration was linked to the idea of a liberal transformation of the entire community. The city became the prototype for the social order as a whole. Here in the city one could witness the realization of constitutionalism at least in principle, a concept which the reformers wanted to extend to the entire state.[10] The political concept behind the term *Gemeindefreiheit* was the belief in the possibility of self-organization of the entire society and the emancipation from the bureaucratic or paternalistic state, which made decisions for its subjects.

In the *Vormärz* period '*Bürgersinn*' – public spirit – became a byword for traditions of the *Bürgertum*, interpreted in an emancipatory manner. *Bürgersinn* did not only refer to political self-determination but in a more comprehensive and quite practical sense the commitment to supra-individual aims and tasks – in other words, a sense of civic duty. This concept went back to the ideal of a largely pre-industrial society with a unified and integrated middle class. It was precisely this integrative thrust which was one of the strong pillars of early German liberalism.[11]

Who were the pillars of local self-administration? For the period of research, for each of the cities involved practically all who held municipal offices were traced and their professional and social status was determined with the help of directories and tax lists. Regardless of the type of city, our research showed that in the first decade of the nineteenth century the seats in the city council of practically every city were filled by wealthy merchants and bankers and in early industrialized places, for example Aachen, by manufacturers. Artisans were hardly able to assert their traditional claim to political representation on these councils any longer. The educated classes were scarcely represented either. In the 1830s artisans, innkeepers or brewers took up posts in the councils of several cities, for example Munich, Karlsruhe and Mannheim. A comparison with tax lists, however, shows that only the wealthy artisans managed to get into key political positions. In places where artisans did not prosper, for example in Cologne and Aachen, they did not participate in the city council or the citizens' assembly.[12]

In the nineteenth century the individual tax payments became the yardstick for opportunities for political involvement. As a result of the influence of the state as well as reform debates within the cities, the old *Bürgerrecht*, which many cities held on to well into the second

half of the nineteenth century – in Munich the holders of the
Bürgerrecht were a clearly defined group even until 1918 – changed
into a system of constitutional rights, which were based on individual
economic achievements. In cities where the *Bürgerrecht* no longer
existed in the nineteenth century, for example Cologne or Aachen,
the census and the three-class electoral systems (*Dreiklassenwahlrecht*)
secured the predominance of wealthy businessmen on the local
councils. In most cities, however, the social differentiations and
economic privileges of the old *Bürgerrecht* were abolished during the
first half of the century, and the *Bürgerrecht* was reduced to the political
right to vote in local elections. It should be pointed out, though, that
Jews continued to be excluded; in most cases they did not win
emancipation until the second half of the century.[13]

In the eyes of contemporary liberals, the limitation of political
participation by means of a census or taxes which citizens were
required to pay to qualify for the *Bürgerrecht* did not conflict with the
demand for equal participation in society's decision-making procedures. For liberals there was no doubt that the possession of the
franchise had to be linked to economic prosperity – in accordance
with the old ideal of personal independence. However, their belief in
progress led, at least in the first half of the century, to the optimistic
assumption that in the not too distant future social conditions were
to be expected under which most, if not all, men would be able to
meet these economic qualifications. In many regions of Germany the
notion of such a 'classless society of middle-income *Bürger*' was
nourished by a still largely pre-industrial social structure in which
the differences in income were not that significant. A considerable
degree of ignorance of the conditions of the lower classes had always
been an integral part of this model.

However, as regards the openness of the *Bürger* society, the extent
to which the tax qualifications for the *Bürgerrecht* or, in resident
communities, the census excluded the lower classes is crucial. In this
respect the cities in Baden went furthest. Here since 1831 approximately four-fifths of all male adults possessed the local *Bürgerrecht*
and, hence, the right to vote. In Heilbronn in Württemberg the
proportion of families with *Bürgerrecht* was also over 70 per cent of all
residents in 1830. Here the 'classless society of middle-income *Bürger*'
was not just an ideal, but a 'social experiment' – particularly in Baden
where the group of people holding the *Bürgerrecht* was consciously
enlarged. The extension of the circle of citizens with voting rights
created the most favourable conditions for the *Bürgertum* in Baden to

establish itself as an independent political force. However, to a certain extent the idea of a broad middle-class society also corresponded to a socio-structural reality. In the cities of the Rhineland, where industrialization was introduced earlier and the proportion of lower-class people in the city's population increased rapidly, the group of those with voting rights (in relation to families) sank rapidly to approximately 20–30 per cent of the population. Here an exclusion policy had already begun in the first half of the century, and was continued and cemented after the Revolution.

Prior to the Revolution, however, even in a city like Cologne, these tendencies towards disintegration were balanced by a political under-standing, in which, on the one hand, corporate city traditions still prevailed – despite all changes of the law – and according to which, on the other, the state was still regarded as the principal political opponent. Both factors made the periodical formation of large alliances between middle-class artisans, shopkeepers, wealthy merch-ants, bankers and manufacturers possible in the first half of the nineteenth century.[14] While in the Southern German *Bürger* communi-ties those alliances represented genuine coalitions on the basis of a largely pre-industrial understanding of society, in Cologne they were most frequently the result of merely tactical considerations. However, in all cities the 'unity of the community of *Bürger*' was an important argument against the state's claim to dominate and rule the cities, and for this reason alone conflicts within the cities were controlled by means of political compromises or economic concessions.[15]

From the 1830s onwards, most cities experienced a process of political mobilization. The campaigns for the elections of a variety of local assemblies (with sometimes several hundred members) led to lasting 'political alertness'.[16] Election committees, meetings of citizens, voluntary associations as well as public festivities, which were frequently attended by thousands of visitors from different cities, banquets in honour of members of the state parliament (*Landtags-abgeordnete*) and petition campaigns were the most important forms of expression of this politicization at a local level, in which a political middle-class public was established. Without these local spheres of political experience for the development of an informed political opinion it is impossible to explain the quick organization of the *Bürgertum* during the Revolution.[17]

Under a 'liberal' banner, the joint opposition to the state could unite many things that appeared incompatible after the Revolution. Even Carl D'Ester, who was the confidant of Karl Marx in Cologne and a member of the communist league was called a man of 'liberal spirit' ('*freisinnig*') when he was elected as a councillor in Cologne in 1846.[18]

The social and political opposites that emerged during the Revolution made it clear that the ideal of a future 'classless society' was no longer tenable. The democratization of society would not result in the emergence of a general '*Bürger* society', but would substantially threaten the social environment of the *Bürgertum*. In the local election debates of the second half of the century the concept of political citizenship was used in a more and more reactionary way against the claims of other social groups. After the Revolution efforts in all cities were aimed at securing the predominance of the propertied class and new communal bylaws restricted the opportunities to participate by increasing the tax qualifications for voting rights.[19] The weighting in the municipal bodies shifted once again in favour of the merchants and, alongside the process of industrialization, more and more in favour of financiers and industrialists as well. Even in the cities of Baden, such as Mannheim and Karlsruhe, the proportion of artisans in the self-administration bodies fell drastically and the local political alliance between merchants and artisans gave way to the power of the leading merchants and industrialists, who – although they were still concerned with constraining the state's possibilities of intervention and supervision – came to a certain *modus vivendi* with the state, which was now expected to support the rejection of lower-class groups' claims to participation.

II

Women were excluded from political participation and the institutional nexus before and after the Revolution. And they were excluded on principle. Although at least in the first half of the century the liberal constitutional movement may have believed in a broad integration of the politically and socially disadvantaged lower classes into a future 'classless society of "middle-income-bracket" citizens', as far as women were concerned, there was no comparable conception foreseeing their emancipation and integration. In relation to women, even the early liberal model for the future had generally already jettisoned the utopia of the classless, legally egalitarian middle-class society. The enfranchisement of women was not even included in the long-term liberal agenda. Because of the continued existence of the idea that society should be formed by the independent male householders the middle-class liberals could principally even more easily imagine the political emancipation of lower-class men – of course not instantly, but by improving their conditions up to the point where they could meet the requirements of an independent male householder – than they could imagine the political emancipation of middle-class women.

Men's and women's worlds were two separate spheres, or at least that was the ideology of the middle-class family. The woman was supposed to be the guardian of the refuge to which the man could retreat from the everyday battle in a 'hostile world'. While she helped to recharge his batteries and guaranteed family cohesion, the man was the woman's link to the social environment.[20] In the social environment of the cities, however, women did not necessarily conform to this conceptual model. Actual relations between the sexes deviated from the normative ideal. The lack of formal political rights by no means prevented women from getting involved in the emerging middle-class public sphere. At an early date women were already organizing themselves in voluntary associations. The work of women's organizations was usually associated with charity. In the area of social welfare in particular, women were developing a broad spectrum of activities in the nineteenth century, beginning with patriotic women's associations in 1813–14, maternal care associations or poor girls' schools (from the mid-1820s onwards).[21]

In the nineteenth century care for the poor was an important part of local self-administration.[22] In some cities, and I will use Cologne as an example, poor law administration was in fact the largest department of municipal administration. The welfare system was regarded as the 'expression of specifically middle-class self-assertion and a capacity of self-organization independent of the state' and the state's influence was seen as an infringement on citizens' freedom.[23] As late as the 1850s the social reformer Wilhelm Adolf Lette represented the liberal opinion that governments must abstain from 'wanting to take decisions from above concerning the social conditions of people's lives like the long arm of the law.'[24] On the other hand, the *local* system of poor relief was hardly an object of liberal criticism in the nineteenth century.

The welfare system in the German cities was modernized in the nineteenth century, i.e. systematic and preventive measures such as poor schools, improvements of the infrastructure, etc. were introduced as an alternative to just helping in acute situations of need. But this changed concept still was connected to the traditions of the old burgher cities. The core of the new concept was a system of social control through so-called 'Armenpfleger' (carers for the poor), who regularly inspected the houses of designated poor families. This system became known in the 1850s as the 'Elberfelder System', but had been practised in many cities as early as the first half of the century. It makes clear the extent to which the role of urban society was still viewed in paternalistic terms.

Comparing the German poor-law system with England, Jürgen Reulecke comes to the following conclusion, when he refers to an official city visit of English local politicians to German cities in the second half of the nineteenth century: 'If one had [. . .] tried to explain the theory of a German "deficit" of public spirit to one of the English observers of the German poor-law system, one would have certainly come across a complete lack of understanding, since they did not see a deficit, but – viewed from their own English mentality – rather a surplus.'[25] This means that apart from concrete disciplinary interests the ideological principle of the municipal welfare system was based on a municipal middle-class way of understanding oneself and was nourished by the awareness of local solidarity. Especially in this sphere the city was still perceived as a corporate association marked by 'community spirit', in which the individual had duties to the community. In the nineteenth century this idea did not only exist in the southern German *'Bürger* communities'; this notion continued to exist even in the residents' communities of the nineteenth century, as for example Cologne. Even there the community was recognized as a place 'in which people need one another and the wealthy take responsibility for the poor in times of need', as the Cologne Patriotic Women's Association put it in 1814.[26] This concept made it the duty of the citizen to help another in times of need, but of course it did not question the social differences. It also did not apply to all the poor of the city, but only to the group of so-called 'shamefaced' poor (*verschämte Hausarme*), often impoverished members of the old middle-class *Bürger* society. The nineteenth century saw harsher treatment than ever of beggars and vagabonds, the 'shameless' poor, who were not afraid to take action when the security of their livelihood was at stake.[27] Beggar hunts and the establishment of penitentiaries and workhouses aimed at the exclusion of these poor people from city society, not their integration. Repression and criminalization were the other face of the communal 'welfare' system, and the workhouse became the 'compulsory measure of middle-class society'.[28] By contrast the 'shamefaced poor' received the 'pleasant burden' (*violence douce*, Pierre Bourdieu) of care services which kept them from utter poverty, but also removed from them the potential for violence which could possibly have turned them into a 'dangerous class'.

Voluntary social work by female citizens was an important part of the network of local welfare, but it was not linked, as it was for male citizens, to any political rights. And yet the women did acquire social power in the charitable societies, which they did not otherwise have in the middle-class public sphere. Indeed, it can even be said that women's charities were a constituent part of middle-class domination of the city. Far better than their men, who were involved in their professions, women could devote themselves personally to the inte-grative task of local welfare. While the man was outside in the 'hostile world', the 'lady of the house' not only presided over the domestic hearth, but also took care to ensure that the domestic society did not crack at the seams in the meantime. [29]

Women's public activities had a profound influence on urban realities in a wide variety of respects, be it through the socio-political impact of the activities themselves or through the events that were necessary to finance these activities, such as raffles, concerts and balls. The women's associations were integrated in the social network that comprised the city's public life, not least through the mobilization of other city associations for the purpose of financial support.

The forms of public activity practised in the first half of the nineteenth century – the organization of benefit concerts, door-to-door collections, the making of lint bandages, donations of jewellery and especially the raffles – also define the pattern of political action on the part of women in the 1848 Revolution. Demands for their own emancipation as women were not formulated in most of the women's associations. A pronounced feminist view was not a prerequisite for involvement in the political process. The public activities of middle-class women were rather based on a sense of responsibility for the 'common weal' within the confines of the middle-class perspective of reality. But at the end of the nineteenth century this became an important argument of the middle-class feminist movement for admit-ting women to municipal offices and granting them the right to vote. The honorary work done in the local welfare system qualified the woman as a citizen with independent political rights. As the women's rights activist Helene Lange put it in 1904:

'Let us imagine [. . .] the question why the topic the woman as a citizen is of practical interest today. The answer would be: because today the woman

actually *is* a citizen; because the woman [...] has emerged from the
dependence of her intellectual and economic being and participates in the
ideological and economic population as a whole; because she has already
begun in the area of social work to take on board as an individual duty
those tasks which officially fall to society as a whole. If this development
is to be a blessing for her herself and society at large, then the system of
laws for public life must also acknowledge her as a citizen.[30]

Helene Lange's argument sums up what the concept of citizenship
meant to her contemporaries even at the beginning of the twentieth
century: independence in the material and figurative sense, honorary
work for 'public welfare' and consequently the right to a voice in the
political decision-making processes. I hope that, against the background of what has been said at the beginning of this essay, the extent
to which this still relates to the old perception of the *Bürger* has been
made clear. But at the same time, the women's voluntary associations
point to a further constituent factor of modern civil society that was
given central significance in the Frankfurt research project.

III

By the end of the eighteenth century, a fundamentally new
kind of constitution of the *Bürgertum* apart from legal regulation had
already emerged in the cities. In the medium of social intercourse,
forms of communication and interaction had been established, which
stood out from the traditional corporate structural principles of
society. 'Free association' was a key slogan of the time, which through
its emphasis on voluntary participation was in direct opposition both
to the paternalistic organization of the state and to compulsory
membership of guilds. [31] The principle behind the concept of association was the notion of self-organization in society. 'Without any help
from the state administrative body [...] but emerging directly from
the needs [...] of the people [...] the associations, organizations and
alliances' should be created, 'in which neither status, wealth nor any
other particular mission, but rather efficiency, capability and endeav-
ouring to be useful to the community have sole validity'.[32] Here the
new middle-class ideal is summed up very programmatically: Society
should be formed by the free association of equal individuals, without
regard of their social status, origin and occupation. The idea of an
association (*Verein*) stood for the place in which the society of *Bürger*
gathered in contrast to the sphere of the state. In everyday life it

underlined the right of the *Bürgertum* to social emancipation. Activities in voluntary associations became a characteristic of 'true public spirit'.[33] This was a concept of life that was not limited to professional or materialistic interests but finds its expression in the meeting of the arts and sciences, in the participation in social life and the concern for the common good. Only thus was it possible to prove one's citizenship in relation to what was understood by the notion at the time.[34] Even if the associations did not pursue any clear political goals in the first half of the century – which was hardly possible given the existing conditions of censorship – their structure alone with internal elections and set rules of procedure on speaking rights and the postulated openness over and above social status showed that here the ideal of a future society was to be modelled and shaped.

Around the beginning of the nineteenth century, in most cities a new kind of association had taken the place of the culture of the reading societies and Masonic lodges of the eighteenth century.[35] A different understanding of the concept of self-education was beginning to emerge, which involved 'self-formation' (*Bildung*) through awareness of one's own creative possibilities. Therefore the enlightening impetus of reading gatherings, organized lectures which was typical of the Lodges and the literary societies, gave way to leisure pursuits, musical practice, the occupation with fine arts or just playing games.[36]

From the 1830s onwards, voluntary associations developed widely. According to Thomas Nipperdey, the willingness to gather in associations gave way to a kind of passion for clubs and societies: 'all middle-class activity was organized in voluntary associations'.[37] The motives for the foundation of such associations were varied, in keeping with the increasingly complex society. 'For one person the representation of his economic interests in a trade association was the decisive link. For another person it was the love of music. And for another perhaps enthusiasm for the new forms of physical exercise.'[38]

These developments occurred surprisingly in parallel in various cities even as far as the names of the associations are concerned. Either the founding of an association in one city followed the example set by others, or the association was organized on a national basis anyway, as in the case of the male choral societies or the gymnastic clubs, in a network of local associations linked, for example, by joint national events. This all shows how much people saw themselves as part of a wider middle-class public. Of course, in the smaller or less dynamic cities fewer associations were founded and in comparison with the larger commercial and industrial cities their foundation often tended to lag behind, as it was certainly the case in capital cities (*Residenzstädte*), where it was more difficult for the social life of the *Bürgertum* to establish itself in the face of a culture which was dominated by the court.

Most voluntary associations did not adopt a self-satisfied attitude; rather they brought to bear their influence in strong measure on the society in which they existed and a large proportion of city cultural life was carried by them. Concert associations held regular musical performances; the municipal theatres were often financed and run by theatre societies; art societies organized exhibitions and supported artists by purchasing their works. Important art galleries and museums, symphony orchestras and theatres emerged from these activities of the *Bürgertum*, for example the Leipzig Gewandhaus Orchestra, the Senckenberg Research Institute in Frankfurt am Main or the Wallraf-Richartz Museum in Cologne. Numerous social, economic and political reform initiatives were carried out by associations of the *Bürgertum* or at least initiated and co-financed by them, such as hospitals and institutes for the deaf and dumb, savings banks and insurance companies and even the construction of the railway.[39] The different political associations, which arose in the cities during and after the 1848 Revolution, soon joined, on a regional and then a national level, to form political parties. Consequently, in this respect also the modern society of the *Bürgertum* was constructed out of the local base.

The personal connections between the individual associations of a city were for the most part 'tight-knit', and in the 'social round' of one association people often met up again with someone they already knew from other social contexts. In Cologne, for example, half of the members of the theatre society also belonged to the art society, which in turn always sold some of the tickets for its exhibitions in aid of the Cathedral Construction Association. Furthermore, the Cologne Steamship Company, many of whose board members were also association members, granted their art society free transportation of pieces of work sent to the exhibitions and the city administration, whose members as a rule were active in various voluntary associations, allowed the use of the city hall free of charge.[40] This shows that the activities of the individual city associations did not stand isolated from one another, but that a kind of network emerged. This close social contact guaranteed middle-class cohesion and made the abstract social term *Bürgertum* 'something which citizens could experience first-hand in their daily lives'.[41]

The computer-aided analysis of the associations' lists of members illustrated this social network. Combined with the information gathered from directories and tax lists as to professional status and economic power of the individual members, it became very clear who was associated with whom in this 'new' middle-class society. A picture of the classes that were excluded also emerged, since the middle-class associations were socially open more often the case in theory than in practice. The acceptance of new members after a ballot (*Ballotage*), or even the high membership contributions alone, secured the social exclusiveness of most of the associations. The fact that economic bankruptcy led directly to exclusion was frequently laid down in the regulations. The membership structure of the associations reflected the structure of the new *Bürgertum*, a class which regarded itself as a new social elite based on individual contributions, which were now first and foremost measured in economic terms.

In the associations that came into existence in the first decades of the nineteenth century the majority of members were wealthy merchants, bankers and manufacturers. The artisan core of the traditional *Bürgertum* was effectively not represented in the new associations. However, in Frankfurt or Cologne for example, Jews, who did not possess the old *Bürgerrecht*, were accepted into the clubs and societies. Even the Cologne Cathedral Construction Association admitted Jewish members. But in some other cities, such as Mannheim or Karlsruhe, Jews were refused membership of the associations. As a result they founded parallel associations themselves. [42]

The social spectrum of the associations that emerged in the 1830s was significantly wider. In many cities, wealthy merchants and middle-class artisans were involved in the same music and art societies. In the sphere of fine arts social dividing lines apparently could be disregarded most easily, and it was possible to maintain an ideal picture of municipal middle-class unity and social harmony, a fact which not least accounted for the huge significance which these associations possessed in city life. By contrast, the Casino, an exclusive men's club which existed in almost every city, only united the economic and political leaders of the city society even in the *Vormärz* period. [43] The fact that this central city association attempted to reduce the fee to achieve a social 'opening' and wide municipal middle-class integration, for example in Karlsruhe, remained an exception.

In the associations of the large commercial and industrial cities it was not the 'educated class' in the narrower sense of the academically educated that was predominant but rather businessmen, wealthy large-scale merchants and bankers, and later also industrial manufacturers and entrepreneurs. In capital cities (*Residenzstädte*) and administrative cities such as Munich, Karlsruhe or Münster, the proportion of civil servants in the associations was comparatively large. In university towns such as Göttingen and Heidelberg, where the academically educated class had a larger numerical proportion of the population, they were also more dominant in the voluntary societies. As the century proceeded the business and industrial middle class increasingly became the essential bearer of social life in all cities,[44] and there can be no question that the educated middle class was dominant in the constitution of modern civil society.

Yet it is misleading to consider 'wealth' and 'education' as two independent forms of constitution of the *Bürgertum*, and to divide it into two different factions, namely a 'property-owning middle class' and an 'educated middle class', according to social status and the field of activity. The contemporary self-characterisation of the *Bürgertum* as the 'propertied and educated classes', was not meant to be complimentary, but rather indicated that both were ideally united in one person.[45] In the nineteenth century, a person without education was not *bürgerlich*, but at best *bourgeois*.[46] But this was education in the wider, more comprehensive sense and was not understood as simply attending school or indicated by degrees or professions. A merchant, for example, saw himself as educated not just because of his school education – which in the business middle class often ended without an official leaving certificate – but also, and more importantly, on the basis of his intellectual and cultural interests, which he cultivated alongside his economic activity.[47] It would therefore be a misunderstanding to think only of holders of academic degrees when, as it is often the case, the associations' rules referred to their members as 'educated men',[48] since the merchants actually meant themselves.

Women were not intended to be members of the associations. This is where the theoretical equality of the associations always ended. Not all associations' regulations excluded women from membership *expressis verbis*, but in those places where the statutes generally referred to 'people', it was men that were meant – this was 'an unmentioned prerequisite'.[49]

The presence of women was allowed and desired above all at festivities. The importance of such celebrations within society and club life is not to be underestimated; after all the associations were also a kind of marriage market for the sons and daughters of the

Bürgertum, but a woman could only ever participate through her husband. If he was an unsociable person and did not join an association, then this connection remained closed to his wife, too.

Theatres, concert halls, art exhibitions and museums were social places open to both sexes and even in domestic social life, which in the nineteenth century was not limited to the 'salon culture' of a few well-known women, the middle-class women assumed important positions as hostesses. Women were even granted limited membership in theatre and art societies and in some choral societies, where female participation was desirable if only for purely musical reasons, i.e. to increase the 'diversity' of the singing.[50] As a rule, however, they did not possess the same rights to vote or have any direct influence in matters relating to the associations themselves. The reason for the fact that women's participation in these associations was limited and that they only had limited influence could have been that association activities were always connected with money. The establishment of a club, the purchase of, for example, music sheets or a piano, or the cost of construction of a theatre building was mostly financed by the members of the association on a share basis. The opportunity for women to own any possessions was very limited in the nineteenth century. Thus the 'general' association remained in the most cases a men's club, a patriarchal community of independent male householders.

In particular, women of the *Bürgertum* were absent when things turned political, because in the eyes of their middle-class contemporaries politics were a men's affair. This can be seen in for example the men's choral and gymnastic societies and most liberal and middle-class democratic associations that arose during and after the 1848 Revolution and did not admit women members. The republican-socialist associations alone and also some dissenting religious groups opened their doors to full female membership. At any rate after the Revolution, female public political activity was often banned, as for example in Prussia by the 1850 associations law.

But we must not forget that for the entire nineteenth century women were active in their own charity associations, where they attached great value to the rules associated with the new middle-class forms of social interaction as an internal democratic organization and the purported openness of its doors and activities to all classes of society. Here women accumulated organizational experience and experience in dealing with the public. At the end of the nineteenth century women derived political demands from these activities.

To conclude, we can see that the programme of modern civil society developed *out* of the traditional burgher cities, not in opposition to them. Within a local framework, the citizens (*Bürger*) demanded the right to determine their own political and cultural history and in this way they acquired the self-confidence and the right to participate in the structuring of society as a whole. They saw the city, first, as a counterpoise to the German states of the time, which were essentially aristocratic, and, secondly as a potential model for a different state and as a possible alternative form of political organization. The established merchants were the most important movers in this process, while the educated classes – particularly the academics and civil servants – were less influential in bringing about these changes than the business community.

The categories of political thinking were in many respects still taken from the repertoire of the 'society of patriarchal male house-holders', who sought to build up the political community analogously with the family, linked political rights and direct influence to personal independence, and combined duties as regards 'public welfare' with these rights. The ideal of 'middle-class unity', from which this practice derived, was in many cities already in conflict with the growing social inequality brought about by industrialization in the first half of the century. But before the Revolution the social dividing lines and the potential for conflict were covered up by a widely shared opposition to the state in almost every city.

During the Revolution, very precisely developed socio-political programmes took the place of a political conceptualization that had made middle-class consent possible, not least owing to a certain vagueness of content. The 'public welfare' argument did not, however, lose its central significance in the authorization programme of middle-class municipal power, but the middle-class elite had lost control over what this 'public welfare' actually should be. During and after the Revolution 'middle-class unity' was dissolved into political and social factions.

After the Revolution the city became the retreat of the politics of the *Bürgertum*. General calls for change were no longer voiced on a national level, but in the cities the *Bürgertum* still wanted to determine the conditions for themselves. Even though this demand – measured against the social and economic changes in the cities – took on an increasingly defensive appearance, the power of the *Bürgertum* in the city was often combined with a decisive reform policy. The municipal government was to be withheld from the lower classes and social democracy, yet municipal society was to be held together by means of the modern service administration. On the basis of an understanding of municipal self-government which was specific to the *Bürgertum*, the municipal authorities developed a system of socio-integrative interventionism earlier and more efficiently than the state.[51]

In the second half of the century this political model had huge potential for dynamism and adaptability. And with its utopian 'surplus' the demands of groups that were still socially discriminated against, as for example women, could be incorporated and justified. The ongoing debates on communitarianism show the continuing attractiveness of a political way of thinking that refers back to the community.

Notes

1. In this essay I have chosen to retain the German word *Bürgertum* wherever possible, as its translation poses almost insoluble problems. For example, the use of the plural "middle classes" in English for the German singular *Bürgertum* dilutes the idea of "middle-class unity" that was essential to our understanding of the German *Bürgertum*. Furthermore, "middle classes" rather refers to "Mittelstand", which is a more hybrid notion than *Bürgertum*; Cf. Willibald Steinmetz, 'Gemeineuropäische Tradition und nationale Besonderheiten im Begriff der "Mittelklasse"', in Reinhart Koselleck and Klaus Schreiner (eds.), *Bürgerschaft*, Stuttgart 1994, 161–238, here 210ff.
2. The project was limited to the question of the constitution of middle-class society in a "public" context. The "private" factors of family and education remained largely unconsidered, with the exception of marriage links. Cf. for the middle-class private sphere Ann-Charlott Trepp, *Sanfte Männlichkeit und selbständige Weiblichkeit. Frauen und Männer im Hamburger Bürgertum zwischen 1770 und 1840*, Göttingen 1996 and Gunilla-Friederike Budde, *Auf dem Weg ins Bürgerleben. Kindheit und Erziehung in deutschen und englischen Bürgerfamilien 1840–1914*, Göttingen 1994. The attempt to consider both private and public factors for an examination of middle-class society was carried out by Albert Tanner, *Arbeitsame Patrioten – wohlanständige Damen. Bürgertum und Bürgerlichkeit in der Schweiz 1830–1914*, Zurich 1995.

3. Bremen, Göttingen, Münster, Dortmund, Leipzig, Cologne, Aachen, Wetzlar, Wiesbaden, Frankfurt/Main, Heidelberg, Mannheim and Karlsruhe, Heilbronn, Augsburg, Munich.

4. For details see the individual monographs. Already published are Hans-Werner Hahn, *Altständisches Bürgertum zwischen Beharrung und Wandel. Wetzlar 1689–1870*, Munich 1991; Karin Schambach, *Stadtbürgertum und industrieller Umbruch. Dortmund 1780–1870*, Munich 1996; Ralf Roth, *Stadt und Bürgertum in Frankfurt am Main. Ein besonderer Weg von der ständischen zur modernen Bürgergesellschaft 1760–1914*, Munich 1996; Ralf Zerback, *München und sein Stadtbürgertum. Eine Residenzstadt als Bürgergemeinde 1780–1870*, Munich 1997; Thomas Weichel, *Die Bürger von Wiesbaden. Von der Landstadt zur 'Weltkurstadt' (1780–1914)*, Munich 1997. An overview of the developments in all project cities: Lothar Gall (ed.), *Vom alten zum neuen Bürgertum. Die mitteleuropäische Stadt im Umbruch 1780–1820*, Munich 1991; Lothar Gall (ed.), *Stadt und Bürgertum im Übergang von der traditionalen zur modernen Gesellschaft*, Munich 1993; Dieter Hein and Andreas Schulz (eds.), *Bürgerkultur im 19. Jahrhundert. Bildung, Kunst und Lebenswelt*, Munich 1996. A first résumé: Lothar Gall, '"Bürger einer Stadt". Selbstverständnis und Lebensweise des Bürgertums im 19. Jahrhundert', *Forschung Frankfurt* 3 (1997), 4–12.

5. In the following, the German "Bürger" is retained, as the English term "burgher" possesses somewhat antiquated connotations – which it did not have in nineteenth-century Germany. The word "citizen" is restricted to a political concept, and thus can serve as a translation only in limited contexts. The same approach has been taken in Ralf Roth, '*Bürger* and Workers. Liberalism and the Labor Movement in Germany, 1848 to 1914', in David E. Barclay and Eric D. Weitz (eds.), *Between Reform and Revolution. German Socialism and Communism from 1840 to 1990*, Providence and Oxford 1998.

6. The old *Bürgerrecht* consisted of a set of economic and political rights. In some cases the rights possessed by an individual varied according to the qualifying sum paid by him. For the project cities see Michael Sobania, 'Rechtliche Konstituierungsfaktoren des Bürgertums', in Lothar Gall (ed.), *Stadt und Bürgertum im Übergang von der traditionalen zur modernen Gesellschaft*, Munich 1993, 131–50, here 133 in general see Ulrich Meier, '*Burgerlich vereynung*. Herrschende, beherrschte und "mittlere" Bürger in Politiktheorie, chronikalischer Überlieferung und städtischen Quellen des Spätmittelalters', in Koselleck and Schreiner, *Bürgerschaft*, 43–89. For the proportion of families with the *Bürgerrecht* within the entire population see Dirk Reuter, 'Der Bürgeranteil und seine Bedeutung', in Gall, *Stadt und Bürgertum im Übergang*, 75–92, here 79.

7. In most cases married women did not acquire the economic privileges of the *Bürgerrecht* until they were widows, but even then political rights were excluded; cf. Andrea Löther, 'Unpolitische Bürgerin. Frauen und Partizipation in der vormodernen praktischen Philosophie', and Ulrike

Spree, Die verhinderte "Bürgerin"? Ein begriffsgeschichtlicher Vergleich zwischen Deutschland, Frankreich und Großbritannien', both in Koselleck and Schreiner, Bürgerschaft, 239–73 and 274–308.

8. Cf. Jürgen Reulecke, *Geschichte der Urbanisierung in Deutschland*, Frankfurt 1985, 62. For the significance of local self-administration for the Bürgertum's perception of itself see Wolfgang Kaschuba, 'Zwischen deutscher Nation und deutscher Provinz. Politische Horizonte und soziale Milieus im frühen Liberalismus', in Dieter Langewiesche (ed.), *Liberalismus im 19. Jahrhundert. Deutschland im europäischen Vergleich*, Göttingen 1988, 83–108; Brigitte Meier and Helga Schultz (eds.), *Die Wiederkehr des Stadtbürgers. Städtereformen im europäischen Vergleich 1750 bis 1850*, Berlin 1994, and Reinhart Koselleck and Klaus Schreiner (eds.), *Bürgerschaft. Rezeption und Innovation der Begrifflichkeit vom Hohen Mittelalter bis ins 19. Jahrhundert*, Stuttgart 1994.

9. Cf. James J. Sheehan, 'Liberalism and the City in the Nineteenth-Century Germany', *Past & Present* 51 (1971) 116–37.

10. Some time ago Thomas Mergel placed the identity of the German Bürgertum in general in the sphere of power, arguing that the Bürgertum was not defined primarily by a common lifestyle and equal economic opportunities, but rather by the ability and the will to rule. According to Mergel the Bürgertum was a 'formation which can and wants to rule. This was the main criterion, not being economically better off'; (Thomas Mergel, *Zwischen Klasse und Konfession. Katholisches Bürgertum im Rheinland im 19. Jahrhundert*, Göttingen 1994, 8, 10f.). Paul Nolte also describes the middle-class ideal as a political vision in the history of the influence of the ancient concept of a burgher; Paul Nolte, *Gemeindebürgertum und Liberalismus in Baden 1800–1850*, Göttingen 1994.

11. Lothar Gall, Liberalismus und "bürgerliche Gesellschaft". Zu Charakter und Entwicklung der liberalen Bewegung in Deutschland, *Historische Zeitschrift* 220 (1975) 324–56, Lothar Gall, *Bürgertum in Deutschland*, Berlin 1989, see also Dieter Langewiesche (ed.), *Liberalismus in Deutschland*, Frankfurt 1988.

12. Regina Jeske, 'Kommunale Amtsinhaber und Entscheidungsträger – die politische Elite', in Gall, *Stadt und Bürgertum im Übergang*, 273–94, here 282ff.

13. Cf. Shulamit Volkov, 'Die Verbürgerlichung der Juden in Deutschland', in Jürgen Kocka and Ute Frevert (eds.), *Bürgertum in Deutschland*, vol 2, Munich 1988, 343–71; see also the essays by Moshe Zimmermann and Steffi Jersch-Menzel in the same volume.

14. Recently Eugenio F. Biagini has shown that the popularity of Victorian liberalism was also based above all on a kind of 'communitaristic' rhetoric and a widely shared opposition to state intervention in the community; Eugenio F. Biagini, *Liberty, Retrenchment and Reform. Popular Liberalism in the Age of Gladstone 1860–1880*, Cambridge 1992. For the new assessment of Victorian liberalism in general see also: Eugenio F.

Biagini (ed.), *Citizenship and Community. Liberals, Radicals and Collective Identities in the British Isles 1865–1931*, Cambridge 1996; James Vernon, *Politics and the People. A Study in English Political Culture 1815–1867*, Cambridge 1993; and James Vernon (ed.), *Re-reading the Constitution. New Narratives in the Political of England´s Long Nineteenth Century*, Cambridge 1996.

15. Cf. Susanne Kill, 'Politische Konstituierungsfaktoren des Bürgertums', in Gall, *Stadt und Bürgertum im Übergang*, 183–202.

16. Paul Nolte, 'Gemeindeliberalismus. Zur lokalen Entstehung und sozialen Verankerung der liberalen Partei in Baden 1831–1855', *Historische Zeitschrift* 252 (1991), 57–93, here 61ff.

17. Cf. also Wolfgang Schieder, 'Probleme einer Sozialgeschichte des frühen Liberalismus in Deutschland', in Wolfgang Schieder (ed.) *Liberalismus in der Gesellschaft des deutschen Vormärz*, Göttingen 1983, 9–21, here 13ff. and Nolte, 'Gemeindeliberalismus', 70.

18. Kurt Koszyk, 'Carl D'Ester als Gemeinderat und Parlamentarier', *Archiv für Sozialgeschichte* 1 (1961), 43–60, here 44.

19. For discussions of the right to vote see Wolfgang Hofmann, 'Preußische Stadtverordnetenversammlungen als Repräsentativ-Organe', in Jürgen Reulecke (ed.), *Die deutsche Stadt im Industriezeitalter*, Wuppertal 1980, 31–56, and Wolfgang Köllmann, 'Von der Bürgerstadt zur Regional-"Stadt"', ibid. 15–30, here 20.

20. Karin Hausen, 'Die Polarisierung der "Geschlechtscharaktere" – Eine Spiegelung der Dissoziation von Erwerbs- und Familienleben', in Werner Conze (ed.), *Sozialgeschichte der Familie in der Neuzeit Europas*, Stuttgart 1976, 363–93. See also Ute Frevert (ed.), *Bürgerinnen und Bürger. Geschlechterverhältnisse im 19. Jahrhundert*, Göttingen 1988.

21. Cf. Carola Lipp (ed.), *Schimpfende Weiber und patriotische Jungfrauen. Frauen im Vormärz und in der Revolution 1848/49*, Bühl-Moos 1986, and Gisela Mettele, 'Bürgerliche Frauen und das Vereinswesen im Vormärz', *Jahrbuch zur Liberalismus-Forschung* 5 (1993), 23–46.

22. In 1827 the Prussian minister for education and the arts, Altenstein called the poor-law administration a "purely middle-class matter"; quotation in Mergel, *Zwischen Klasse und Konfession*, 105. For the entire nineteenth century, poor-law administration remained with the local authority; cf. Dieter Langewiesche, '"Staat" und "Kommune". Zum Wandel der Staatsaufgaben in Deutschland im 19. Jahrhundert', *Historische Zeitschrift* 248 (1989), 621–35, here 623, cf. also 634.

23. Quote from Jürgen Reulecke, 'Formen bürgerlich-sozialen Engagements in Deutschland und England im 19. Jahrhundert', in Jürgen Kocka (ed.), *Arbeiter und Bürger im 19. Jahrhundert*, Munich 1986, 261–85, here 281. See also Franz-Ludwig Knemeyer, 'Polizei', in *Geschichtliche Grundbegriffe*, vol 4, Stuttgart 1978, 875–97, here 892. For local poor-law systems see also Ludovica Scarpa, *Gemeinwohl und lokale Macht. Honoratioren und*

Armenwesen in der Berliner Luisenstadt im 19. Jahrhundert, Berlin 1995; Thomas Küster, *Alte Armut und neues Bürgertum. Öffentliche und private Fürsorge in Münster von der Ära Fürstenberg bis zum Ersten Weltkrieg (1756– 1914)*, Münster 1995; Susanne F. Eser, *Verwaltet und verwahrt. Armenpolitik und Arme in Augsburg vom Ende der reichsstädtischen Zeit bis zum Ersten Weltkrieg*, Sigmaringen 1995.

24. Quote from Reulecke, 'Formen bürgerlich-sozialen Engagements', 278; also Jürgen Reulecke, 'Die Armenfürsorge als Teil der kommunalen Leistungsverwaltung und Daseinsvorsorge im 19. Jahrhundert', in Hans Heinrich Blotevogel (ed.), *Kommunale Leistungsverwaltung und Stadtentwicklung vom Vormärz bis zur Weimarer Republik*, Cologne 1990, 71–80.

25. Reulecke, 'Formen bürgerlich-sozialen Engagements', 273.

26. Historical archives of the City of Cologne; no. 400-III-24C-1.

27. Cf. Norbert Finzsch, *Obrigkeit und Unterschichten. Beiträge zur Geschichte der rheinischen Unterschichten Ende des 18. und zu Beginn des 19. Jahrhunderts*, Stuttgart 1989, 46, 62. Cf. also Finzsch's differentiation of "roaming", "resident", "deviating" and "socially conforming" poor; ibid. 14ff., for the change in middle-class understanding of poverty, cf. 111. The concept of "social discipline" (referring to the early modern age, but applicable also to the nineteenth century) was discussed by Martin Dinges, 'Frühneuzeitliche Armenfürsorge als Sozialdisziplinierung', and Robert Jütte, '"Disziplin zu predigen ist eine Sache, sich ihr zu unterwerfen eine andere" (Cervantes). Prolegomena zu einer Geschichte der Armenfürsorge', both in *Geschichte und Gesellschaft* 17 (1991), 5–29 and 92–101. See also Christoph Sachße and Florian Tennstedt (eds.), *Soziale Sicherheit und soziale Disziplinierung. Beiträge zu einer historischen Theorie der Sozialpolitik*, Frankfurt 1986.

28. Bernd Weisbrod, 'Wohltätigkeit und "symbolische Gewalt" in der Frühindustrialisierung. Städtische Armut und Armenpolitik im Wuppertal', in Hans Mommsen and Winfried Schulze (eds.), *Vom Elend der Handarbeit. Probleme der Unterschichtenforschung*, Stuttgart 1981, 334–57, here 354.

29. See also Christoph Sachße, 'Social Mothers: The Bourgeois Women´s Movement and Welfare-State Formation. 1890–1929', in Seth Koven and Sonya Michael, (eds.), *Mothers of a New World: Maternalistic Politics and the Origins of Welfare States*, New York 1993, 136–58. By regarding (and underestimating) the social welfare activities of women "only" as an extension of work in the family to other families Ute Frevert overlooks the fact that the entire welfare system in the cities was based on this "family"-principle; Ute Frevert, *Frauen – Geschichte. Zwischen bürgerlicher Verbesserung und Neuer Weiblichkeit*, Frankfurt 1986, 70.

30. Iris Schröder, 'Soziale Frauenarbeit als bürgerliches Projekt. Differenz, Gleichheit und weiblicher Bürgersinn in der Frauenbewegung um 1900', in Klaus Tenfelde and Hans-Ulrich Wehler (eds.), *Wege zur Geschichte des Bürgertums*, Göttingen 1994, 209–30, here 224.

31.   Thomas Nipperdey, 'Verein als soziale Struktur in Deutschland im
       späten 18. und frühen 19. Jahrhundert', in Hermann Heimpel (ed.),
       Geschichtswissenschaft und Vereinswesen im 19. Jahrhundert, Göttingen 1972,
       1–44; also Otto Dann (ed.), *Vereinswesen und bürgerliche Gesellschaft in
       Deutschland*, Munich 1984; Etienne François, *Sociabilité et société bourgeoise
       en France, en Allemagne et en Suisse, 1750–1850*, Paris 1986. For the most
       recent overview of literature and research documents see Heinrich Best
       (ed.), *Vereine in Deutschland. Vom Geheimbund zur freien gesellschaftlichen
       Organisation*, Bonn 1993, cf. also Wolfgang Hardtwig, *Genossenschafte,
       Sekte, Verein in Deutschland*. Vol. I: *Vom Spätmittelalter bis zur französischen
       Revolution*, Munich 1997; second volume to follow on associations in
       the nineteenth century.

32.   Cologne Art Society, Annual Reports 1839–1872, here 1846; historical
       archives of the City of Cologne no. 1386, nos. 438–440.

33.   Elisabeth Fehrenbach, *Verfassungsstaat und Nationsbildung 1815–1871*,
       Munich 1992, 31.

34.   Cf. Lothar Gall, *"Der hiesigen Stadt zu einer wahren Zierde und deren
       Bürgerschaft nützlich". Städel und sein "Kunst-Institut"*, Frankfurt 1992, 13.

35.   Of course, the Masonic lodges did not completely disappear as
       associations, but they lost some significance in the face of the new
       associations and societies. In the new "sociable" concept, the contrast-
       ing natures of "work" and "social life" became central, a distinction
       which had not yet played a role in types of association like the reading
       societies and Masonic lodges; indeed, the freemasons had explicitly
       called their gatherings "work".

36.   Cf. Dieter Hein, 'Soziale Konstituierungsfaktoren des Bürgertums', in
       Gall, *Stadt und Bürgertum im Übergang*, 151–82, here 155, and Dieter Hein,
       'Kunst und bürgerlicher Aufbruch', in Jutta Dresch and Wilfried
       Rößling (eds.), *Bilder im Zirkel*, Karlsruhe 1933, 25–35, here 30. General
       literature on this change: John Ormrod, 'Bürgerliche Organisation und
       Lektüre in den literarisch-geselligen Vereinen der Restaurations-
       poche', in Günther Häntzschel (ed.), *Zur Sozialgeschichte der deutschen
       Literatur von der Aufklärung bis zur Jahrhundertwende*, Tübingen 1985, 123–
       49.

37.   Nipperdey, 'Verein als soziale Struktur', 3.

38.   Hein, 'Soziale Konstituierungsfaktoren', 172.

39.   Gall, 'Bürger einer Stadt', 11.

40.   Cf. Cologne Art Society, Annual Reports 1839–1872, here 1844–1851;
       historical archives of the City of Cologne City No. 1386, Nos. 438–440;
       and Peter Gerlach, 'Köln und die bildende Kunst für die Bürger', in
       Peter Gerlach and Wilfred Dörstel (eds.), *Kölner Kunstverein. Einhundert-
       fünfzig Jahre Kunstvermittlung*, Cologne 1989, 37–73, here 46.

41.   Cf. Hein, 'Soziale Konstituierungsfaktoren', 160 and 172.

42.   Ibid. 156–62. On the basis of their share of the population, Jews were
       also not represented in the associations of Cologne. The main reason

for this was, however, the fact that most Jews in Cologne were less wealthy . As lower middle-class butchers and copperplate engravers they found little opportunity to enter the associations, as did non-Jewish artisans.

43. Most of the time practically all municipal office holders were members. In the cities the "Casinos" formed an effective sub-structure of the "formation of an informed opinion" and of decision-making. Membership was an important prerequisite for the individual to move up the middle-class social ladder.

44. For Munich Cf. Ralf Zerback, *München und sein Stadtbürgertum: Eine Residenzstadt als Bürgergemeinde*, Munich 1997, 82ff. and 205ff., and in general Hein, 'Soziale Konstituierungsfaktoren'.

45. The French equivalent "ceux qui ont fortune et instruction" makes this clearer, although, behind the "instruction" there is a different (narrower) meaning of education compared to how it is understood in German. In the last volume of the four-volume essay collection *Bildungsbürgertum im 19. Jahrhundert*, Jürgen Kocka also disputes the existence of an "educated middle class" as an independent social formation; Jürgen Kocka, 'Bildungsbürgertum – Gesellschaftliche Formation oder Historikerkonstrukt?' in Jürgen Kocka (ed.), *Bildungsbürgertum im 19. Jahrhundert*, Part IV, *Politischer Einfluß und gesellschaftliche Formation*, Stuttgart 1989, 9–20, here 19. The term "Bildungsbürger" (educated middle-class citizen) was not invented until 1920; cf. Ulrich Engelhardt, *"Bildungsbürgertum". Begriffs- und Dogmengeschichte eines Etiketts*, Stuttgart 1986, 189.

46. Cf. also Franz J. Bauer, *Bürgerwege und Bürgerwelten*, Göttingen 1991, 288f.

47. Cf. the example of the Bassermann family of Mannheim; Lothar Gall, 'Die Bassermanns. Eine Bürgerfamilie zwischen Ancien Régime und moderner Welt', in M. Rainer Lepsius (ed.), *Bildungsbürgertum im 19. Jahrhundert. Part III*, Stuttgart 1992, 102–12, here 108f.

48. As for example: Munich Museum of the 1830s, Harmoniegesellschaft Augsburg 1830, cf. Gall, Vom alten zum neuen Bürgertum, 13.

49. Ute Frevert, 'Männergeschichte oder die Suche nach dem "ersten Geschlecht"', in Manfred Hettling (ed.), *Was ist Gesellschaftsgeschichte?* Munich 1991, 41–3, here 39.

50. With respect to women's participation the associations can be divided into two groups: If associations were to serve the moral and aesthetic refining process and "ennoblement" of life, then women were involved to a certain degree. If, on the other hand, an association, as for example the male choral society or the gymnastic society, was thought as a place for informal social interaction free from social constraints, as a counterbalance to an increasingly formal and finer middle-class life, then contemporaries could or would not imagine the presence of women.

51. Langewiesche, '"Staat" und "Kommune"', 623, cf. also 634; cf. also
     Horst Matzerath, '"Kommunale Leistungsverwaltung". Zu Bedeutung
     und politischer Funktion des Begriffs im 19. und 20. Jahrhundert', in
     Blotevogel, *Kommunale Leistungsverwaltung*, 3–24, here 24. From the 1860s
     onwards the *Honoratiorenverwaltung* was challenged by the demands of
     a rapidly growing urban industrial society. As Richard Evans has shown,
     the most dramatic demonstration of the failure of "amateur"
     government was the cholera epidemic in Hamburg in 1892. But it
     should be pointed out that in the mass meetings held immediately after
     the epidemic the Hamburg Social Democrats did not demand state
     intervention but universal suffrage for the Hamburg citizens' assembly
     and the abolition of the compulsory 30-Mark fee, arguing "that if we
     had been represented in the Hamburg Citizens' Assembly there would
     have been no need to have carried 10,000 people to the cemetery";
     Richard J. Evans, *Death in Hamburg. Society and Politics in the Cholera Years
     1830–1910*, Oxford 1987, 539. A recent overview with literature on some
     problems of urban local government in Imperial Germany: Friedrich
     Lenger, 'Großstädtische Eliten vor den Problemen der Urbanisierung.
     Skizze eines deutsch–amerikanischen Vergleichs 1870–1914', *Geschichte
     und Gesellschaft* 21 (1995) 313–37.

SYLVIA SCHRAUT

Burghers and other Townspeople – Social Inequality, Civic Welfare and Municipal Tasks during Nineteenth-Century Urbanization

In this essay I should like to discuss some questions about the connection between municipal and state governmental influences on welfare and social inequality in Germany during the nineteenth century and to examine the role of citizen movements in the formation of municipal tasks and the modern welfare state. I should also like to investigate the role played by the city constitution, state legislation and the civil association movement, and the way private welfare, often carried out by women, was connected with the deployment of the women's movement in towns. Such questions, which first require clarification of the term 'burgher' and of communal welfare and its development during the nineteenth century, will only be addressed in the context of four selected large cities – Hamburg, Munich, Leipzig and Mannheim – representing different types of urbanization in various regions of Germany.

According to *Zedler's Encyclopaedia* from the first half of the eighteenth century, burghers lived in towns and earned money through trade and craft.[1] With citizenship they had more or less defined privileges, which enabled them to take part in the political and administrative tasks of their town. But this did not mean all townspeople were burghers, because only those inhabitants who owned property and contributed to the municipal revenue counted as such, and the legal privileges of burghers could vary considerably from town to town.[2] Female burghers possessed no voting rights and could not take on municipal governmental functions. This was so common that the encyclopaedia did not point it out. *Zedler's Encyclopaedia* also defined in various ways what a town actually was. It offered as one definition the township with self-ruling rights, or an assembly of people who cohabited peacefully in accordance with self-constituted laws and contracts, or for example, simply a community, or a so-called civil society.[3]

Town and burgher traditionally belonged close together, yet at the beginning of the nineteenth century, the so-called bourgeois era (*bürgerliches Zeitalter*), no innovative social impulses emerged from the towns. Rather the state with its interest in all inhabitants of the country drove social development forward. A series of governmental laws, the legal liberation of the agrarian population from ties to the land and free trade prepared the ground for industrialization. The triumphal progress of industrialization during the second half of the nineteenth century made the towns once more centres of social change and modernization.

In 1800 the great majority of the German people lived in the country and subsisted from agriculture; in Prussia in 1816, for example, only 10 per cent of the inhabitants resided in communities with more than 5,000 people. Until 1871 more than 30 per cent of Germans lived in communities with city rights. By 1910 6 out of 10 people were living in towns, 2 of 10 in a city with more than 100,000 inhabitants. In 1871 there existed only 8 cities in Germany; their number rose to 48 within the next 40 years.[4]

Provoked by the immense growth in the population, the towns – specifically the ruling bourgeoisie within them – had to take on new social tasks and to find new ways of solving the resulting social problems. They had not only to introduce and develop a communal infrastructure; they had to find solutions that allowed the increasing number of labourers and their families to find habitation and to ensure the health of the inhabitants. Numerous impulses to the solution of social questions were developing in the second half of the century, in the first instance not through the state, but through the urban industrializing centres of Germany. Most social and political movements emerged in urban centres at this time, coincidentally with, or as a reaction to, municipal problems. Finally, the socially defined group of municipal burghers developed into the political bourgeoisie, which struggled for political power.

Two of the central problems were public health care and support for the lower social classes.[5] Another kind of poverty was on the rise during the nineteenth century. Sick and old inhabitants remained dependent on aid as they had been before industrialization. Now they were joined by the members of the new working class, who lived merely from their wages, and who demanded municipal support in periods of economic crisis, when they were sick or out of work. At the beginning of the century it was the state that set minimum standards in welfare for the poor to care for all inhabitants of the country, without having the capacity to realize it in most cases. But during the nineteenth century centres of urban development and industrialization had to work out concrete models to solve social problems. At the end of the century the state, through Bismarck's social reforms, tried to adopt solutions for the entire country that had already been put in place by the cities.

Traditionally support for poor people was guaranteed by a combination of municipal and denominational welfare. The municipal organs were interested in providing a minimum of welfare for the burghers, but refused to accept responsibility for the welfare of inhabitants without citizenship. Sick or impoverished strangers were returned to their place of birth. Particularly in the case of larger towns, which during the nineteenth century accommodated an increasing proportion of foreign workers, it was very important that expenditure was reserved for those sick and poor who should legitimately have access to municipal support. Decisions about awarding citizenship were clearly influenced by strategies to minimize the number of people who were guaranteed communal support. This behaviour stood in contrast to that of the absolutist state of the late eighteenth century. More than ever in the early nineteenth century, urban interests stood in opposition to those of the state, which tried to institute widespread medical care and to build up poor relief for all the inhabitants of the country. Certainly governmental welfare schemes often failed because of the costs and during the first third of the nineteenth century a single standard for all medical institutions needed to be set. Meanwhile the municipal authorities had to care increasingly not only for the welfare of poor burghers, but for the resident inhabitants as a whole. In many German states towns lost their struggle against impoverished immigrants because the governmental authorities did not permit the expulsion of poor people from the towns. But with regard to the rights of burghers and municipal self-government the laws of the individual German states varied profoundly. In Bavaria, for example, the so-called home right (*Heimatrecht*) was prevalent almost until the end of the nineteenth century. This meant that strangers, poor and sick persons dependent on welfare, were sent back to their place of birth. In Saxony the *Heimatrecht* was implemented until 1870 and only after five years' affiliation to the citizenry could people enjoy municipal support. In Prussia the state increasingly tried to hold municipalities responsible for support in case of poverty or sickness for all inhabitants, not only for the burghers. Prussian law linking public support to residence brought in adequate regulations after 1842. It was exemplary for numerous other German states, and adopted in 1871 by the German Empire with the exception of Bavaria. According to this law one could claim support from a town by right after two years of uninterrupted residence.

Beyond the legal situation, the towns tried to keep welfare as cheap as possible. In order to minimize the costs they began to define exactly what municipal welfare meant. Numerous theoretical discussions about the state of poverty and possible auxiliary measures were published. Poverty was often seen not in connection with economic conditions and available jobs but as a result of unstable moral conduct.[6] Another way of putting limits on the costs of welfare was to give exact determination and limitation to public benefits, as far as government law allowed. How should poor people be supported and above all which burghers should define the nature of welfare and the categories of recipients? This question connects citizenship, municipal franchise and leadership with municipal welfare. In towns there lived not only burghers, but also those who took part in the political management of the towns, those who at least voted for the ruling burghers, those who were to be supported in case of poverty or sickness, and those without citizens' rights who were sent back to their home towns in cases of need. In addition many civil servants lived in cities without being real burghers. The situation was indeed complex.

The general tendency in Germany for local differences to predominate can be demonstrated in cities like Hamburg – the old northern Hanseatic city; Mannheim – the last residence city of the Palatinate, relocated in the nineteenth century; or Munich – the Bavarian residence in the south. As the second largest city of Germany, Hamburg was one of the few places where both municipal and state government were identical until the last third of the nineteenth century and where no external authority limited the force of urban self-government. Until 1860 members of the magistracy were installed for life and they co-opted new members from among the bourgeoisie without any electoral participation of the burghers.[7] Only the exclusive group of inhabitants who were able to earn their money from self-employment, who possessed capital, houses or real estates, were counted as citizenry, although their political influence on the magistracy was meagre. Only 3,000–4,000 men out of 100,000 inhabitants belonged to the citizenry.[8] Together with their families they comprised 13–17 per cent of the inhabitants. Thus the vast majority of the inhabitants of Hamburg had no say in municipal affairs and they mostly lived as employed workers. Yet the ruling class felt responsible for providing welfare not only for the burghers, but also for almost all the inhabitants. By the late eighteenth century the senate had taken the administration of welfare away from the Lutheran Church and installed a system of municipal public supply for the poor, the Allgemeine Armenanstalt (General Poor Relief). This central welfare body, composed of members of the magistracy and co-opted burghers, organized a system of support, which divided the town into small parts; and it commissioned 180 honorary wardens to take care of the poor, all known personally to them.[9] Thus the system connected a tight but peripheral organization with honorary work of the burghers. Welfare in Hamburg finally divided the inhabitants into families who granted support and those who received it. About 5–6 per cent of the families of the citizenry might have been involved in the distribution of municipal social aid. On the opposite site were 2,000–3,000 households each year that profited from public support during the first decades of the nineteenth century. This connected rich and poor families, ensuring mutual awareness of living circumstances. Contemporaries regarded the system installed by the bourgeoisie of Hamburg as exemplary and extremely efficient.

This was not true of every large town of Germany. In Mannheim, the former Palatine residence, for example, welfare did not function at the beginning of the nineteenth century.[10] The town, in economic crisis and with about 15,000 inhabitants, was given to Baden, one of the new German states created by Napoleon in 1802, and the new state government almost totally abolished municipal self-government under its new occupancy. This decision, which probably should have provoked opposition from the citizenry in the first instance, also affected public welfare. Because Mannheim had lost its possessions in the countryside, the state took over responsibility for aid to the poor, but it did not allow the citizenry to interfere significantly. In the beginning of the nineteenth century the economic situation in Mannheim was really miserable. This was obvious, when the poor were counted. A commission decided that 2,400 persons, one out of six inhabitants, were below the level of subsistence. In the following decades by no means all the poor could obtain public support, but the cost of public welfare, essentially paid by the territorial government and by voluntary collections of the middle classes, was enormously high. During the 1830s municipal congregationalism was strengthened in Baden too, and the burghers of Mannheim fought for influence in public welfare organization, in the face of government control of the municipal welfare organizations. Ultimately the city council obtained the right to participate in welfare decisions, but the new privilege was linked to the obligation to pay for the deficit of welfare tasks. The recently involved city council became innovative in detecting ways of reducing the costs of municipal supply for the poor and thus of municipal subsidies. The accommodation of domestic and craft helpers in case of sickness offered an opportunity to intervene. Experience had shown that employers increasingly took the chance to divest themselves of their legal liability and in the end the municipal authorities had to supply the helpers. Finally the city council devised new ways of finding solutions to the financial questions. It initiated health insurance for the relevant persons, with the employers bearing the costs. Therefore the general public hospital was engaged to provide outpatient and inpatient care for the employed. First initiated on a voluntary basis, the insurance fund met with resistance. To the surprise of the city council the employers did not welcome the new system. In 1842 the city council secured from the ministry of the interior the permission to impose an obligatory insurance for the employed journeymen living in Mannheim. That new system obliged all employees, domestic servants, journeymen and apprentices in crafts and trades to become members of the insurance scheme. Some employees and employers opposed it, but the city council finally instituted the obligatory insurance and the new organization obviously stood up to the test. By the middle of the nineteenth century the city council no longer had to force employers to use the insurance: the new factory owners themselves asked for membership for their labourers. Finally in the 1860s probably 15–20 per cent of the inhabitants were integrated into the municipal health insurance. The obligatory insurance showed results in many aspects. Not only did it bring a cost-covering insurance system for the employed population of the town. Another result was that the public hospital was separated from welfare for the poor. In this way the insurance scheme saved its members from the stigma of asking for municipal social aid. Thus obligatory insurance on the communal level anticipated a solution that was established at state level about half a century later.

Innovation did not characterize the welfare system of Munich, the third largest city of Germany. In Munich – as in many early large towns of the German Empire – different types of towns overlapped each other. It was a commercial town, a monarchical capital, a territory and a civil service town characterized by a large administrative apparatus. At the beginning of the nineteenth century about 40,000 inhabitants lived in Munich, but about half of the population belonged to the so called 'Exemten', meaning that they and their families were officials of government, the military, the churches or similar institutions. They all undoubtedly resided in town, but belonged to traditionally territorial authorities, and most of them would have greeted the award of citizenship as an impertinence rather than as a privilege.[11] The importance of the inhabitants of Munich who did not belong to the citizenry remained considerable in the growing town, and even in the middle of the century only half of the inhabitants were not employed by the government or the monarchy.[12] In the middle of the century more than a quarter of the 'real' inhabitants were self-employed or belonged to the family of a self-employed tradesman and houseowner. The heads of these families were entitled to vote on the municipal level and determined the composition of the city council and the welfare system. Thus in comparison to Hamburg, the Munich city council was supported by a much larger part of the citizenry. In contrast to bourgeois-ruled Hamburg, the city council of Munich, which depended on the self-employed house-owning urban middle classes, was at pains to reduce the number of inhabitants who were to be supported by municipal welfare. The policy of the municipal authorities was to send strangers back to their home towns if they were in need of aid.[13] In the middle of the century, for example, only 4 per cent of the inhabitants qualified for support in cases of poverty or sickness. Yet at the end of the nineteenth century the differences between the two municipal systems of welfare were remarkable. Bourgeois-ruled Hamburg paid on average 4 Marks for one inhabitant's welfare, which was basically financed through municipal revenues. Meanwhile in Munich the city council, constituted of members of upper and lower middle classes, paid only 2.70 Marks per capita. Moreover, up to the last third of the century the costs of welfare were defrayed through a separate tax, which was to be paid by every person, burgher or not, who rent accommodation in Munich. Thus many strangers had to pay without being entitled to municipal aid. The clear exclusion of the majority of inhabitants in welfare cases by the city council of Munich opened the door to private welfare, which did not make citizenship a prerequisite.[14]

Energetic private social clubs and associations developed in the town, which offered to noble society and the upper classes without citizenship opportunities for social contact and engagement. In this way the associations initiated by the religious communities had great importance. In 1838, for example, a Protestant welfare association was founded. Its predominantly female members and staff were recruited mostly from the well-educated middle classes and families of government officials, the political bourgeoisie who were not burghers of Munich. On the Catholic side there were corresponding men's and women's associations, which often recruited their members from Catholic families of government officials and which were patronized by the royal family. All these associations developed programmes of intensive social work from the 1840s until the German Empire was founded. They competed with the municipal welfare associations. Besides these, in Munich, as in other towns, women's associations especially were engaged in welfare.[15] The maintenance associations, which provided care for wounded soldiers during the Napoleonic Wars were early forms of women's welfare associations. Also in Munich in 1814 women came together in order to help sick or wounded defenders of the fatherland, as they said 'following the example of their sisters in other German territories'.[16] At the end of the so-called liberation wars, and not only in Munich, such welfare associations, which were orientated towards the interests of the broader territory, although located in towns, disappeared. But when the association movement increased during the following decades, women's welfare work that was orientated towards urban social developments once again boomed. In 1829 in Munich a so-called 'women's association to support poor married women in childbirth' was founded.[17] The aims of the association were advanced by the membership, which included the wives and daughters of the nobility, civil servants and the bourgeoisie, and also the wives of urban artisans. Members of the royal family assisted, and thus enhanced the image of an association that transcended social boundaries.[18] Numerous other social associations might be listed. Not only in Munich can one find intensive private associations' activity organized in the service of the poor and invalids. Similar organizations were founded in many towns, particularly in the residences of the territories. It was only here that urban associations existed which brought together socially conscious members of the nobility, state social policy and religiously motivated welfare activity in the context of civic social work, thereby extending welfare assistance to those urban inhabitants who were not entitled to municipal aid. The private welfare associations thus revealed forward-looking characteristics that crossed the borders of urban territory. Their supporters saw the local need as sufficient reason to intervene. They were not constrained by the narrow legal definition of what the authorities considered to be their responsibility. They also aimed their welfare work at poor members of the same confession or, if they were not linked to religion or the church, at the impecunious inhabitants of the same territory or even of the German Empire. Private welfare associations were criticized by urban authorities for this transgression of the town limits.

Conflicts were exacerbated when religious social associations developed into organizations of political opposition or when they founded alliances with them. One example is the German Catholic opposition movement. Following public discussions about the obligations of religion and the churches in Germany, in which political and social protest were articulated, the German Catholic movement grew in the 1840s. This is not the place to discuss the religious beliefs and motives of the German Catholics, but for us the deeply urban character of the movement is important. This led to the foundation of many German Catholic communities in predominantly Protestant cities, or religiously mixed areas with a Protestant majority. In 1844/5 one could find German Catholic associations, for example, in Breslau, Berlin, Leipzig, Dresden and many other cities. As Sylvia Paletschek demonstrated in her analysis of this movement, membership often stemmed from the lower middle or proletarian classes. But the leaders were often liberal upper-class citizens, who became famous politicians in the revolution of 1848.[19] In Leipzig, for example, Robert Blum was an initiator and later deputy of the German democratic parliament at Frankfurt. But where are the connections with social inequality and welfare in German towns? Following the example of the German Catholic movement numerous women's associations were founded, linking religious work with urban social work. The aim of German Catholic liberal women's associations was to collect money for religious work, for supporting poor or sick persons or educating children. Thus they wanted to integrate traditional religious social work into the new religious communities, but they also founded schools for maidservants (Danzig) and for female workers (Magdeburg). The Hamburg chapter supported Fröbel's kindergarten movement. In Dresden the association aided families of persecuted Forty-Eighters. The generally close contact between urban social work, political liberalism and the forerunners of the women's movement is shown in the women's newspaper *Deutsche Frauenzeitung*, edited in Leipzig by Luise Otto. Actually one can see the connection in the person of Luise Otto herself. The editor of the *Frauenzeitung* was born in Meißen and belonged to the liberal and democratic opposition of 1848. She was one of the founders of the German women's movement. She sympathized with the German Catholic movement and was friends with German Catholic or democratic women and women from liberal women's associations, such as Eugenie Blum, the wife of Robert Blum, the democratic member of the German parliament, who was killed in Vienna during the revolution. The liberal women's associations of Hamburg, Hanau, Breslau and Dresden regularly reported on their activities in the *Frauenzeitung*. One of the employees of the paper was Emily Lecerf, who was on the management of a Dresden women's aid association and a German Catholic. The movement could not survive the conservative reaction that followed the failure of the revolution of 1848, but its inheritance can be seen in the women's movement that followed in the 1860s.

Summarizing the development of municipal welfare tasks in the middle of the nineteenth century, one can see that in many towns welfare work ran into trouble because migration was growing and the economy looked bleak, while at the same time the state demanded increasing social support for the urban inhabitants. Political associations came under government pressure and the welfare association movement had to demonstrate how it could survive. When the population increased rapidly during the last decades of the nineteenth century, municipal welfare institutions seemed to be failing irrevocably. In economically bad years expenditure on poor inhabitants devoured sometimes up to half of the public revenue, and because of the legal requirement after 1870 municipal authorities were obliged to assist all entitled poor. In response they tried to arrange welfare more effectively and to determine exact assistance for claimants. This was only possible by increasing the number of honorary helpers. The industrial town of Elberfeld was pioneering in its welfare reform of 1852/3.[20] The municipal authorities of Elberfeld expanded the system of honorary collaboration instituted and tested in Hamburg, and considerably enlarged the number of honorary social workers. Now every social worker had to take care of only 5–10 poor families, and in finding new social workers the system co-operated with the lower middle classes. The new organization reduced the costs of public welfare considerably. The Elberfeld model was therefore adopted by numerous German towns. But of course cost saving depended less on modern administration than on the social origin of the new social workers. Those social classes that now took part in honorary welfare work were able to earn a living only with great effort. They were prepared to support the poor, but doubtlessly they were not very well prepared to aid able-bodied paupers. Generally speaking, the nature of municipal welfare institutions in nineteenth-century towns can be described as follows: the higher, more exclusive and thereby more undemocratic the social strata that controlled the town council, the more generous the municipal poor relief.

The cases of Dresden and Leipzig around 1880 may illustrate this.[21] In the capital of Saxony the Elberfeld system had been installed in 1880, where a welfare committee had been constituted with some councillors and some eligible burghers. They organized welfare by using tax money. At least 400 elected honorary social workers out of the lower and upper middle classes took over controlling and caring for the poor. A newly founded welfare association 'against poverty and begging' with about 5,000 members co-ordinated municipal and private welfare, representing about fifty associations. On the other hand, public welfare in the rich commercial town of Leipzig had been organized since the early nineteenth century by an exclusive association authorized by an autocratic magistracy which co-opted its members. The welfare society was an association of gentlemen who administered public welfare, as they said, 'authorized by the confidence of the other burghers'. The society, with forty-five members, outlived the changes in the municipal code of Saxony in 1832 and 1873 and co-opted its members without any democratic election. This noble consortium was probably made up of a majority of men from the bourgeoisie or the educated middle classes. Money for welfare was collected from the wealthy burghers. Honorary social workers were selected from the citizens. If one compares the social benefits in Dresden and Leipzig, it becomes apparent that welfare in Leipzig was more expensive and that more inhabitants received public aid. In Dresden every seventeenth person was supported, in Leipzig every tenth. Comparisons of supported households in both towns show which social groups did not get help, if welfare was organized according to the Elberfeld system.[22] In both towns older people, widows and single women both with and without children received above-average relief, but in Leipzig many men of working age were supported by public welfare too. Obviously, in this town the welfare association made decisions based on the actual social situation of the claimants and did not confuse employability with employment, which was common when using the Elberfeld system. In considering this, the contemporary experts criticized the conditions in Leipzig. 'In our time', a commentator of the Saxonian statistical office wrote, 'when vagabondage, aversion to work and professional begging and claiming are everyday occurrences and can hardly be managed without severe authoritative measures, a free association of honorary men cannot manage the public welfare of a large town without governmental power, without a well-organized workhouse for the poor'.[23] This comment demonstrates the usual reservations of municipal authorities towards private welfare, but considering the need to economize on public aid for the poor it was correct. After the establishment of the Elberfeld system in Leipzig too, public welfare became cheaper.

While communal authorities began to reduce the costs of municipal welfare by implementing the Elberfeld system, private welfare associations found more and more support from the state authorities. In Saxony and Baden, for example, governments initiated a system of welfare associations promoted and co-ordinated by the state and especially used women's associations to enhance welfare for the poor. Female participation in political life was unthinkable in the middle of the nineteenth century, but female welfare work was not criticized as indecorous. Engagement in welfare associations did not subvert the gender roles of upper-class women. Honorary work in private welfare associations offered a highly valued opportunity for public activity. Early in 1836 the queen of Saxony, for example, called for the foundation of women's associations to enhance welfare for the poor, but she was primarily thinking of rural associations. During the second half of the nineteenth century Louise, duchess of Baden, a daughter of the king of Prussia, initiated a well co-ordinated women's association, the 'Badischer Frauenverein', which soon had branches in every large town of Baden. The 'Badischer Frauenverein' maintained a widespread private system of welfare, which encompassed all fields of social aid, and which was later carried out by municipal welfare authorities.[24] The local branches functioned through the financial support and honorary activities of the daughters and wives of the richest families in town. If the duchess called, no woman of the upper class could refuse. And because of ducal protection no municipal authority could deny assistance. At first the communal officials often did not trust the association; later most of them supported the private welfare work of the 'Badischer Frauenverein', which had founded an alliance with the state in the person of the duchess and which worked very effectively. Moreover the 'Badischer Frauenverein' developed more and more activities in support of education and job training of women of the lower classes. The success and widespread appreciation of the association is demonstrated by its membership figures. In 1890, for example, almost every fifteenth adult woman in Mannheim was a member. Similarly effective alliances between private women's welfare associations and the state are not known in other states of Germany, but the alliance of the state, personalized through female members of the ruling family, with women's welfare associations can also be found in other states.

Because the women's auxiliary associations worked so effectively, eventually the officials of the municipal welfare authorities decided to integrate women into their own work. One pioneer was the German association of welfare for the poor, the 'Deutscher Verein für Armenpflege und Wohltätigkeit'. The association was established in 1881 at the behest of urban political authorities from big cities like Berlin, Leipzig or Dresden.[25] Until the end of the nineteenth century the important charities and most municipalities with more than 20,000 inhabitants became members of this umbrella organization. Its aim was to co-ordinate disparate reform ambitions and to provide a forum for discussion. Therefore the association organized annual congresses and published the lectures. In its first booklet the association published a report of the so-called 'Vaterländischer Frauenverein' in Prussia about the connection between municipal social work and private social work carried out by women's associations.[26] Yet, when the founding assembly of the association met, the question of how far women could be integrated into official social work was discussed. The founding assembly did not reach a decision, because the reservations of some of the participants could not be overcome. But the members agreed to endorse the integration of women's welfare work into municipal social work. In 1885 the association discussed once more the work of the 'Vaterländische Frauenvereine', and in 1896 it was part of the agenda of the meeting arranged to attract women into municipal social work, indicating that professional social workers agreed with the integration of women into these areas. The assembly demanded the inclusion of women in public welfare administration with the same rights and duties as men. Finally, in 1905, the club of gentlemen and professional social workers invited a woman as official commentator. As the discussion showed, professional social workers welcomed women as assistants, but male honorary helpers did not agree. The

gentlemen feared being unable to speak freely if women took part in
the local social help meetings and they believed municipal social help
would become more expensive if women had the power to decide
things.[27] But beyond such considerations the entry of women in
municipal welfare work was no longer opposed.

The social municipal work of women, first honorary, later – at the
beginning of the twentieth century – paid, showed a side effect of
female private welfare associations, which was not only useful for the
poor, but also assisted the progress of women. Welfare activity gave
women of higher classes the chance to learn public political behaviour.
Women of the lower classes got the opportunity to undertake paid
welfare work. Moralizing female amateurs were followed by well-
educated nurses and professional female welfare workers.[28] Female
welfare work was a forerunner of the aims of the women's liberation
movement, to open up to women medical careers that had been
traditionally occupied by men. For example, long before women were
allowed to study at German universities, women's welfare associations
engaged female doctors who had studied abroad.[29] But urban medical
welfare establishments of the women's liberation movement not only
worked to establish medical careers for women, but gave labourers
and their families the chance to get medical help without paying for
it. Because this aid was not part of municipal help, it did not diminish
their electoral rights. It was this fact that once more brought women's
welfare associations into the limelight at the end of the nineteenth
century. People no longer criticized possible wastefulness; rather they
interpreted women's welfare organizations as societies supporting
the socialist movement. A welfare institution in Mannheim, which
provided a home for women during their confinement, exemplifies
this.[30] On the initiative of the bourgeoisie of Mannheim in 1887, a
home was opened where maternity care was available free of charge
for poor married women. The house was supported through an association of women of the bourgeoisie. Soon the so-called 'Asyl' was used
by many working-class women.[31] About one in four births took place
there at the beginning of the twentieth century, and the house became
the largest institution of its kind in southern Germany.[32] Of course,
this was not only because the medical treatment was free of charge,
but the success was attributed to the manner of admittance. Using
the house was not counted as municipal welfare. Women with and
without claims to municipal help were supported, and using the
medical facilities of the 'Asyl' had no consequences for the electoral
rights of the new fathers. This may explain why the 'Asyl' worked so

successfully, but it may also explain why the directors of the house had to defend their work against conservative accusations that they supported the socialists. This however opens a new topic at the end of the nineteenth century and introduces a new social movement and new social conflicts in the area of municipal welfare. It was the Social Democratic movement that demanded a change from the apparent dishonour attached to the poor burghers for accepting municipal help to higher wages and the right to secured living circumstances, and which became the arena of contention in the context of the fight for entry into municipal councils. The state responded with the reform programme of Bismarck. These reforms finally relieved the over-charged communal authorities from their burden,[33] but the triumphal progress of Social Democracy could not be halted by the new obligatory insurance system.

Notes

1. J. H. Zedler (ed.), *Grosses vollständiges Universal-Lexicon aller Wissenschafften und Künste*, Halle and Leipzig 1732/54, citizen: 1875ff.

2. W. Krabbe, *Die deutsche Stadt im 19. und 20. Jahrhundert : eine Einführung*, Göttingen 1989, 8–23, 48–67.

3. Zedler, *Universal-Lexicon* 1744, town: 768ff.

4. See Ch. Sachße and F. Tennstedt, *Geschichte der Armenfürsorge in Deutschland*, Stuttgart 1980; V. Böhmert, *Das Armenwesen in 77 Deutschen Städten und einigen Landarmenverbänden*, 3 volumes, Dresden 1886–1888; W. Fischer, *Armut in der Geschichte*, Gottingen 1984.

5. J. Reulecke, *Geschichte der Urbanisierung in Deutschland*, Frankfurt am Main 1985, 203–4.

6. U. Frevert, *Krankheit als politisches Problem 1770–1880*, Göttingen 1984.

7. D. Duda, *Die Hamburger Armenfürsorge im 18. und 19. Jahrhundert. Eine soziologisch-historische Untersuchung*, Weinheim 1982, 32ff.; E. Klessmann, *Geschichte der Stadt Hamburg*, Hamburg 1981, 436ff; I. Bauer, *Armut, Arbeit und bürgerliche Wohltätigkeit*, Hamburg 1987.

8. A. Kraus, *Die Unterschichten Hamburgs in der ersten Hälfte des 19. Jahrhunderts*, Stuttgart 1965, 24.

9. Duda, *Hamburger Armenfürsorge*, 52ff.; Kraus, *Die Unterschichten Hamburgs*, 46ff.

10. M. Krauss, *Armenwesen und Gesundheitsfürsorge in Mannheim vor der Industrialisierung: 1750–1850/60*, Sigmaringen 1993.

11. R. Zerback, 'Unter der Kuratel des Staates – Die Stadt zwischen dem Gemeindeedikt von 1818 und der Gemeindeordnung von 1869', in R. Bauer (ed.), *Geschichte der Stadt München*, Munich 1992, 274–306, here 277.

12. F. B.W. von Hermann, *Beiträge zur Statistik des Königreichs Bayern, 1. Bevölkerung*, Munich 1850, 86–9.

13. M. Doege, *Armut in Preußen und Bayern*, Munich 1991; Th. Guttmann, *Armut in der Großstadt*, Munich 1996.

14. I. Tornow, *Das Münchner Vereinswesen in der ersten Hälfte des 19. Jahrhunderts, mit einem Ausblick auf die zweite Jahrhunderthälfte*, Munich 1977; R. Zerback, *München und sein Stadtbürgertum*, Munich 1997, 296ff.

15. Sachße and Tennstedt, *Geschichte der Armenfürsorge in Deutschland*, 222–44.

16. E. Volland and R. Bauer (eds.), *München – Stadt der Frauen*, Munich, 1991, 15.

17. Tornow, *Das Münchner Vereinswesen*, 138ff.

18. Zerback, 'Unter der Kuratel des Staates', 179.

19. S. Paletschek, *Frauen und Dissens: Frauen im Deutschkatholizismus und in den freien Gemeinden 1841–1852*, Göttingen 1990.

20. E. Münsterberg, *Das Elberfelder System* (Schriften des deutschen Vereins für Armenpflege und Wohltätigkeit, H. 23), Leipzig 1903; Ch. Sachße and F. Tennstedt, *Geschichte der Armenfürsorge in Deutschland. Band 2: Fürsorge und Wohlfahrtspflege 1871–1929*, Stuttgart 1988, 23ff.

21. V. Böhmert, 'Das Armenwesen der Städte Dresden und Leipzig nach der Armenstatistik vom Jahre 1880', *Zeitschrift des K. Sächsischen Statistischen Bureau's* 23 (1883), 1–85.

22. Ibid. 27.

23. Ibid. 8.

24. S. Asche, 'Fürsorge und Emanzipation – oder Rassenhygiene', in S. Jenisch (ed.), *Standpunkte*, Tübingen 1993, 132–42 and 242–4; K. Lutzer, '"... stets bestrebt, dem Vaterlande zu dienen ..." Der Badische Frauenverein zwischen Nächstenliebe und Patriotismus', in Frauen & Geschichte Baden-Württemberg (ed.), *Frauen und Nation*, Tübingen 1996, 104–17 and 243–5.

25. E. Münsterberg, *Generalbericht über die Tätigkeit des deutschen Vereins für Armenpflege und Wohltätigkeit während der ersten 25 Jahre seines Bestehens 1880–1905* (Schriften des deutschen Vereins für Armenpflege und Wohltätigkeit, H. 72), Leipzig 1905, 1–28.

26. Ibid. 95–9.

27. Ibid. 98.

28. H. Radomski, *Die Frau in der öffentlichen Armenfürsorge*, Berlin 1917; Ch. Sachße, *Mütterlichkeit als Beruf, Sozialarbeit, Sozialreform und Frauenbewegung 1871–1929*, 2nd edn. Opladen 1994.

29. K. Hoesch, *Ärztinnen für Frauen, Kliniken in Berlin*, Stuttgart 1995, 50ff.

30. H. B. Brennecke, 'Errichtung von Heimstätten für Wöchnerinnen', *Deutsche Vierteljahrsschrift für öffentliche Gesundheitspflege* 29 (1896), 56–95.

31. A. Eckert, 'Das Wöchnerinnenasyl Luisenheim in Mannheim', *Deutsche Vierteljahrsschrift für öffentliche Gesundheitspflege* 39 (1906), 295–303.

32. S. Schraut, 'Wie edel ist also der Gegenstand Eurer Beschäftigung. Zwei Jahrhunderte Hebammenwesen in Mannheim', in I. Thomas and S. Schraut (eds.), *Zeitenwandel*, Mannheim 1995, 82–98.

33. For Munich, see R. Freund, *Armenpflege und Arbeiterversicherung*, Leipzig 1895, 42.

FRIEDRICH LENGER

Building and Perceiving the City: Germany around 1900

'The psychological basis of the metropolitan type of individuality consists of the intensification of nervous stimulation, which results from the swift and uninterrupted change of outer and inner stimuli.' These were the words used by Georg Simmel, the philosopher and sociologist, in a lecture on *The Metropolis and Mental Life* in 1903 in order to describe the abundance of irritations that to him were not only typical of city life but were changing the nature of the urban inhabitant. In contrast to the inhabitant of the small town, metropolitan man for Simmel was no longer capable of reacting to his environment with his feelings (*Gemüt*) but was in need of an intensified intellectuality. 'Intellectuality is thus seen to preserve subjective life against the overwhelming power of metropolitan life'; or as it reads in the original with an imagery that is lost in the translation: 'die gesteigerte Verstandesmäßigkeit diene "als ein Präservativ des subjektiven Lebens gegen die Vergewaltigungen der Großstadt"'.[1] Besides this heightened intellectuality it was the blasé attitude that formed the inevitable consequence of the richness and the continuous change of nervous stimuli in the big city.

The essence of the blasé attitude consists in the blunting of discrimination. This does not mean that the objects are not perceived . . . [But] they appear to the blasé person in an evenly flat and grey tone; no one object deserves preference over any other. This mood is the faithful reflection of the completely internalized money economy. By being the equivalent to all the manifold things in one and the same way, money becomes the dreadful leveller. For money expresses all qualitative differences of things in terms of 'how much'?

This analysis, which tends to equate money economy with metropolitan life, may sound like a story of decay, one which originates in and keeps as its counterpart the small town founded upon personal relationships. But Simmel's view of the big city is more ambivalent than that. He recognizes quite clearly that the big city opens up room for the development of individuality and subjectivity that is unknown to the small town. To quote him for a last time: 'The small-town life in Antiquity and in the Middle Ages set barriers against movement and relations of the individual towards the outside, and it set up barriers against individual independence and differentiation within the individual self. These barriers were such that under them modern man could not have breathed.'[2]

Thus to Simmel modern man is the big city man. His analysis can be read both as a theoretical model and as a document of the ways in which the city was experienced and perceived around 1900. That he contrasted the modern city with older, often medieval small towns was in no way unique. Other authors of his generation such as Ferdinand Tönnies and Werner Sombart did just the same. Later commentators on big city life such as Siegfried Kracauer or Walter Benjamin, however, presupposed the existence of the metropolis as a given. Thus the newness of the phenomenon obviously had to do with the interpretation of the big city itself. It seems advisable therefore to outline briefly the basic features of big city growth in turn-of-the-century Germany in the first section of this essay. The second part then deals with the qualitative side of this development, with questions of urban planning and urban development, urban administration and communal politics, settlement patterns and infrastructural change. While the focus here is on the perceptions of administrators and others, the way in which the big city was experienced and perceived around 1900 is addressed separately in the third part of the article. Within the broader field of an alleged German anti-urbanism sociology, literature and the arts are the fields that will be considered at some length.

I

In Germany the percentage of people living in big cities – defined as having at least 100,000 inhabitants – rose from less than 5 per cent to more than 20 per cent between 1870 and 1910. The number of big cities increased from eight to forty-eight during the same timespan. Since the overall population grew from about 40 millions to roughly 65 million in this period, this was a truly spectacular process at the end of which about 60 per cent of the German population lived in cities.[3] Among the more important causes of city growth were certainly the strong population growth and the rapidity of German industrialization. Urbanization therefore was a far more dramatic process in Germany than in France whose population grew far more slowly if at all. More complex is the relationship between urbanization and industrial development.

To understand it, some distinctions introduced by Werner Sombart around the turn of the century still have some heuristic value. He contrasted medieval and early modern towns which for him were largely consumer cities, with the producer cities of the modern age, giving special weight to the industrial towns dominated by mining and heavy industry. Sombart found that the reason for the enormous growth of industrial towns lay mainly in the introduction of steam technology, which was accompanied by the emergence of the large plant as the typical unit of production. This had caused a process of local concentration, which with the introduction of the coke furnace was directed largely towards the mining areas. Around this heavy industrial core all kinds of supplementary and additional industries had been established, most notably machine building and metalworking. A direct contribution of industrial development to urbanization in Sombart's view was limited to these industrial towns. Within them more than two-thirds of employees were working in the industrial sector. And he was sure that in certain smaller industrial communities not covered by the statistics immediately to hand, the respective percentages would be even higher. He called them partial cities because, 'typically the entrepreneurial profit gained there is not consumed there. . . . The partial industrial town is thus a pure workers' town, inhabited, besides the industrial proletariat, by just so many directors and civil servants as are necessary for the technical management of the plant.' In contrast, the complete industrial town always displays 'the tendency . . . to grow into a big city'.[4] The big city, however, was a multifunctional phenomenon, being a centre of industrial production as well as of commerce but above all also a centre of consumption.

That the direct impact of industrialization was limited to industrial towns can also be seen by the fact that only in areas dominated by heavy industry did new towns emerge in larger numbers. The Ruhr area is only the best-known example of this. At the same time other types of towns experienced an enormous growth too. Cities with an important harbour like Hamburg, commercial and administrative centres such as Düsseldorf or Cologne, even Wiesbaden – called 'Pensionopolis' by Max Weber – experienced an increase in the number of their inhabitants which, while not a direct consequence, was not independent of industrialization either. This more general city growth was not uniform, however, but was closely connected to the development of the railway system.[5] Its expansion strengthened the polycentric structure of the German urban system, which together with the extraordinary speed of development and the important role of industrial towns forms the major specifics of German urbanization in a comparative perspective.

> 53000 Berliner sterben im Jahr
> und nur 43000 kommen zur Welt.
> Die Differenz bringt der Stadt aber keine Gefahr,
> weil sie 60000 Berliner durch Zuzug erhält.
> Hurra![6]

This stanza of a poem by Erich Kaestner, which I could not translate adequately, refers playfully to one of the ever recurring stereotypes of anti-urban critiques, i.e. the charge that cities by themselves were not capable of at least maintaining their population but that they were dependent upon a continuous influx from the countryside. By the late nineteenth century this charge had long lost its earlier justification. While infant mortality remained especially high in the cities, their growth depended as much upon the surplus of births over deaths within the cities as upon immigration.[7] In fact, immigration itself contributed strongly to what demographers term natural growth because it was primarily young singles who moved into the cities where they then started families.

Among all migrants those who stayed permanently formed a minority, however. They were clearly outnumbered by those who came and went within one year. The number of all migrations within the German Empire has been estimated at 20 million for 1907 and 22 million for 1910. These numbers indicate that on the one hand migration to other countries, while important, only accounted for a small proportion of all migrations and that on the other hand the migration from the countryside into the rapidly growing towns also forms only part of the whole story. Focusing on the cities themselves it is easy to see that the numbers of in- and outmigrants moved along parallel lines, while the difference between the two remained comparatively small. In larger towns with at least 50,000 inhabitants there were about 250 migrations per 1,000 inhabitants each year during the 1880s, a figure that rose in accordance with economic cycles to more than 350 in the years before the First World War.[8] These numbers indicate an enormous mobility; they do not, however, substantiate the claim that about a third of the urban population was on the move each year. To a considerable degree migration still followed seasonal patterns. Just think of the building workers who found work in the towns in spring and left again in autumn; they usually did not give up their rural bases. According to estimates for some especially well-researched towns those arriving and leaving within a year or often much shorter periods may have been responsible for half of all migrations.[9]

What can be said about the migrants more generally? First of all, they were more often male than female and that is why the industrial towns especially had an unbalanced gender structure. Secondly, single people migrated far more often than complete families. And thirdly, most migrations covered only rather modest distances. Berlin alone attracted migrants from a somewhat larger radius, while the recruitment of the labour force from the far distant provinces of eastern Prussia, as it was practised by the mining companies of the Ruhr, was otherwise uncommon. Only in the years before the First World War did long-distance migration became more important, a type of migration usually associated with the exploitation of opportunities in the labour market for the better qualified. On the whole, however, the distribution of migrations over the year still followed an agrarian rhythm on the eve of the Great War. The modern form of daily commuting was not very well developed; it seems to have replaced other forms of migration rather rapidly from the 1920s onwards.[10] To summarize: the majority of urban migrants came from the city hinterlands, and their main characteristic was their relative youth. Singles younger than thirty were responsible for most cases of migration and it was these young workers and domestic servants who often only stayed in one town for a couple of days or for just a few weeks. Thus, while mobility around the turn of the century depended on social status, it seems more appropriate to view it as a phase in the lifecycle of broad social strata rather than the lifelong fate of a proletarian reserve army.

The sheer amount of mobility irritated quite a few contemporaries. Later historians, too, have tended to interpret the mobility of urban inhabitants as proof of Simmel's diagnosis of uprootedness as a feature of big city life. In doing so, they have overlooked the fact that those millions of migrations were much less disorderly than has often been assumed. We have already noted that a considerable proportion of short-stay migrants was rooted in the rural surroundings. But those who stayed in the city for good had usually acted upon information provided by friends and relatives. Only in very exceptional cases will they have been without any contact at the place to which they were migrating. Establishing a link between geographic mobility and a specific metropolitan type of person, the cultural historian Karl Lamprecht argued on the eve of the First World War that, 'with the unrest around them the masses became restless and inwardly unstable as well; a reciprocal effect of inner motivations and outer mobility emerged giving rise to a new type of human being, the type of big city sensitiveness. . . . Out of the atmosphere of greater freedom', Lamprecht continued, 'there arose the longing for stronger enjoyment, noble and not noble: the licentiousness of sexual life, the stimulating visit to the music hall, the enjoyment of the multicoloured splendour of the shop windows . . .'.[11] – Actually many facets will have contributed to the attractiveness of the big city, described recently by the ethnographer Gottfried Korff as the 'place of the enlarged horizon of opportunities', as a 'place where one could achieve something'.[12] It is quite difficult to determine how many migrants succeeded in bettering themselves, because the careers of those who left the city again remain unknown, with the sources typically available for the turn of the century. Those who stayed for good moved up quite often, but maybe their relative success was the main reason for staying in the first place.

We would like to know much more about the motives and the occupational fates of those migrating into the big cities of turn-of-the-century Germany. Even if migration was not unstructured the urban environment was alien in many ways. Fritz Wiechering, the son of a peasant in Dielingen, born in 1896, later recalled his move to the nearby town of Herford as an 'entry into an alien world'. He went there at the age of fourteen in order to become trained as a schoolteacher. Raised in a peasant world that despised all urban trappings the future teacher now felt ashamed because of his dialect, because of his lack of table manners, but also because he wore shirts of handmade linen and an old-fashioned suit. How deeply humiliated he felt becomes clear when one reads that one day he lied to his parents that his shirts had been stolen and then pressed them into buying him 'real' shirts and a modern suit.[13] Franz Wieber, later in his life a prominent leader of the Christian trade union movement and my second example here, came from a completely different background.

He was born in 1858 in a small village not far away from the river Fulda and went to Frankfurt at the age of thirteen. 'Now I suddenly stood in the big city of Frankfurt. What there was to be seen, what a splendour and what a glory. Only millionaires can be living there – that was at least what I thought.' That Wieber experienced the city quite differently than the son of a Westphalian peasant had a number of reasons, not least social ones. Wieber took it for granted that he would go to the 'Dalles'. That was, as he explained, 'an open square where everybody took one's stand if looking for a job. It was – so to speak – the open labour market. The employers came and picked those people they wanted to have.'[14] Wieber's entrance into the urban scene will have been far more typical than that of the future teacher. It was also quite typical that he returned home after a while, handed over his pay to his father and later on migrated to Bochum where two of his brothers were already working. For him too, migration was anything but aimless or unstructured.

II

But what about the cities, which so far we have only been dealing with as places of rapid growth and as magnets to attract migrants? What did they look like? How did they develop? Who ran them? And how were they perceived by their inhabitants? If one wants to deal with these types of questions one has to take seriously the heterogeneity of single cities and of city types. Industrial villages like Hamborn or Oberhausen, which were growing into big cities, had little in common with traditional urban centres such as Munich, which was described by Thomas Mann towards the end of the Wilhelmine Empire as a 'big city watering place with a flowering hotel industry and a kind of "city beautiful association" at the top'.[15] Cities like Munich or Wiesbaden blocked industrial development or relegated it to the outskirts. The majority of cities did not have these opportunities, although they too tried to influence their economic structure, not least by incorporating smaller communities. It was quite typical that when these incorporations were arranged the infrastructure provision and the economic character of certain quarters were fixed.[16] But, of course, the inequality between different parts of town in so far as environmental risks or the quality of services were concerned existed independent of incorporations. This marked inequality was not something given, however, but was the concrete result of political decisions at the local level.

Among the problems that arose from the enormous city growth and which confronted urban parliaments and urban administrations the spatial development of the city ranked among the most pressing. Most nineteenth-century towns could be crossed on foot within half an hour. Once the town walls had been demolished, however, the horse-drawn and later electric tramways permitted an ever-larger spatial expansion. Suburbanization and city building went hand in hand with new patterns of social segregation. While earlier on the location of a flat within the house had defined the social status of the inhabitant, who either lived facing the yard or facing the street, underneath the roof or in the *bel étage*, now different social strata were increasingly located in different quarters. Of course, working-class areas and quarters for the poor had existed for a long time but towards the end of the nineteenth century the widespread separation of home and workplace led to an ever clearer distinction between different quarters and to a higher social homogeneity within them. The starkest examples of this are the industrial towns of the Ruhr area. They often did not have a core but were formed by a variety of settlements centred on single mines and single mills.[17] Besides its spatial dimension segregation also had a temporal aspect. Thus Werner Sombart could write in a book on the proletariat in 1906: 'How their day begins we only discover when we return exhausted from a night of dancing or from a game of poker or when walking to the station to catch the early train.'[18]

Contemporary urban planners like James Hobrecht wanted to counter what they considered a dangerous alienation between social classes. His 1862 map for Berlin was permeated by the idea that the deep building blocks that it defined should only be covered by buildings at the edges and that the rest of them should be filled with gardens and yards. The houses to be built should contain larger flats for middle-class families on the two lower floors and smaller and cheaper ones on the upper floors and within the wings. Out of spatial closeness social harmony would emerge, and in that respect Hobrecht's thinking was clearly informed by older patterns of social segregation. The way in which his plan was put into effect before 1919 is a telling example of the very limited possibilities of urban planning before the First World War. The streets basically followed Hobrecht's lines. What became decisive, however, was that he had no way of influencing the way in which the separate blocks were built on. Since the houseowners had to contribute to the costs of road-making according to the width of their building, they wanted their often very narrow plots to be built on as deeply as possible. Thus numerous multi-storey backhouses replaced the gardens envisioned by Hobrecht and the yards were kept to the absolute minimum that was legally possible.[19]

The fate of Hobrecht's plan shows that the planning ambitions were clearly subordinate to the profit interests of landed proprietors. The utmost intervention that cities in Imperial Germany dared to introduce was the restriction of the height and type of buildings for certain well-defined quarters, a kind of zoning that went beyond the mere separation of industrial quarters from the others.[20] Even more important, however, were the huge differences of the aims cities could pursue with their planning. While an industrial town like Oberhausen which was cut through by a multitude of railway lines was desperately trying to establish a physical town centre, planners in other cities discussed whether the aesthetic principles of urban architecture should be taken from Camillo Sitte or Otto Wagner.[21]

Within this architectural debate Otto Wagner represented the modernists. To him, functional necessity was the sole governess of art and his work as an architect celebrated the structures and materials of modern technology. Beyond its architectural monuments this modern technology had changed urban life fundamentally around 1900, and it did so in ways that still dominate our present. This is true for the electric lighting of cities – causing quite a sensation at the time of its introduction – as well as for the provision of gas, electricity and water, for waste disposal as well as for urban transport, which in the largest cities already included the underground before the First World War. It is similarly true for the immediate environment of the apartment itself. Karl Kraus greeted all these innovations in 1911, saying: 'I demand of a city in which I shall live asphalt, street cleaning, a front-door key, hot-air heating and warm water supply.' And he added in a phrase that cannot be translated: 'Gemütlich bin ich selbst.'[22]

Two aspects of infrastructural development were especially noteworthy. On the one hand, there was controversial discussion about which tasks should be fulfilled by the cities themselves and which ones were better left to private entrepreneurs.[23] On the other hand, it is remarkable how many infrastructural innovations owed their existence to the fear of epidemics, how strongly the discourse of medical and natural sciences informed the perception of the big city and its problems.[24] In both areas, in what was called by contemporaries *municipal socialism* on the one hand, and in the realm of urban hygiene on the other, the larger cities of Imperial Germany displayed a remarkable capacity for reforming themselves, because or in spite of their being ruled in the interest of the bourgeoisie by a powerful administration.[25]

'Through bad drinking water contagious diseases such as cholera, typhoid fever etc. [. . .] can be spread. To care for good drinking water is thus among the prime duties of a good urban administration.'[26] This sentiment, expressed here by an influential social science encyclopaedia in 1911, was self-evident to both medical experts and urban administrators around 1900. But well into the 1890s an older understanding identifying the origins of contagion in so-called miasmata had given priority to the disposal of waste water, which was led into brooks and rivers. The biggest German cities had introduced canal systems as early as the 1850s. Hamburg, for example, had been among them, but was to suffer nevertheless from an enormous cholera epidemic in 1892 that cost the lives of almost 10,000 people. Richard Evans has related this to the archaic structure of the local city government but I would like to stress two different points.[27] On the one hand, it seems as if it had needed the Hamburg catastrophe to prove Robert Koch's earlier discovery of the cholera bacillus. Only now did the filtering and clarification of waste water become widespread. On the other hand, it is astonishing how quickly the new insight gained ground. Less than two years after the Hamburg epidemic one could read in a popular encyclopaedia, 'that the indescribably wretched water and housing conditions of Hamburg would have justified an even worse outbreak of the epidemic'.[28] What seems interesting beyond the immediate context of explaining diseases is the self-evident combination of 'water and housing conditions'. Urban hygiene was a concept that linked irresolvable medical and social dimensions of urban life. It covered all aspects of urban planning and development, it comprised infrastructural modernization as well as the equipment of apartments or specific settlement structures.

> The property-owning classes must be shaken from their slumber; they must finally understand that even if they make considerable sacrifices, these will be . . . but a modest insurance sum, by which they protect themselves against the epidemics and the social revolutions that have to come if we do not stop reducing the lower classes in our big cities to barbarians, to beastly existence by their housing conditions.[29]

This rather famous *Admonition in the Housing Question*, penned by the economist and social reformer Gustav Schmoller in 1887, expressed quite clearly the middle-class fears of epidemics on the one hand,

and the fear of social revolution on the other. These fears centred above all on the housing question. While the causes of housing shortages were discussed quite seriously, the dangers concerning health and morals clearly took centre stage. To stress middle-class anxieties and insistence on the autonomous process of perceiving the housing problems in turn-of-the-century Germany is not to deny the existence of these problems. Take Berlin as an example. Statisticians defined a flat as overcrowded only if – given one heatable room – five or more people lived there or – given two heatable rooms – eleven or more people lived there. Even if we apply this rather generous definition, 13 per cent of all flats with just one heatable room were overcrowded in 1895 in Berlin and in neighbouring Charlottenburg.[30] So the existence of a serious housing problem is not in doubt. But it is remarkable nevertheless that the rural housing conditions, which were even worse, did not attract comparable attention. Thus it seems reasonable to conclude that it was the proximity of the urban lower classes that caused anxieties and motivated reforms.

The aims of the housing reformers had originally been concentrated on sufficient air supply for each inhabitant. But increasingly a different and less individualistic conception dominated the discussion. This was the idea of housing fit for families.[31] It comprised the demand for separate dwellings for each family as well as the separation of the bedroom from other rooms. If these spatial preconditions for middle-class family life were created, there could be hope for the civilization of the urban lower classes. As the prominent housing specialist Carl Johannes Fuchs put it in 1911: 'If the worker returns from work tired, and does not find any comfort, no family peace, he will go the pub.'[32] But the pub was not the only threat to an idealized family life that the reformers detected. Even more threatening seemed the widespread habit of working-class families taking in lodgers to alleviate the rent burden. Especially for the mothers of small children there was hardly any other possibility of earning any money. The public debate around 1900 was utterly obsessed with possible sexual relationships between these lodgers and the female members of working-class families. Middle-class fears of epidemics and social revolutions, it seems, went hand in hand with fears of the presumably 'wild' sexuality of the immoral urban lower classes.[33]

The latter is but one example of a general shift in the perception of urban problems, a shift away from medical to social problems that can be observed towards the end of the nineteenth century. This shift gave rise to quite a few institutions that had their part in giving the cities in turn-of-the-century Germany a modern outlook.[34] In some respects one finds here elements of the later welfare state. Inseparable from its caring intentions was the disciplining impulse. That could be shown in infant welfare as well as in the early juvenile welfare measures.[35] Seen from the point of view of the reformers these measures were not unqualified successes. Working-class mothers, for example, accepted the educational offers of middle-class reformers only when they were combined with tangible benefits, as was the case with the distribution centres for milk.[36] And, of course, there tended to exist a rebellious youth culture well into the twentieth century.

III

This by no means complete survey of some of the problems confronting the larger German cities around 1900 and of the ways in which these problems were perceived may have prompted some sympathy for those contemporaries who felt uneasy about big city life. But before dealing with their views, often subsumed under the label 'anti-urbanism', it must be stressed that those architects, medical doctors, welfare workers, legal experts and administrators who shaped the larger German cities around 1900 were by no means just fear-ridden reformers. On the contrary, one finds in them quite often an almost unrealistic optimism, an enormous confidence in their own ability to master the huge problems mentioned above.[37] This puts into perspective the results of the comparative work undertaken by Andrew Lees in the mid-1980s, which found once more an especially hostile attitude towards the city in Germany.[38] To engage in the numerous urban reform organizations or to accept an honorary position in the city administration was in itself an expression of trust in the viability of the big city. Beyond the local level such pride in the modernization of German cities was expressed in countless exhibitions and conferences.[39]

But while it is necessary to look at the numerous urban practitioners, thus putting the anti-urbanists in a proper perspective, this is not to deny the existence of quite a few critics of urban society. Excluding the explicitly political debate one may distinguish four more or less separate groups. The first group could be called the followers of a popular agrarian romanticism, a position prominent for example in the movements to preserve the countryside and the regional arts and crafts traditions (*Heimatschutz- u. Heimatkunstbewegung*).[40]

Secondly, one could identify a heterogeneous discourse on the city as the grave of the race.[41] Towards 1900 the city is attacked here from three different sides. On the one hand, the city is accused of eliminating an important factor of selection by protecting the weak. Along similar Darwinian lines the city appears as a vile instrument of selection itself by first drawing the best and strongest from the countryside into its orbit and then exposing them to the decadent influences of the city. And finally the well-being of the race is viewed as being threatened by the inclination of the more successful urbanites to limit the number of their children. These first two lines of an anti-urban critique occasionally overlapped. It is almost impossible to determine precisely how widespread these beliefs were. Through such papers as the *Kunstwart* and others they were certainly familiar to large parts of the educated middle class. Here, as Ute Planert shows in a recent book, they could form part of an anti-modern syndrome that comprised anti-Semitism as well as anti-feminism and anti-urbanism.[42]

Apart from these beliefs, which were important because they were quite widespread, there are others that are intellectually more interesting. The examples are therefore taken from sociology on the one hand, and from literature and art on the other. 'If the bus and today the electric streetcar, the elevated railway or the underground are symbols of the modern metropolis', Werner Sombart wrote in 1903 in an attempt to sum up the nineteenth century, 'there was some kind of a symbol of the old estate-like ways, as it has been maintained up to the middle of the nineteenth century: the night-watchman with spike and horn. [. . .] Today one whistles a shrill signal where one used to sing!'[43] Such an opposition evoked the organic naturalness of past times against the dead technology of the present. Sombart's hostility towards modern technology included the telephone, the gramophone and – here he was in agreement with Simmel – the pocketwatch. But while Sombart despised it as part of modern technology, Simmel considered the pocketwatch a symbol of the new experience of time characteristic of the big city, an experience that to him paralleled the calculating character of a capitalist money economy.

The three aspects we have noted in Sombart's and Simmel's encounter with the big city – the confrontation of mass culture and mass society; the question of the psychological effects of life within the urban mass society upon the individual; and the sentimental conjuring up of a better past – are all to be found again when we turn briefly to literary comments upon the big city. The theme of urban society as mass society has already been addressed indirectly via Kaestner's poem quoted above. Its first stanza reads:

> Laßt uns Berlin statistisch erfassen!
> Berlin ist eine ausführliche Stadt,
> die 190 Krankenkassen
> und 960 ha. Friedhöfe hat.

While Kaestner ironically suspends the individual fate in statistical numbers, the individual is at the centre of Rainer Maria Rilke's *Notebooks of Malte Laurids Brigge*:

> To think that I cannot give up the habit of sleeping with an open window! The electric streetcars rage through my room with ringing fury. Automobiles race over me. . . . An electric car rushes up excitedly, then away overhead, away over everything. Someone is calling. People are running, overtaking each other. A dog barks. What a relief: a dog! Towards morning even a cock crows; and that brings immeasurable solace. Then all at once I fall asleep.

Rilke also contrasts technology and nature, big city and country life in a rather romanticizing way. When he has his protagonists say, 'Have I said before? I am learning to see. Yes, I am beginning. It still goes slowly; but I intend to make the most of my time', he not only postulates a new perception suited to the metropolis but he also contrasts the unified personalities of earlier generations with the segmentation of roles in urban society. 'For one thing, it has never occurred to me before how many different faces there are. There are quantities of people, but there are even more faces, for each person has several.' Rilke's novel goes beyond contrasting the metropolitan present and the rural past, however, and reflects implicitly and explicitly the consequences of an altered mode of perception for the writer. 'The telling of stories, the real telling, must have been before my time. I have never heard anyone tell stories.'[44] It is hardly surprising, then, that the relationship between urban perceptions and narrative structures continues to be discussed intensely by scholars of literature. It has to be noted, however, that the critique of the city as we find it in Rilke is not representative of German literature around 1900. Particularly if one turns to urban poetry one finds fascination and horror expressed almost simultaneously.[45]

Something similar can be said about modern painting. Meidner, Feininger, Heckel, Beckmann and Kirchner all took up the challenge of the new urban infrastructure and painted gasometers, water towers, road bridges and the like. Walter Grasskamp has suggested that artificial lightning in particular must have aroused the painters' professional interest, but at least thematically other issues were more important to them.[46] The loss of individuality and original characters within urban mass society occupied centre stage. Consider, for example, the paintings of Ernst Ludwig Kirchner, a man who expressed most intensely the possibility already mentioned by Simmel, 'that one may possibly feel nowhere as lonely and abandoned as in the bustle of the big city'.[47] Kirchner's urban inhabitants have almost no faces, they look past each other, and if they move they do so almost automatically with the equal steps of the masses. Women are almost always portrayed as prostitutes, thus signalling that the relationship between the sexes within the big city can no longer be based on love but has turned into a mere monetary relationship.[48]

Otto Dix and George Grosz took up this theme repeatedly during the war and post-war period. They did so in a way that has recently been characterized – unconvincingly – as a brutal attack against women that anticipated some of the atrocities of the Nazi era.[49] While in their paintings the urban moloch and the brutalizing effects of the war cannot be separated, Ludwig Meidner's self-portrait *I and the City* as early as 1913 depicts a person whose nerves are wrecked by the metropolis, somebody who is – to speak with Simmel – not sufficiently blasé for big city life.[50]

Notes

For a more extensive treatment cf. Friedrich Lenger, 'Großstadtmenschen', in Ute Frevert and Heinz-Gerhard Haupt (eds.), *Der Mensch des 19. Jahrhunderts*, Frankfurt 1999, 261–91, 367f.

1. Georg Simmel, *Die Großstädte und das Geistesleben*, reprinted in id., *Aufsätze und Abhandlungen 1901–1908*, vol. 1 (Georg Simmel-Gesamtausgabe, vol. 7), Frankfurt 1995, 116–31, at 118.
2. Georg Simmel, *The Metropolis and Mental Life*, in *The Sociology of Georg Simmel*, edited, translated and with an introduction by Kurt H. Wolff, New York 1950, 409–24, 409ff. and 414; cf. on Simmel and the city above all David Frisby, *Simmel and Since. Essays on Georg Simmel's Social Theory*, London 1992, 98–117.

3. The numbers are taken from the excellent survey by Jürgen Reulecke, *Geschichte der Urbanisierung in Deutschland*, Frankfurt 1985.

4. Werner Sombart, *Der moderne Kapitalismus*, vol. 3: *Das Wirtschaftsleben im Zeitalter des Hochkapitalismus*, part 1, Munich 1927, 407; cf. id., 'Der Begriff der Stadt und das Wesen der Städtebildung', *Archiv für Sozialwissenschaft und Sozialpolitik* XXV (1907), 1–9. Unless otherwise noted the translations are my own.

5. For a good survey in English cf. e.g. J. J. Lee, 'Aspects of Urbanization and Economic Development in Germany 1815–1914', in Philip Abrams and E.A. Wrigley (eds.), *Towns in Societies. Essays in Economic History and Historical Sociology*, Cambridge 1978, 279–93.

6. Erich Kaestner, 'Berlin in Zahlen' (1931), reprinted in Waltraud Wende (ed.), *Großstadtlyrik*, Stuttgart 1999, 150.

7. Cf. e.g. Wolfgang Köllmann, *Bevölkerung in der industriellen Revolution. Studien zur Bevölkerungsgeschichte Deutschlands*, Göttingen 1974.

8. Cf. for a brief summary in English Dieter Langewiesche and Friedrich Lenger, 'Internal Migration: Persistence and Mobility', in Klaus J. Bade (ed.), *Population, Labour and Migration in 19th- and 20th-Century Germany*, Leamington Spa 1987, 87–100, and most recently Steve Hochstadt, *Mobility and Modernity. Migration in Germany 1820–1989*, Ann Arbor, MI 1999.

9. Cf. e.g. Friedrich Lenger, *Zwischen Kleinbürgertum und Proletariat. Studien zur Sozialgeschichte der Düsseldorfer Handwerker 1816–1878*, Göttingen 1986, 65–93.

10. In addition to the summary by Langewiesche and Lenger (n. 8) cf. Friedrich Lenger and Dieter Langewiesche, 'Räumliche Mobilität in Deutschland vor und nach dem Ersten Weltkrieg', in Axel Schildt and Arnold Sywottek (eds.), *Massenwohnung und Eigenheim. Wohnungsbau und Wohnen in der Großstadt seit dem Ersten Weltkrieg*, Frankfurt 1988, 103–26.

11. Karl Lamprecht, *Deutsche Geschichte der jüngsten Vergangenheit und Gegenwart*, vol. 1: *Geschichte der wirtschaftlichen und sozialen Entwicklung in den siebziger bis neunziger Jahren des 19. Jahrhunderts*, Berlin 1912, 503.

12. Gottfried Korff, Mentalität und Kommunikation in der Großstadt. Berliner Notizen zur 'inneren' Urbanisierung, in: Theodor Kohlmann/ Hermann Bausinger (eds.), Großstadt. Aspekte empirischer Kulturforschung, Berlin 1985, 343–361.

13. Quoted from Josef Mooser, 'Kleinstadt und Land im Industrialisierungsprozeß 1850–1930. Das Beispiel Ostwestfalen', in Manfred Hettling et al. (eds.), *Was ist Gesellschaftsgeschichte? Positionen, Themen, Analysen*, Munich 1991, 124–34, here 124.

14. Quoted from the reprint in Hartmut Pietsch (ed.), *Industrialisierung und soziale Frage in Duisburg*, Duisburg 1982, 57ff.

15. Thomas Mann, *Betrachtungen eines Unpolitischen*, Frankfurt 1988 (1st ed. 1918), 132.

16. For a well-documented example cf. Franz-Josef Brüggemeier, *Leben vor Ort. Ruhrbergleute und Ruhrbergbau 1889–1919*, Munich 1983, 36ff.

17. Cf. e.g. the important study by Heinz Reif, *Die verspätete Stadt. Industrialisierung, städtischer Raum und Politik in Oberhausen 1846–1929*, 2 vols., Cologne 1993.

18. Werner Sombart, *Das Proletariat. Bilder und Studien* (Sammlung sozialpsychologischer Monographien, ed. Martin Buber), Frankfurt 1906, 37.

19. On the much-discussed Hobrecht plan, cf. in English Brian Ladd, *Urban Planning and Civic Order in Germany, 1860–1914*, Cambridge, Mass. 1990, esp. 79ff.

20. Cf. e.g. Stefan Fisch, 'Die zweifache Intervention der Städte. Stadtplanerische Zukunftsgestaltung und Kontrolle der Wohnverhältnisse um 1900', in Jürgen Reulecke and Adelheid Gräfin zu Castell Rüdenhausen (eds.), *Stadt und Gesundheit. Zum Wandel von 'Volksgesundheit' und kommunaler Gesundheitspolitik im 19. und frühen 20. Jahrhundert*, Stuttgart 1991, 91–104.

21. On Oberhausen cf. Reif, *Verspätete Stadt* (as n. 17) and for a brief discussion of Sitte and Wagner, Rainer Hank, 'Topik und Topographie. Seelenlandschaft und Stadtlandschaft im Wien der Jahrhundertwende', in Manfred Smuda (ed.), *Die Großstadt als 'Text'*, Munich 1992, 217–38, esp. 226–33.

22. Karl Kraus, *Aphorismen. Pro domo et mundo*, (*Schriften*, vol. 8), Frankfurt 1986, 179–301, here 209.

23. The most recent discussion of municipal socialism in English is Jan Palmowski, *Urban Liberalism in Imperial Germany. Frankfurt am Main, 1866–1914*, Oxford 1999.

24. Cf. e.g. Ladd, *Urban Planning* (as note 19), Reulecke and Castell Rüdenhausen (eds.), *Stadt* (as note 20) and Beate Witzler, *Großstadt und Hygiene. Kommunale Gesundheitspolitik in der Epoche der Urbanisierung*, Stuttgart 1995.

25. For an evaluation in comparative perspective cf. Friedrich Lenger, 'Großstädtische Eliten vor den Problemen der Urbanisierung. Skizze eines deutsch-amerikanischen Vergleichs 1870–1914', *Geschichte und Gesellschaft* XXI (1995), 313–37.

26. Th. Weyl, 'Städtereinigung', *Handwörterbuch der Staatswissenschaften*, 3rd ed., vol. 7, Jena 1911, 773–80, at 774.

27. Cf. Richard Evans, *Death in Hamburg. Society and Politics in the Cholera Years 1830–1910*, Oxford 1987.

28. 'Cholera', *Meyers Konversations-Lexikon*, 5th ed., vol. 4, Leipzig 1894, 101–8, at 104.

29. Gustav Schmoller, *Ein Mahnruf in der Wohnungsfrage* (1887), quoted from the partial reprint in Hans J. Teuteberg and Clemens Wischermann (eds.), *Wohnalltag in Deutschland 1850–1914*, Münster 1985, 377f.

30. Cf. ibid. 131.

31. Cf. e.g. Clemens Wischermann, '"Familiengerechtes Wohnen": Anspruch und Wirklichkeit in Deutschland vor dem Ersten Weltkrieg', in Hans Jürgen Teuteberg (ed.), *Homo habitans. Zur Sozialgeschichte des ländlichen und städtischen Wohnens in der Neuzeit*, Münster 1985, 169–98, or Clemens Zimmermann, *Von der Wohnungsfrage zur Wohnungspolitik. Die Reformbewegung in Deutschland 1845–1914*, Göttingen 1991.

32. Carl Johannes Fuchs, 'Wohnungsfrage', *Handwörterbuch der Staatswissenschaften*, 3rd ed., vol. 8, Jena 1911, 873–928, at 891.

33. For a good discussion in English cf. Lutz Niethammer, 'Some Elements of the Housing Reform Debate in Nineteenth-Century Europe. Or, On the Making of a New Paradigm of Social Control', in Bruce M. Stave (ed.), *Modern Industrial Cities. History, Policy, and Survival*, Beverly Hills, Ca. 1981, 129–61.

34. Cf. many contributions to Hans Heinrich Blotevogel (ed.), *Kommunale Leistungsverwaltung und Stadtentwicklung vom Vormärz bis zur Weimarer Republik*, Cologne 1990, and to Reulecke and Castell Rüdenhausen (eds.), *Stadt* (as n. 20).

35. Cf. e.g. Detlev J. K. Peukert, *Grenzen der Sozialdisziplinierung. Aufstieg und Krise der deutschen Jugendfürsorge von 1878 bis 1932*, Cologne 1986.

36. Cf. Ute Frevert, '"Fürsorgliche Belagerung": Hygienebewegung und Arbeiterfrauen im 19. und frühen 20. Jahrhundert', *Geschichte und Gesellschaft* XI (1985), 420–46.

37. Cf. e.g. Friedrich Lenger, 'Bürgertum und Stadtverwaltung in rheinischen Großstädten des 19. Jahrhunderts. Zu einem vernachlässigten Aspekt bürgerlicher Herrschaft', in Lothar Gall (ed.), *Stadt und Bürgertum im 19. Jahrhundert*, Munich 1990, 97–169.

38. Andrew Lees, *Cities Perceived. Urban Society in European and American Thought, 1820–1940*, Manchester 1985.

39. Cf. e.g. Ladd, *Urban Planning* (as note 19) and Hermann Beckstein, *Städtische Interessenpolitik. Organisation und Politik der Städtetage in Bayern, Preußen und im Deutschen Reich 1896–1923*, Düsseldorf 1991.

40. Cf. besides Lees, *Cities* (as note 38) Klaus Bergmann, *Agrarromantik und Großstadtfeindschaft*, Meisenheim am Glan 1970.

41. Cf. the excellent summary by Rolf Peter Sieferle and Clemens Zimmermann, 'Die Stadt als Rassengrab', in Smuda (ed.), *Großstadt* (as note. 21), 53–71.

42. Cf. Ute Planert, *Antifeminismus im Kaiserreich. Diskurs, soziale Formation und politische Mentalität*, Göttingen 1998.

43. Werner Sombart, *Die deutsche Volkswirtschaft im 19. Jahrhundert und im Anfang des 20. Jahrhunderts. Eine Einführung in die Nationalökonomie*, 8th ed., Darmstadt 1954, 19f. (first published in 1903); cf. on Sombart's view of the city Friedrich Lenger, *Werner Sombart 1863–1941. Eine Biographie*, 2nd ed., Munich 1995, esp. 136–70.

44. Rainer Maria Rilke, *The Notebook of Malte Laurids Brigge*, introduced by Stephen Spender, Oxford 1984, 4. 6 and 139 (written in 1910).

45. Cf. the selection ed. by Wende, *Großstadtlyrik* (as n. 6).

46. Cf. Walter Grasskamp, 'Die Malbarkeit der Stadt. Die Krise der Vedute im deutschen Expressionismus', in Smuda (ed.), *Großstadt* (as n. 21), 265–84.

47. Simmel, *Metropolis* (as n. 2).

48. Cf. the convincing interpretations by Jutta Hülsewig-Johnen, 'Gesichter der Stadt. Überlegungen zur Menschendarstellung in den Großstadt-bildern des Expressionismus', in Smuda (ed.), *Großstadt* (as n. 21), 239–63.

49. Cf. Maria Tatar, *Lustmord: Sexual Murder in Weimar Germany*, Princeton, 1995, chs 4 and 5.

50. For a reproduction of decent quality cf. the catalogue by Eberhard Roters and Bernhard Schulz (eds.), *Ich und die Stadt. Mensch und Großstadt in der deutschen Kunst des 20. Jahrhunderts*, Berlin 1987, 89.

FRANZ-JOSEF BRÜGGEMEIER

Normal Pollution: Industrialization, Emissions and the Concept of Zoning in Germany, 1800–1970

In this essay I should like to combine a well-established area of historical research with a rather new one: urban history and environmental history. Of course, these two areas have much in common and aspects of pollution have a long tradition in urban history. But they were mainly seen as a side aspect and it was only very recently that environmental problems moved into the centre of historical research. As a consequence, our knowledge about them is still fairly limited. In this essay I shall, therefore, place special emphasis on the Ruhr region since from an environmental history point of view it is the best researched area in Germany and, furthermore, reveals, in a concise way, important elements of the more general development.

The Ruhr basin occupies an area approximately 60 kilometres long by 30 kilometres wide. The river that gives it its name – the Ruhr – lies in the southern part of the region; the river Rhine defines the western boundary, while the Emscher runs approximately parallel to the Ruhr, separated by distances ranging from about 6 to 20 kilometres.[1] Geographically the region is rather flat, with some small hills in the south. The soil is not very fertile and the climate is wet and moderate. Up until the late nineteenth century, the population was relatively small and largely agricultural; urbanization was limited. The largest towns in 1850 were Essen and Dortmund, each with populations of about 10,000 people.[2]

Whatever industrial development existed before 1850 lay in the hilly southern areas. Here coal seams lay just below the earth's surface,

and coal mining and several small iron works had existed since the
eighteenth century. The scale of mining was modest, with 12,000 miners
producing 1.5 million tons of coal in 1850. In the latter part of the
century the situation changed dramatically: by 1910 the number of
miners exceeded 400,000 and the production of coal had reached more
than 110 million tons.[3] In the early twentieth century a single modern
mine produced more coal than the whole area had produced sixty years
earlier. In addition, by 1900, huge integrated steel works dominated
the riverbanks. The Krupp Works in Essen, for instance, employed more
than 30,000 workers. The population of the town rose to more than
300,000 inhabitants, turning the sleepy countryside almost overnight
into an urban conglomerate. On the eve of the First World War, the
population of the Ruhr region had reached almost 3 million.[4]

The processes of urbanization and industrialization had far-reaching
consequences for the environment. Coal mining, coal processing, and
iron and steel industries imposed the greatest burdens. They consumed
large areas of land, erasing an agricultural landscape and extensively
polluting air, land and water. Because of the scale and the speed of
these changes and the predominance of heavy industry the Ruhr was
a special case. At the same time, the development in this and other
industrial areas is instructive for the whole of Germany, since the basic
institutions, laws and procedures that prevailed here also applied to
the rest of Germany. In industrial areas and especially in the Ruhr,
however, these mechanisms combined to produce a special result: they
emerged as areas where industry rather than nature or the environment was protected. While attempts to establish nature reserves or
national parks[5] had not been generally successful in Germany before
the First World War, industrial regions effectively became areas where
industry was protected, at the expense of nature. Rather than reducing
pollution and changing industry and technology accordingly, the
history of environmental policy in these regions can be seen as an
attempt to create a nature that was fit for industry.[6]

This is well illustrated by a 1916 ruling of the German Supreme
Court (*Reichsgericht*). In this case, the owner of some fruit trees had
sued for compensation from a nearby coke plant for damage to his
orchards. Normally, it was very difficult to ascribe such damage to a
particular cause and to prove beyond doubt that a specific factory was
to blame. Trees could be damaged by a variety of causes, and in most
cases there existed a great number of factories that could be responsible. In this instance, however, there was no doubt. In its ruling,
the court stated as a fact that the coke plant emitted noxious gases

and that these gases had destroyed the trees. The ruling, however, was surprising in that it contained no provision for compensation. Instead, the court asked the plaintiff how he could expect his trees to bear fruit, given their location in an industrial area. The judges noted that other factories in the vicinity did the same. Polluting factories, the court declared, were normal for the Ruhr. It was the cultivation of trees that was abnormal.[7]

It is difficult for us today to understand such decisions. They require explanations, especially in the context of the emerging discipline of environmental history. Since this is still a very young discipline and since at the same time the environmental issues under discussion often strike us as being of catastrophic dimensions, there was a tendency especially in the early days to develop all-embracing, fundamental explanations. The Christian understanding of nature, for example, was cited, in particular the biblical task of subduing the earth. Others blamed the development on modern, so-called mechanistic science, which in their eyes started with Newton, or they saw capitalist profit-oriented thinking as the decisive frame of reference.[8] Yet others saw such cases as proof of the fact that until recently there had been no awareness of environmental problems. These arguments do have a point. But they are much too abstract and generally unhelpful when it comes to explaining legal rulings like the one just mentioned.

At the same time there is a tendency in environmental history, at least in Germany, to concentrate on case studies. Some of these studies are very interesting, and the stories they tell are often fascinating and hard to believe.[9] They do, however, often leave the reader helpless and in need of explanations. What we need, therefore, are explanations which lie somewhere in between these two extremes. In my essay I would like to develop one such explanation by looking at industrial regions such as the Ruhr, and asking why they came to be so heavily polluted. I shall devote particular attention to the case of zoning, a concept familiar to urban historians and important, for example, when studying social segregation. I would like to argue that, in Germany at least, from about the middle of the nineteenth century zoning played a key role in dealing with environmental problems – an aspect which has as yet not been sufficiently recognized. And in connection with this I should like to introduce a further concept of considerable importance, that of *Ortsüblichkeit*, which can best be translated as 'local standards'. In the course of the argumentation it will become evident – and this is my third point – that debates on environmental problems and efforts to reduce them have taken place to a surprising extent since the very beginning of industrialization.

Contaminating enterprises such as tanneries and knacker's yards existed long before industrialization, and traditionally there had been attempts to locate them away from densely populated areas. These efforts continued at the onset of industrialization, and there are plenty of examples in Germany of chemical factories being erected on or relocated to sites outside towns.[10] But this approach created an increasing number of problems. The towns grew so rapidly, that outlying factories soon found themselves surrounded by houses. At the same time the number of factories increased, so that they could not all be built at a safe distance. Not that the owners wanted this. They wanted to be close to the towns, the workforce and the transport routes. Furthermore, this type of relocation contradicted the state's liberal economic policy. Finally, there was the danger that the instrument of relocation would be exploited to impede the setting up of factories or to prevent new ones altogether, a particular phenomenon of the first half of the nineteenth century.[11] The state authorities, therefore, began to interfere and increasingly blocked attempts to designate separate areas in or outside towns for factories on the one hand and for housing on the other.

However, the efforts on the part of the towns continued and led at times to the adoption of radical positions. A good example of this is a decree issued by the community of Steglitz near Berlin in 1890. In Steglitz a chemical plant had applied for a licence, the granting of which the community representatives were determined to impede. They knew from other places what a damaging effect such factories could have and how little could be done to oppose them, once permission had been granted. So they issued a decree which effectively declared Steglitz to be an industry-free zone. The decree prohibited the establishment of factories or plants in the locality, which could cause 'the inhabitants danger, disadvantage or annoyance by harmful fumes, thick smoke or unusual noise'.[12] The Berlin ministries were horrified by these regulations. They feared that other towns would follow suit, impeding the development of industrialization. Not all places attempted to hinder the process by introducing a general ban. Some towns, however, tried to implement a policy of zoning by declaring special areas for industry, workers' housing areas and middle-class districts. They did not intend to prohibit new industrial settlement generally, rather they wanted to channel it. But even this approach caused the Berlin government concern, because it was not clear to what extent industry might be held back by such a policy. So the authorities made Steglitz withdraw the decree.[13]

About thirty years earlier a similar discussion had taken place in Dresden. Here, too, there had been attempts to introduce a zoning policy, in this case at the request of the entrepreneurs themselves. This sounds surprising, considering that the aim was to keep factories out of certain areas. But the Dresden factory owners were, so to speak, thinking dialectically. They were prepared to accept the declaration of housing areas, if in compensation other areas were reserved for industrial plants. For they assumed that conditions in the industrial districts would be particularly advantageous for themselves. By that time, there had already been a considerable amount of controversy about pollution caused by factories, often leading to lengthy legal proceedings and in some instances to compensation awards. While the payments were not high, the frequent cases of disagreement were a thorn in the flesh of the factory owners. They wanted to avoid them and therefore pleaded that industry in the factory districts should enjoy immunity against complaints about smoke and soot. Inhabitants of these zones should lose their right to lodge complaints, and the factories should be generally freed from any obligation to pay compensation.[14]

These sound like strong demands, but in the debates of the time they were backed up by an interesting argument. Progress in modern industry – as the Prussian Supreme Court concluded in 1852 – had shown that while factories were beneficial, they necessarily also had drawbacks. It was a crucial and novel aspect of the spreading factory system, so the Supreme Court argued, that disadvantages like emissions were a basic component of production and not one that could easily be avoided. This was not a question of failure on the part of the factory owner, the judges declared, it was rather an inevitable consequence of industrial production. And since factory owners could not really avoid these emissions, there should be no obligation for them to pay damages. The state and society as a whole, so the argument continued, wanted factories to be established. They wanted to profit from their production and welcomed the jobs they provided. It was therefore not fair for society to enjoy the advantages they brought but to attribute all the responsibility for the drawbacks to the factory owners. Rather, the disadvantages had to be shared by all.[15]

A short time before, in 1848, this argument had led to a compensation demand being dismissed, although there was no doubt about the fact that the defending entrepreneur had caused the damage of which he was accused. Following the argumentation outline above, this ruling was consistent. But, as a commentator remarked, it would amount to 'the mutual destruction of property being regarded as the normal state of affairs. This would jeopardize the continuing existence of civil society.' [16]

Realizing these consequences of its verdict, the Prussian Supreme Court soon revised its position. In Dresden too, the demands of the factory owners went too far for the liking of the officials. Industry was, in their opinion, striving for 'complete immunity', that is to say, for a position outside established legislation. The authorities did not comply with the factory owners' wishes, and this was why the Dresden attempt failed, but it had indicated a direction which in the following decades would prove to be the most important one. Gradually the drive to establish factory districts succeeded in spite of all opposition. At first these districts lacked planning, but later they were more systematic. In practice this approach was shown to offer numerous advantages. It was possible to concentrate factories in certain regions, keeping them at a distance from others. In addition, conditions particularly advantageous for industry were introduced here. This did not entail suspending the rights of local inhabitants, as the Dresden factory owners had demanded, because in principle local residents retained the right to file complaints against industrial emissions. But in practice this right became increasingly worthless, as the court decision of 1916 showed. Courts and authorities proceeded more and more to apply different yardsticks in factory districts, referring to the above-mentioned concept of *Ortsüblichkeit*, i.e. local standards.[17]

The concept of local standards has played an important role in Germany from the beginning of industrialization, since even the first factories provoked controversy and opposition from local inhabitants. Nowadays when such conflicts arise precise regulations are issued and, for example, emission limits define what factories have to adhere to. Both these options created enormous difficulties for most of the nineteenth and well into the twentieth century. Factory owners, public authorities, technicians and scientists knew far too little to be able to issue precise regulations, and moreover it was very difficult to determine limits, let alone control them. Such limits have to be quantified and above all they have to be measured with appropriate apparatuses. These were developed only slowly, so alternative solutions had to be found, among them the concept of local standards.

In the early stages of industrialization, the argument of local standards could be used to hamper the setting up of factories, since they were still an exception.[18] As factories increased in number the situation changed. Their presence became more and more 'normal', their emissions spread and the standards of normality in the affected regions changed. We can see this in the example of the Hermann-shütte near Dortmund.[19] This ironworks had been built in the 1850s and had caused its neighbours annoyance right from the beginning with its smoke and foul waste water. The licence for the ironworks, granted in 1841, stated explicitly that such damages had to be indemnified, and this did happen. The cemetery gardener for example received 150 Marks each year because his flowers and plants withered, and in 1897 a total of fifty-four people received payments of between 1 and 750 Marks.[20]

Around this time, however, the attitude of the ironworks changed. A little later, in 1899, a resident who owned several houses in the immediate vicinity was to experience this when she complained that she could hardly find tenants on account of the dirt spread by dust and smoke. She called in a lawyer and demanded compensation and redress for her grievances.[21] Both claims were turned down categorically by the ironworks, with explicit reference to the concept of local standards. At first the neighbourhood of the works had been agrarian in character, they explained, and that was why compensation had been paid. In more recent years, however, numerous other factories had settled in the area. The old village had been converted into an industrial site, in which other standards applied. Industrial emissions were no longer the exception, they had become the rule and were thus 'normal'. To quote the ironworks, persons 'living in the vicinity of large industrial plants have to put up with those causes of annoyance which do not exceed the measure of norm and necessity and which are shown to be an inevitable inconvenience'.[22]

The houseowner took the ironworks to court. This case also came before the Reichsgericht (Imperial Court) in Berlin. To help it reach a decision the court called in numerous experts, one of whom, Professor Brockmann from Bochum, expressed the prevailing opinion in a particularly succinct manner. Right at the outset Brockmann made reference to the underlying problem contained in the commissioned report. He was to judge whether the damages caused by the works corresponded to the local conditions. That presented him with difficulties, since this was not a purely technical issue, for which there existed exact standards; on the contrary, 'personal views and relative concepts' – as he put it – greatly influenced the forming of an opinion. To illustrate this problem he described in detail how he himself lived.

> I have been living in Bochum for the past twenty years, and when west
> wind prevails I have to inhale a yellow-brown, thick atmosphere heavy with
> smoke, soot and ashes (from the Bochum steel works); the north wind
> wafts revolting fumes (from several collieries) into my nostrils; if the wind
> comes from the south I enjoy the fumes from the iron foundries, the
> gasworks, chemical factories, etc. Soot and smoke bother me wherever I
> go, and loud noises and earth tremors of all kinds disturb me at work
> during the day and chase away my sleep at night. This is all very bother-
> some and unpleasant, but has to be tolerated in industrial areas.

Having heard his description of the truly infernal conditions and his
apparently heroic readiness to accept the situation, we should not be
surprised to learn that in the course of his four site visits Professor
Brockmann was not able to determine

> what would be likely to cast doubt on my appraisal of the situation in favour
> of industry; to judge from the files I would have expected worse conditions.
> . . . Hoerde [nowadays part of Dortmund] is a town dominated by factories
> and ironworks to the highest degree and is no health or summer resort.
> Whoever moves to Hoerde will be aware that he has to expect an atmos-
> phere contaminated by the extensive factory sites of the iron industry. All
> sorts of smells will irritate his nose, and loud noises will cause his ears to
> vibrate, because [this is a place, where] you find heavy masses of iron and
> steel in motion and not padded cushions filled with air.[23]

His enquiries confirmed the complaints and reports made by the local
residents, but in comparison with his own home in Bochum they hardly
seemed worth mentioning. What was more important, he argued,
where such conditions prevailed, was that appropriate safety measures
should be implemented and here, he stated, the plaintiff was very
definitely found wanting. The windows did not close tightly; the gutters
did not incline enough, so that soot and ash could not be washed away
by the rain; it was too long since the curtains had been washed, and
the living room was utterly cheerless. 'In short, one sees there is no
real determination to combat the existing adversities.'[24] These were
indeed considerable, but on the whole did not exceed the level prevailing in Hoerde.

The court largely followed his opinion. It concluded, however, that
one of the technical processes used in the ironworks deviated so much
from the norm and was so harmful that it was no longer employed
elsewhere. The court case was not therefore dismissed outright, and
the factory had to pay a (very small) part of the damages. The argument
of local standards (*Ortsüblichkeit*) thus did not amount to a completely

free warrant. Even in industrial zones industry had to comply with minimum standards and to avoid a catastrophic amount of damage. However, it did continue to enjoy special privileges and could expect the local residents, as required in Hoerde, to put up with soot and ash in the living room, to wash curtains and clothing frequently, and even to accept that trees would perish.

But that was not all. It was not enough that the inhabitants adapted to industry. Furthermore attempts were even made to adapt nature itself to the new conditions. These attempts went back to the nineteenth century and were especially widely discussed in a conflict that began around 1850, lasted until the turn of the century and took place near Freiberg in Saxony. In this case, widespread damage was caused by a state-owned smelting works. Over several decades, numerous committees were set up to sponsor scientific experiments, leading to the construction of ever higher chimneys, but also to the suggestion that the farmers choose fruits and animals that were suited to industrial emissions.[25] This was no easy task, and in Freiberg the results were disappointing. The fruits chosen did not live up to the expectations; the use of quicklime – to neutralize the sulphurous gases – proved ineffective; and generally the costs involved were too high. But in spite of these setbacks the idea of adapting nature to the new situation gained ground and was particularly strongly supported by a commission examining air pollution in the Ruhr region in the 1920s.

The reason for the investigation of this commission was the occupation of the Ruhr by the French in 1923. This occupation gave rise to a general strike. Industrial production stopped overnight, and with it the contamination of water, air and soil. The results were astounding, especially for nature. The general strike began in spring, at the beginning of a new vegetation cycle. For the first time in decades nature did not suffer from emissions and showed amazing changes, as we hear from a biologist's report.

> As soon as the extraction and production of coal, coke and steel stopped, air conditions in the Ruhr region improved clearly, noticeable even for humans, so that one could no longer discern a difference from non-industrial areas. The change had an amazingly favourable effect on the vegetation. This effect was best seen in the root crops, the leaves of which stayed green right into the autumn, whereas previously they had often withered by early summer. . . . The potatoes, which are regarded as being very sensitive to smoke, showed a willingness to flower such as had not been known for a long time. . . . All the other field crops grew equally well in 1923. Inasmuch as they had already been growing above ground over

winter and had been affected by smoke at a young phase, they recovered almost completely. . . . Bare spots gradually receded. In contrast to other years, when only two cuts were possible, as many as three cuts were made with yields seldom seen. . . . Growth in the gardens was so abundant that in many places there was more than enough food for their owners' consumption and substantial amounts still could be sold, which had been unthinkable before. . . . The crops, which were normally always stained with a thin layer of soot, flue dust and tar particles were remarkably clean.

Even the annual rings on the trees (Figure 1) were thicker in 1923 than in previous or later years.[26]

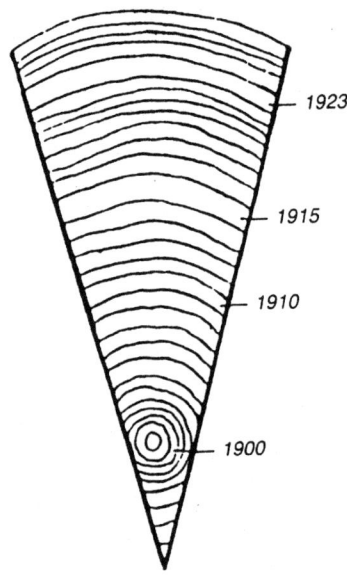

Figure 1   Cross-section of tree showing annual growth rings.

The passive resistance stopped in the autumn. Production recommenced, much to the relief of the populace, which as a consequence of the general strike had lost its income and suffered enormously. The stoppage of industrial production had been good for nature, but it had been far from good for the inhabitants of the Ruhr. For them, smoking chimneys promised an end to the deprivations. It had, however, become abundantly clear how very harmful industrial emissions were for the vegetation of the Ruhr. To investigate this issue and to recommend solutions the aforementioned commission was set up in 1924.

The commission confirmed that fumes, especially the sulphurous acids they contained, caused considerable damage and led to wholesale tree blight[27] (Figures 2 and 3). But there was little that could be undertaken to correct this situation, the commission found, because there were no methods available to remove the sulphurous acids. This statement was not correct. Such methods existed and were already in use, in gasworks for example, to purify the gas of such substances, thus making it available for household use. But this type of treatment was expensive, and neither it nor other possible means were considered further. On the contrary the commission concluded resignedly: 'The fight against smoke pollution caused by heavy industry appears to have little chance of success.'[28] It envisaged only one alternative: breeding and cultivating acid-resistant trees.

In its opinion, 'the only way to preserve forest stands lies in the direction of planting acid-resistant tree types, and any attempt to preserve the sensitive conifers should be abandoned as futile'.[29] It had been known for a long time that deciduous trees were more resistant to smoke fumes than conifers, and individual types were regarded as particularly smoke-proof. As a result, tree nurseries were set up to cultivate these trees and to sell them at a discount to forest owners and

Figure 2   Trees damaged by pollution in the Ruhr Area (28 years old)

*Figure 3   Trees in an unpolluted area (26 years old). The white trees show the height
reached by the trees in Figure 2, i.e. approximately 20 per cent.*

the town councils. Similar efforts were being made elsewhere, by for
example, the Association of German Engineers. This association had
itself set up a commission to investigate smoke pollution and by the
end of the 1920s its members wanted to not only breed acid-resistant
trees but also industry-proof plants generally. They proposed to search
for a factory with high emission rates on an isolated site, to cultivate
around the factory a large number of different plants and then to determine the survival rates. In the meantime, however, the slump of 1929
had broken out and the plan failed owing to a lack of money.[30]

But this only meant that particularly ambitious attempts to adapt
nature to industry could not be realized. In practice the inhabitants
of industrial areas were still expected to adapt their behaviour, their
choice of garden plants and their farming practices to the demands
of industry. This attitude persisted under National Socialism and was
explicitly confirmed by a further ruling of the Reichsgericht (Supreme
Court) in 1937. In this case a farmer from Oberhausen had sued a
steelworks, but instead of being awarded the expected compensation
he was asked by the court, 'to run his farm according to local conditions and to choose a type of cultivation which is as resilient as possible
to contaminating influences'. Even then, however, only partial damages
would be allowed, since in an industrial area like the Ruhr the remainder
had to be 'tolerated without indemnity'.[31]

After the war this was still the prevailing line of argument. In 1951, at the beginning of the *Wirtschaftswunder*, the German economic miracle, a resident of Duisburg lodged a complaint about the acid smoke emitted from a nearby chemical plant. Here too the authorities admitted the damage caused, but at the same time they dismissed the case on the grounds that – and the reasoning is now familiar – in an industrial town like Duisburg 'one has to accept contamination such as this, since it must always be reckoned with here'.[32]

To sum up the argument: effectively, since the nineteenth century, certain districts within towns or whole regions such as the Ruhr had emerged with very high levels of pollution. An important reason for this development was the notion of *Ortsüblichkeit*, i.e. normal local standards, and in connection with this, the concept of zoning. As mentioned earlier, this concept was originally opposed by the state authorities, but became such a practical solution that from the middle of the 1890s onwards the Prussian Government gave up its resistance. For zoning not only benefited industry by allowing factories to concentrate in particular areas; it also prevented them from infiltrating others. Take the southern Ruhr region for example, which has remained even up until today an upper-class residential area within an attractive countryside. It was here that Alfred Krupp sought refuge

Figure 4   The house that Alfred Krupp built in the grouds of his factory.

in the 1870s. He had only just built himself a fine house with a con-
servatory and a small park in the middle of his factory grounds (Figure
4).[33] In this way he had wanted to demonstrate his close ties with his
workers, but he soon realized that the smoke, smog and noise made
life unbearable in his new and pretty house. So he built his Villa Hügel
overlooking the Ruhr, a huge house in the style of an English mansion.
Together with the other residents of the area he made sure through
a written agreement with the town of Essen that no polluting industry
would ever be permitted there.[34] In other cities comparable areas
existed. In Berlin, for example in Dahlem and Grunewald, or along
the banks of the Alster in Hamburg, industry was also kept away from
health and holiday resorts and from better-class housing areas in
general.

In other words, pollution was limited to specific localities and
regions, and localization and regionalization formed a key aspect of
environmental politics right up to the 1970s. In this way it was largely
possible to save large areas of Germany from heavy pollution. In
return, other regions suffered far more, but this seemed to be accept-
able, because the predominant opinion held the effects to be admittedly
unpleasant and regrettable, but not really alarming, at least as far
as human health was concerned. It is true that there had been warnings
of possible health hazards all through the nineteenth century, but it
was difficult at that time to produce unambiguous proof. Thus,
concentrating contamination regionally appeared to be a justifiable
solution, although the proponents of the zoning concept were all too
conscious of the fact that they were thus privileging certain classes
of society.

As early as the 1860s for example, there were demands to prohibit
factories being set up in Berlin's favoured residential area, the so-
called Tiergarten, because this district of the city provided 'government officials with quiet housing'.[35] Elsewhere, it was said, 'people
with an abnormal, sedentary way of life'[36] should be spared the injurious
effects of industrial emissions, and the inhabitants of Steglitz expressed
– in the dispute about the chemical factory mentioned above – more
clearly who was actually meant by this strange formulation. They
wanted to prevent the chemical factory from settling in their community so that it could continue to survive as a pleasant suburb 'for
a large number of civil servants, writers, merchants etc., whose health
requires that after the day's burdens and toil they live in fresh and
pure air'.[37] It was the general opinion that workers on the other hand
had become accustomed to bad air so that, as an observer put it, 'by

no means all parts of the population need the same protection'.[38] In fact, it was often argued that the influx of workers would create far greater problems than the setting up of factories themselves and that the real task consisted of preventing this influx of the working classes.

These lines of argument and mechanisms prevailed well into the 1960s. Only then did things start to change, as I can only briefly describe at the close of this essay. An important factor for this change was the growing anger about pollution levels. Even in the Ruhr region, where the population had had to put up with so much for so long, complaints were increasingly being voiced. Added to this was the more reliable scientific research, enabling health risks to be identified more effectively than before. Pressure grew for measures to be taken against pollution, and this took the form, among others, of building even higher chimney stacks, so as to discharge smoke and gases at greater heights, dispersing them over larger areas and thus diluting them. Such efforts can be traced back to the nineteenth century, but by the 1970s they were undertaken much more systematically and at far greater expense. The chimneys sometimes exceeded heights of 200 to 250 metres and they achieved the desired effect. In the Ruhr region the situation improved. This approach, however, also had an undesirable effect. The pollutants did not disappear in the 'infinite sea of the sky' – as it had long been hoped. Rather they descended elsewhere, distributing the load. Accordingly, complaints increased in areas such as the Black Forest or Bavaria, which until then had largely been spared industrial pollution. Such pollution was also caused by factories, and by industry in general, spreading into the countryside as a result of the economic miracle after 1950. Thus the principle of localization and regionalization was doubly violated, on the one hand by building higher chimneys, on the other by factories spreading into agricultural areas.[39]

By the early 1980s it had become all too obvious that the familiar approach of concentrating contamination in certain areas no longer promised to be a viable solution. The inhabitants of such areas were no longer prepared to put up with the situation and besides, industry had spread far beyond these regions. One result of this development was the tree blight, which provoked considerable outcry, especially in Germany, and mobilized public opinion. Within a few years, scientists argued, large parts of the German forests would die out, and the remaining woodlands would probably all but disappear in the 1990s. The pictures of blighted trees were impressive and delivered to the public clear proof of the fact that the policy of high chimney stacks had failed.

Ecologically speaking, the outcome of the policy of high chimney
stacks was problematic, while from the point of view of environmental
politics the tree blight also had positive results. It made crystal clear
the point that pollution could no longer be concentrated within certain
regions, that diluting pollutants was not a viable option, and that
attempts to create a nature fit for industry had failed. On the contrary,
contamination had spread, and new measures were called for, much
of which has now passed into legislation. Within a few years the large
power plants and factories had to employ filters and implement other
measures to reduce emission levels. The results are impressive, as
Tables 1 and 2 show, but they were not only the consequence of new
policies.[40] One also has to bear in mind that many factories closed
down, especially in the Ruhr region, because of the deep crisis of coal
mining and heavy industry in general. Comparable charts could be
shown for other harmful substances, not only for air, but also for water
and soil. The debate on tree blight has had a decisive influence on
these changes and on the introduction of new approaches in environmental politics. This in itself is a fascinating story, which I cannot go
into here, not the least because so far very little research has been
done on it.[41] But I would like to mention an ironic aspect to this story
which has gone largely unnoticed in the public debate.

A few years ago a book was published in Germany about the state
of European forests.[42] The authors had surveyed various countries
and carefully examined the tree growth over the past decades. Their

Table 1   Trend of Emissions in the Rhine-Ruhr-Area (Germany) – Annual
Averages Sulphur Dioxide.

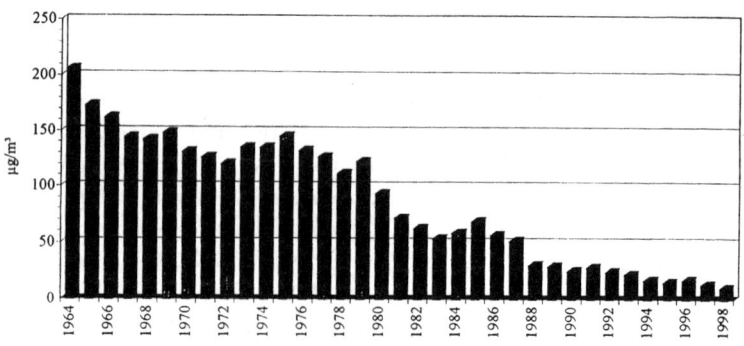

Source: Landesumweltamt Nordrhein-Westfalen, 1999.

Table 2 Trend of Emissions in the Rhine-Ruhr-Area (Germany) – Annual Averages Lead in Suspended Particulates.

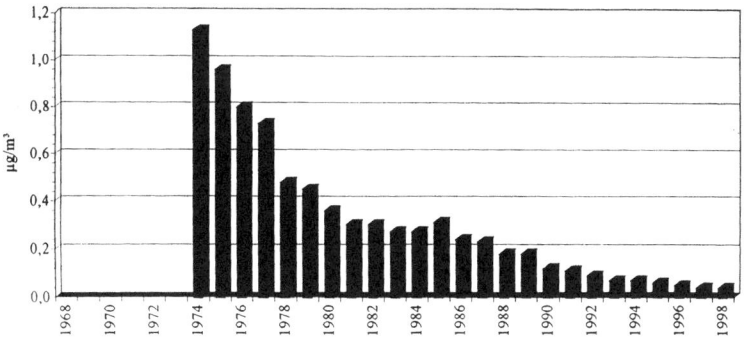

Source: Landesumweltamt Nordrhein-Westfalen, 1999.

findings are astonishing: there is no question of forests generally dying out. On the contrary, during the past decades trees have grown at an unusually strong and fast rate – with the exception of individual locations with particularly unfavourable conditions or where, as in parts of the modern Czech Republic, factory pollution is extremely high. Otherwise trees are growing at a faster rate than before – and here we probably have a further example of how myths can exercise great influence and create their own reality. Nevertheless, the inhabitants of the Ruhr basin can undoubtedly be thankful for the myth of the dying forests and its consequences, because it helped to clean their air.

Notes

1. N. J. G. Pounds, 'The Ruhr Area: A Problem in Definition', *Geography* 36 (1951), 165–78.
2. H.-G. Steinberg, *Die Entwicklung des Ruhrgebiets. Eine wirtschafts- und sozialgeographische Studie*, Düsseldorf 1967; W. Dege, *Das Ruhrgebiet*, Berlin, 3rd ed., Stuttgart 1983; N. J. G. Pounds, *The Ruhr. A Study in Historical and Economic Geography*, London 1953.
3. K. Tenfelde, *Sozialgeschichte der Bergarbeiterschaft an der Ruhr im 19. Jahrhundert*, Bonn/Bad Godesberg 1977.

4. W. Fischer, *Herz des Reviers. 125 Jahre Wirtschaftsgeschichte des Industrie- und Handelskammerbezirks Essen-Mülheim-Oberhausen*, Essen 1965; P. Wiel, *Wirtschaftsgeschichte des Ruhrgebiets, Tatsachen und Zahlen*, Essen 1970; W. Weber, 'Entfaltung der Industriewirtschaft', in W. Köllmann et al. (eds.), *Das Ruhrgebiet im Industriezeitalter*, Düsseldorf, vol 1, pp. 199–319; E. C. McCreary, 'Essen 1860–1914. A Case Study of the Impact of Industrialization on German Community Life', Ph.D. Yale University.

5. W. Schoenichen, *Naturschutz, Heimatschutz. Ihre Begründung durch Ernst Rudorff, Hugo Conwentz und ihre Vorläufer*, Stuttgart 1954; A. Knaut, *'Zurück zur Natur'! Die Wurzeln der Ökologiebewegung*, Greven 1993.

6. For a more detailed discussion of the argument presented here see F.-J. Brüggemeier and Th. Rommelspacher, *Blauer Himmel über der Ruhr. Geschichte der Umwelt im Ruhrgebiet 1840–1990*, Essen 1992; F.-J. Brüggemeier, *Das unendliche Meer der Lüfte. Luftverschmutzung, Industrialisierung und Risikodebatten im 19. Jahrhundert*, Essen 1996.

7. H. Bergerhoff, *Untersuchungen über die Berg- und Rauchschädenfrage mit bes. Berücksichtigung des Ruhrbezirks*, Bonn 1928, 107–9.

8. L. White, 'The Historical Roots of Our Ecological Crisis', Science 155 (1967), 1203–7; C. Amery, *Das Ende der Vorsehung. Die gnadenlosen Folgen des Christentums*, Reinbek 1972; C. Merchant, *Death of Nature. Women, Ecology and the Scientific Revolution*, San Francisco 1987; I. Diamond and G.F. Orentein (eds.), *Reweaving the World: The Emergence of Ecofeminism*, San Francisco 1990; for more recent literature see the journal *Capitalism, Nature, Socialism. A Journal of Socialist Ecology*.

9. J. Calließ, J. Rüsen and M. Striegnitz (eds.), *Mensch und Umwelt in der Geschichte*, Pfaffenweiler 1989; G. Jaritz and V. Winiwarter (eds.), *Umweltbewältigung. Die historische Perspektive*, Bielefeld 1994; R. Henneking, *Chemische Industrie und Umwelt. Konflikte um Umweltbelastungen durch die chemische Industrie am Beispiel der schwerchemischen Farben- und Düngemittelindustrie der Rheinprovinz (ca. 1800–1914)* (*Zeitschrift für Unternehmensgeschichte*: Beiheft 86), Stuttgart 1994; A. Andersen, (ed.), *Umweltgeschichte. Das Beispiel Hamburg*, Hamburg 1990.

10. I. Mieck, '"Aerem corrumpere non licet". Luftverunreinigung und Immissionsschutz in Preußen bis zur Gewerbeordnung 1869', *Technikgeschichte* 48 (1967), 36–78; Brüggemeier, *Das unendliche Meer*, 79ff.

11. See *Entwurf eines allgemeinen Gewerbe-Polizei-Gesetzes nebst Motiven*, Berlin 1837.

12. GSta Merseburg Rep. 120 BB II a 1 Nr. 1 adh. 1, Bl. 130.

13. Ibid., reports by the Ministry of Commerce (11.2.1891) and the Ministry of the Interior (13.7.1891), Bl. 152f.

14. See Lent and Hendel (1889), Oertliche Lage der Fabriken in den Städten, Referate und Diskussion und Resolution der 14. Versammlung zu Fall 13.9.1888, DVföG 11: 59f.

15. See *Justiz-Ministerialblatt für die Preußische Gesetzgebung und Rechtspflege* 14 (1852), 259–61.

16. C. E. Koch, *Allgemeines Landrecht für die Preußischen Staaten*, 4 vols, Berlin and Leipzig 1884, 393.

17. See Brüggemeier, *Das unendliche Meer*, chs. 6 and 10.

18. See R. Ogorek, 'Actio negatoria und industrielle Beeinträchtigung des Grundeigentums', in H. Coing and W. Wilhelm (eds.), *Wissenschaft und Kodifikation des Privatrechts im 19. Jahrhundert*, vol. 4, Frankfurt/M. 1979, 40–78; U. Gilhaus, '*Schmerzenskinder der Industrie*'. *Umweltverschmutzung, Umweltpolitik und sozialer Protest im Industriezeitalter in Westfalen 1845–1914*, Paderborn 1995.

19. See Brüggemeier and Rommelspacher, *Blauer Himmel*, 37f.

20. Hoesch Archiv DHHU 2112, letter of the gardener, 24 June 1896.

21. Ibid., DHHU 1580, letter from the lawyers, 22 April 1899.

22. Ibid., Statement by the ironworks, 29 May 1899.

23. Ibid., report by Brockmann, 15 July 1903.

24. Ibid., between May and July Brockmann inspected the ironworks and its neighbourhood three times.

25. See A. Andersen, *Historische Technikfolgenabschätzung am Beispiel des Metallhüttenwesens und der Chemieindustrie, 1850–1933*, Stuttgart 1996; Brüggemeier, *Das unendliche Meer*, ch. 7.

26. Bergerhoff, *Untersuchungen*, 72–6.

27. Siedlungsverband Ruhrkohlenbezirk (ed.), *Denkschrift über die Walderhaltung im Ruhrkohlebezirk*, Essen (1927), 35

28. Id., *Bisherige Tätigkeit des Ausschusses für Rauchbekämpfung beim Siedlungsverband Ruhrkohlenbezirk*, Essen (1928), 17.

29. Ibid. 16.

30. See Bundesarchiv Koblenz R 154, 92.

31. See *Juristische Wochenschrift* 66 (1937), 1237ff.

32. HStAD Reg. Düsseldorf BR 1015/22, Schreiben vom 9. Oktober 1951, Bl. 131f.

33. K. Tenfelde (ed.), *Bilder von Krupp. Fotografie und Geschichte im Industriezeitalter*, Munich 1994, 56/5.

34. See F.-J. Brüggemeier, *Leben vor Ort. Ruhrbergleute und Ruhrbergbau 1889–1919*, 2nd edn, Munich 1984, 36–8.

35. GStA Merseburg Rep 120 BB II 1 Nr. 69, statement by the advisory committee in technical affairs, 14. March 1861.

36. See *Entscheidungen des Oberverwaltungsgerichts* 18 (1890), 317.

37. *Magdeburger Zeitung*, 9 October 1890.

38. See A. Weiland, 'Die Frankfurter Zonenbauordnung von 1891 – eine "fortschrittliche" Bauordnung?', in J. Rodriguez-Lores and G. Fehl (eds.), *Städtebaureform 1865–1900. Von Licht, Luft und Ordnung in der Stadt der Gründerzeit*, 2 vols, Hamburg 1985, 383.

39. See R. Weichelt, 'Die Entwicklung der Umweltschutzpolitik im Ruhrgebiet am Beispiel der Luftreinhaltung 1949–1962', in R. Bovermann and St. Goch and H. J. Priamus (eds.), *Das Ruhrgebiet – ein starkes Stück NRW*, Essen 1996, 476–98; Th. Rommelspacher, 'Zwischen Heimatschutz

und Umweltprotest. Konflikte um Natur, Umwelt und Technik in der BRD 1945–65', in *Forum Geschichtskultur, Information 1/1998*, Essen 1998, 22–9; Brüggemeier and Rommelspacher, *Blauer Himmel*; K. G. Wey, *Umweltpolitik in Deutschland. Kurze Geschichte des Umweltschutzes in Deutschland seit 1900*, Opladen 1982.

40.   Minister für Umwelt, Raumordnung und Landwirtschaft des Landes NRW, *Luftreinhaltung in Nordrhein-Westfalen. Eine Erfolgsbilanz der Luftreinhaltungsplanung 1975–1988*, Düsseldorf 1989, 198.

41.   See E. Müller, *Innenwelt der Umweltpolitik. Sozial-liberale Umweltpolitik – (Ohn)macht durch Organisation?*, Opladen 1995; H.-P. Vierhaus, *Umwelt-bewußtsein von oben. Zum Verfassungsgebot demokratischer Willensbildung*, Berlin 1994; Wey, *Umweltpolitik*.

42.   H. Spieker et al. (eds.), *Growth Trends in European Forests*, Berlin 1996.

HANS-ULRICH THAMER

Urban Society and Urban Politics in Germany between the Wars

In the last decade modern urban history has received a fresh impetus: we can observe a remarkable intensification, as well as a specialization and differentiation, of historical research. Corresponding to the expansion of political and social functions of the modern cities historians revealed new fields of research, from local health policy to welfare policy, from leisure culture to criminality. In addition, our view on historical subjects became broader and more different-iated. Particular groups within the major social classes as well as the social consequences of local politics attracted scholarly attention.

From the last decades of the nineteenth century one of the most outstanding features of urban politics was the growing interest in municipal services. The formulation and realization of a growing spectrum of public services designed to improve the living conditions of city dwellers and to defuse the social problems and conflicts caused by urbanization and industrialization became the major focus of urban politics and public interest.[1] Even foreign visitors came to German cities in order to study the new policy of municipal services and social provision for the future (*Daseinsvorsorge*). The American Frederic Howe wrote on the eve of the First World War:

The German cities are thinking of tomorrow as well as of today, of the generations to follow as well as the generation that is now upon the stage. Germany almost alone among the civilized nations sees the city as the permanent centre of the civilization of the future, and Germany almost alone is building its cities to make them contribute to the happiness, health and well-being of the people.

The constitution of the Weimar Republic marked an important change.[2] While the cities proved the efficiency and the flexibility of their practice in municipal social provisions during the war and in the immediate post-war years, the constitution of a democratic social welfare state, which enforced the tendency towards centralization, reduced the autonomy of cities. This reduction began with the financial reform of Matthias Erzberger in 1919, which put the municipal budget into a condition of dependence on the national assignment. This dependence grew dramatically during the economic crisis of the late 1920s and was fuelled by the policy of austerity decreed by the government of Chancellor Brüning. The consequences were a severe decline of local self-government and of public services. The crisis of local self-government as well as other phenomena of political and social crisis gave the National Socialist movement the chance to misuse the surviving foundations of local government for their ideological policy.

This story of permanent decline was one of the reasons why urban history has not held much attraction for historical research in comparison to the pre-war years, which marked the climax of a social reform movement that partly took its rise from the cities. Although the political life of the German cities in the 1920s and early 1930s gave rise to some important and famous mayors and influential heads of local authorities, contemporary urban history seemed to be of minor attraction. Not only because the welfare state (*Sozialstaat*) became more important than the social city (*Sozialstadt*), but as a result of a permanent decline of political and cultural urban identity, which started in the years between the wars.

However, this seems to be a narrow and one-sided view, harking back to a glorious bourgeois past of the nineteenth century and to the climax of urbanization. This view fails to take account of the urban capacity for improvisation as well as the varieties of urban politics and strategies that were developed in order to answer the urgent social problems of the 1920s. It also overlooks the specific forms of an intertwining of the public and private spheres in the German welfare state, which constituted itself in the Weimar Republic and established a tradition of a mixed economy of welfare. Within this network of a neo-corporate constitution and social-political interests one can study the consequences of local administration and politics as if in a social laboratory.

My purpose is to demonstrate some of the main problems of urban politics between the wars by reference to the important field of welfare politics in the German cities. First of all I want to turn to the problem of municipal activities, the free rein they could hold and the embarrassments they were confronted with during the Weimar Republic. Secondly, I want to ask what they contributed to the development of the welfare state. Furthermore I am interested in the social conflicts within the urban communities as they are reflected in the process of the implementation of the local welfare system. For this reason I will concentrate my view on the urban welfare politics of three German cities during the 1920s and 1930s, which have been the object of a research project conducted at Münster University over the past years.[3] These cities – Nuremberg,[4] Frankfurt and Leipzig[5] – were characterized by many identical structural factors, but also by some significant differences. They belonged to the group of the ten largest cities of the German Reich, they had a mixed confessional structure with a Protestant majority, and they were all centres of industry and services with a similar socio-professional structure. While in Nuremberg the industrial sector took the lead, Frankfurt saw a preponderance of commercial and banking businesses, which permitted a certain financial stability even in times of crisis. The industry of Nuremberg and Leipzig on the other hand, which produced finished articles, suffered from a high dependency on economic trends. Nevertheless, the social problems and defects were more or less similar. The constitutional urban system showed differences between Frankfurt and Leipzig on the one hand and Nuremberg on the other hand. The local authorities in Frankfurt and Leipzig were headed by a town council (*Magistrat*), while in Nuremberg we find the south German type of a *Ratsverfassung*, i.e. a one-chamber constitution, designed to reduce conflicts between the town parliament and the head of the municipal administration. More important though were the different forms of political behaviour and culture, which in a very profound way affected political decisions in social politics. While the political atmosphere in Frankfurt and Nuremberg was dominated by liberal-socialist alliances, the urban political community of Leipzig was divided into bourgeois and proletarian camps. The potential for political consensus was extremely small, whereas in Frankfurt and Nuremberg there existed a basic consensus between the parties of the Weimar coalition and the local authorities, which allowed a policy of social compromise. The balance between confrontation and co-operation reflected the policy of the Social Democratic Party (SPD) as well as the behaviour of bourgeois groups. In Leipzig the SPD defined itself as the guardian of the proletarian milieu and remained in a majority position, which seemed to be confirmed by the fact that socialists were expelled from the urban political decision-making process. In Nuremberg and Frankfurt the Social Democrats followed a reform line and participated in local politics, especially in the realm of social politics and welfare administration.

Three spheres of urban social politics will demonstrate the potential for conflicts and co-operation, of centralization and participation: public welfare, labour market politics, and housing welfare. The first will demonstrate the conflict between public and private welfare, the second the conflict between social city and social state, the third the conflict between public welfare and private economic interests.

In line with recent research in social history and social politics, I will divide the period in two. I will look first at the improvisation and consolidation of the welfare state between 1914 and 1929, before considering the authoritarian and totalitarian deformation of welfare politics between 1930 and 1938, although the deep political break of 1933 in the realm of social politics did not mean a clear rupture at first.

The First World War as a Catalyst

The outbreak of the First World War in August 1914 marked an important turning point in the history of the German welfare state and urban welfare politics. The war had the effect of a catalyst on the development of a modern system of public service. The politics of national reconciliation (*Burgfrieden*) made the establishment of the welfare state in the local sphere possible. The integration of the Social Democrats into the local administration of all three cities (in Frankfurt and Nuremberg with the perspective of a long-running experience, in Leipzig[6] only temporarily) permitted the development of a broad system of public services, from housing welfare to the support of war veterans and surviving dependants to food supply. The system of support was expanded to the group of the new poor.[7] These were the *Kleinrentner* and *Sozialrentner* who had been reduced to poverty by the results of the war (a condition later compounded by the inflation) and not through any fault of their own. Local authorities permitted the foundation of semi-public organizations for war victims and the poor and even allowed them to participate in the administration of their aid (*Mitbestimmungsrecht*). The last two points in particular, self-organization and participation, granted for reasons of socio-political stabilization and to maintain loyalty during the war, were essential components of the later constituency of a democratic social state created by the Weimar Republic. Another line of continuity was constituted by the organization of new welfare authorities in the cities, separated from the traditional poor law administration. The last point to mention is the adjustment of the co-operation between the private services, especially the confessional organizations like Caritas or Innere Mission, and the public authorities, later characterized as a dual system. Behind this formula from the beginning and during the war, we find different arrangements, from delegation to mere subordination. For example, authorities like Nuremberg used financial and political means to influence directly the policy and actions of the private welfare organizations, while at the other end of the spectrum we find the Catholic city of Münster simply handing over all social services to private welfare organizations.[8]

The Organization of Local Welfare Administration

The construction of a local system of welfare administration was visible proof of the establishment of the welfare state at a local level. The first step was taken during the war, and in the immediate post-war years this trend of makeshift construction caused by material and social need continued. The accumulation of the social problems was a common phenomenon, confronting all three cities with the same problems, namely the continuation of the *Kriegsfürsorge*. This was because the old poor law proved to be insufficient against the background of the mass problems of need and new clients, the *Kleinrentner* and *Sozialrentner* of the old and new middle classes, groups that had never belonged to the poor. In spite of all the misery, local welfare authorities demonstrated their efficiency in the years between 1918 and 1923. Although the central social state regained its competence in social affairs, the local authorities had many opportunities and a free hand to identify the type of welfare that would be appropriate for local social and cultural conditions. Frankfurt and Nuremberg made great efforts to co-ordinate and to strengthen their administration in the branches of poor law, which consisted of the support of veterans and the disabled, and, as a new field of social service, *Jugendfürsorge*, youth welfare. While in general terms aid was granted by the principles of individualism, welfare administration was centralized for policy purposes and decentralized in practice by the organization of welfare committees (*Bezirksfürsorgeausschüsse*). In contrast to this, in Leipzig the authorities preferred to adopt a reactionary stance and to distance themselves from the general trend, something which social experts criticized for its fragmentation. The reason for this backwardness of municipal social politics in Leipzig can be found in the political sphere: the bourgeois (*Magistrat*) local authority and a left-wing majority in the local parliament were unable to reach a compromise and remained in a situation of political paralysis. It took many years of political and juridical quarrels until Leipzig was able to create in 1929 the same organization of social policy as Nuremberg and Frankfurt had established immediately after the war. There is another reason for this delay: the personal factor. Neither the mayor nor the head of the administrative departments in Leipzig was engaged in social politics. They showed no political initiative. Their colleagues from Frankfurt and Nuremberg,[9] however, were among the leading figures of the German Städtetag, on behalf of social policy, or the Deutscher Verein für öffentliche und private Fürsorge, which combined all service organizations in a welfare trust. They were well-known welfare experts and were part of a political and academic discourse.

Although we have no means of evaluating the practice and efficiency of welfare politics from the perspective of the various types of the clients, we can describe at least the social origins of the indigent as well as of the honorary welfare assistants. As I have already mentioned, the existence of masses of new poor, who had been reduced to poverty by the lost war and by inflation, was one of the characteristic social phenomena of the post-war period. It was also one of the reasons for the delegitimization of the Weimar Republic, which was saddled with this burden. The victims of war demanded the realization and fulfilment of all social promises, although they represented only 25–30 per cent of welfare clients. But their political weight surpassed their quantitative importance because they formed part of those social groups presumed loyal to the state. They were well organized and they were supported by local pressure groups as well as by political parties: the *Sozialrentner* by the SPD, and the middle-class *Kleinrentner* by right-wing parties like the DNVP (Deutschnationale Volkspartei). Although no city could neglect the demands of the new poor, Frankfurt and Nuremberg tried to minimize the particular efforts made for these groups who demanded special help organized by a specific administration branch, while the local authorities persisted in their policy of equal treatment. In Leipzig, on the other hand, political antagonism was favourable to the realization of such demands, because these two sections of the new poor were organized in an effective union.

The support of the *Sozialrentner* and *Kleinrentner* was the crucial point of a severe conflict between cities and state. While the Reich Welfare

Decree of 1924 granted an increased support (*gehobene Fürsorge*), the cities continued their egalitarian refusal of all forms of a hierarchy or differentiation in support. They viewed the Reich's solution to the problem as an attack on their autonomy and their finances.

Let us return to our social classification of welfare administration and the welfare workers (*Fürsorger*). They worked in an honorary capacity, in most cases as members of private welfare organizations. They were chosen by the authorities as members of a regional welfare committee within a city. While they were recruited in the pre-war period from the bourgeois strata, the democratization of the municipal elections after 1918 changed the method of recruitment. This happened almost immediately in Frankfurt and Nuremberg, but there was a specific delay in Leipzig, where the shift of the political majority to the left caused a radical social transformation of the group of the *Fürsorge*. In Leipzig in 1926 33.7 per cent of the voluntary welfare workers came from the working classes, only 13.7 per cent from the middle classes, and 6.4 per cent from the economic bourgeoisie, which means that their social recruitment now reflected the socio-professional structure of the city as a whole. This also meant that the bourgeois classes had lost their social superiority within urban politics.

The Dualism of Public and Private Welfare Organizations

The other characteristic structure of the German welfare state, the dualism of public and private welfare organizations, was dominated by the same ambivalence of co-operation and conflict even on a local level. The Reich Welfare Decree of 1924 marked the end of improvisation, and also the growing influence of the central private organizations (Caritas, Innere Mission, Zentralwohlfahrtsstelle der Juden, Rotes Kreuz, Paritätischer Wohlfahrtsverband) on national legislation and on ministerial bureaucracy especially in the Ministry of Labour and Social Policy, led by the Catholic Centre Party. Their growing influence can be read in the Welfare Decree, where they succeeded in embodying the principle of subsidiarity in law. This meant that private organizations could take precedence over public welfare. In the reality of everyday welfare politics on the local level the decree did not prevent a permanent conflict by this principle of subsidiarity. One of the main issues between the confessional organizations and public authorities, besides school politics, can be found in the realm of youth welfare. While the churches and the confessional organizations cultivated the fear of a total municipalization – a nightmare that could be used as a propaganda instrument – the social democratic cities like Nuremberg could never have transformed this vision into reality, even if they had intended it. At all times the private confessional organizations succeeded in maintaining their superiority by reason of their knowledge and tradition in the realm of youth welfare. The only way for the local authorities to diminish the influence of the private sector was by using the instrument of subsidies. When granting financial support, local authorities tried to link it with some conditions, even in personal matters. The consequences of this antagonistic situation can be described as dialectic. At first the private bodies strengthened their organizational structures, reinforcing their identities behind the barricades of the Trust Laws, which permitted them to bargain with the other side and to find a way of a peaceful coexistence. However, the same bureaucratic face and welfare practice for which the public welfare administration was criticized increasingly still remained. The left-wing majority in Leipzig acted even more unyieldingly. They attacked the welfare practice of the confessional organizations by all means, not just financial ones. All they could offer the private bodies was the option to participate in local welfare committees, as prescribed by law.

Unemployment Relief

The other field of conflicting social interests provoked by the welfare state can be seen in unemployment relief. The Law of Labour Exchanges and Unemployment Insurance of 1927 (Gesetz über Arbeitsvermittlung und Arbeitslosenversicherung), which sealed the process of centralization of welfare policy, did not relieve the local welfare establishment from financial and social obligations. The reason for this was that the support granted by the Reich was so small that local authorities, who were confronted directly with the everyday needs of the unemployed, had to sustain them with payments in kind or with relief employment organized by works run by the city.

This kind of municipal economy provoked the harsh protests of the conservative parties and of the private sector. They tried to reduce this public engagement, which was regarded as a dubious form of competition that prejudiced small businesses. A case of corruption in Frankfurt in 1926 offered the political opportunity to get rid of this public competitor, at least temporarily. Another instrument of unemployment relief gave rise to bitter attacks by private interests and radical political parties. This was the so-called 'produktive Erwerb-slosenfürsorge'. These were relief works, designed to prevent social radicalization, and which enabled the cities to realize public buildings or other projects, exploiting the cheap labour available from the ranks of the unemployed. There are many stadiums, streets and even lakes which are the result of this unemployment programme – rare examples of public buildings in the Weimar Republic. The mass unemployment during the Great Depression, brought the Reich as well as the *Länder* and cities to the edge of ruin. From 1929 they had to struggle with a dramatic increase in the number of the *Wohlfahrtserwerbslosen* ('unemployed receiving benefits'). At the beginning of 1932 even those communities that had practised an austerity policy reached the end of their financial capacity. This forced them to adopt a risky credit policy, often used later by the National Socialists in order to extort local authorities.

Municipal Housing Offices and Local Interests

Let us take a brief look at a third field of public welfare, which was just as controversial as the other two. The housing problem, which had been regarded as a severe social problem since the end of the nineteenth century, turned out to be a central object of welfare politics in the 1920s. Initially a popular field of social reform policy, bourgeois local politics after the First World War was forced to introduce strong regulation in spite of its own liberal credo and social interests. As matters did not improve during the Weimar Republic, the cities were forced to continue and even to expand the controlled housing economy.[10] Again we find the socio-political difference between the two social-liberal cities, Frankfurt and Nuremberg on the one hand, and Leipzig on the other. Although the Social Democrats accepted the laws of the market as the basis of their housing policy, in both Frankfurt and Nuremberg the authorities resisted the harsh politics of middle-class interests of small business and house owners. In Leipzig we can see two antagonistic strategies. The first one is to be found at the beginning of the Republic and under a left-wing majority. The organization of a municipal housing office was declared to be the beginning of a socialist urban policy. In addition, the socialists founded a municipal house-building company. The financial support from the Reich was intended only for housing support for workers and small traders. This meant a radical break with the pre-war practice and provoked the bitter protest of the private building trade and house owners, which influenced the politics of the *Bürgerblock* in the local parliament. As the political majority after the elections of 1924 shifted to the right, this marked a total U-turn in housing policy. But as the political majority would change frequently in the next years, the zigzag course therefore continued. We can quantify the effects of these policies. The house-building quota of Leipzig was lower than that of Frankfurt, where much smaller units were built. Even today we can observe the positive results in Frankfurt, destined to be the famous model of social housing policy. The city could attract very creative and famous architects, such as Ernst May, politically backed by a social-liberal consensus, which supported municipal as well as private house building. But even this successful housing policy could not resolve the housing problem completely, above all because of the beginning of the economic depression that brought all progress to a halt.

From Democratic to Authoritarian Welfare Policy

The Great Depression marked the decisive turning point even in the realm of welfare policy.[11] It was the change from a democratic to an authoritarian policy, from local self-government and autonomy to a further centralization under a conservative-authoritarian style. Sometimes this change coincided with a change in political leadership. In Leipzig Carl Goerdeler, who would become one of the heads of the German resistance movement against Hitler after 1938, became mayor in 1930 and decided to end the excesses of parliamentarism and to reduce political participation to an authoritarian minimum. He was also determined to save money, to reduce social support and welfare policies, and to diminish political participation within the welfare administration and committees. He founded a *Hauptausschuß*, a central committee, to formulate political decisions and to replace the local parliament. From 1930 he reduced the meetings of the parliament and conferred only with the leaders of the parliamentary groups. His strict policy of austerity meant a reduction of social support, but he sustained all activities of the Freiwilliger Arbeitsdienst (Labour Service), promoting a labour service obligation. This political change from democratic to authoritarian municipal politics, including welfare, established the pattern for the first period of the Nazi administration and permitted the transition to office of

Goerdeler as one of the representatives of a conservative and authoritarian policy. He represented a group of municipal politicians who were tolerated by the Nazi Party for a certain time and who themselves helped to stabilize administrative and political functions after the Nazi's seizure of power.

Goerdeler was even one of the authors of the German Gemeinde Ordnung of 1935, in which he tried to codify his authoritarian, statist but constitutional views on policy. In the everyday practice of Leipzig, though, he was soon forced to concede that the irrational dynamic of the Nazi movement was stronger than his conservative bastions.[12]

It would be an oversimplification to neglect the changes which characterized Nazi politics and which marked the difference from Goerdeler and others. The mayor himself realized these differences in the fields of economic and municipal politics. But these differences also marked the realm of social policy, which was transformed not only in an authoritarian, but above all in a racist, way. It was a small step from the idea of austerity to the idea of segregation of all the disabled, 'imbeciles' and 'inferiors', who seemed incurable and who were regarded as a burden that should no longer be sustained in the national community (*Volksgemeinschaft*). Those 'Gemeinschaftsfremde' would be supported by private welfare, by the churches, afterwards by the pseudo-scientific help of physicians and eugenicists. Soon the concept changed to one of dynamic radicalization, which meant a policy of extermination. Goerdeler hoped to be able to defuse the racist demands of local party groups by integrating racist health care ideas into public administration and by appointing a physician, who, although a partisan of eugenics, was also a professional. Later on, after his resignation, this municipal administration of health and race care became an agency of segregation and deportation.

One of the first measures of the Nazi Party in local welfare administration was to purge the regional welfare committees of all the *Fürsorger* delegated from the parties on the left. This meant that 1,000 of the 3,500 *Fürsorger* at the beginning of 1933 were dismissed and substituted by members of the NSDAP. Later on the Nazi Party used this purged administration to install its system of 'Blockwarte' within the welfare administration.

The transformation of the dual system of welfare took place in two ways. First came the marginalization of private organizations, which had to care for the 'imbeciles' and other 'inferiors'. This was followed by the replacement of the dual system by the party organization of the Nationalsozialistische Volkswohlfahrt (NSV), which functioned as a competitor and pursued a covert policy of undermining the welfare administration. Thereby, all institutional forms of welfare administration were dissolved and the propaganda thesis of centralization and simplification of administration tried to hide the reality of a loss of bureaucratic rationality. In the same way the propaganda of *Volksgemeinschaft* had to hide the fact that the new social policy meant a radical break with a democratic and humane tradition of welfare.

To sum up, Nazi welfare policy did not mean a continuation of the tradition of welfare and a social state, nor was it a step to a further modernization, owing its deeply irrational and inhuman character, which destroyed all forms of political rationality and human values.

Notes

1. C. Sachße and F. Tennstedt, *Geschichte der Armenfürsorge in Deutschland*, vol. 2: *Fürsorge und Wohlfahrtspflege 1871 bis 1929*, Stuttgart 1988, 15–42; F. Tennstedt, 'Der deutsche Weg zum Wohfahrtsstaat 1871–1881. Anmerkungen zu einem alten Thema aufgrund neu erschlossener Quellen', in A. Wollasch (ed.), *Wohlfahrtspflege in der Region. Westfalen-Lippe während des 19. und 20. Jahrhunderts im historischen Vergleich.* Paderborn 1997.
2. W. Abelshauser (ed.), *Die Weimarer Republik als Wohlfahrtsstaat. Zum Verhältnis von Wirtschafts- und Sozialpolitik in der Industriegesellschaft*, Stuttgart 1987.
3. H. U. Thamer and J. Ch. Kaiser, in Zusammenarbeit mit G. Bußmann-Strelow, J. Paulus, P. Brandmann, M. Funk, 'Kommunale Wohlfahrtspolitik zwischen 1918 und 1933 im Vergleich (Frankfurt, Leipzig, Nuremberg)', in J. Reulecke (ed.), *Die Stadt als Dienstleistungszentrum. Beiträge zur Geschichte der 'Sozialstadt' in Deutschland im 19. und frühen 20. Jahrhundert*, St. Katharinen 1995.
4. G. Bußmann-Strelow, *Kommunale Politik im Sozialstaat. Nuermberger Wohlfahrtspflege in der Weimarer Republik*, Nuremberg 1997.
5. P. Brandmann, *Leipzig zwischen Klassenkampf und Sozialreform. Kommunale Wohlfahrtspolitik zwischen 1890 und 1929*, Cologne 1998; J. Paulus, *Kommunale Wohlfahrtspolitik in Leipzig 1930 bis 1945*, Cologne 1998.
6. Brandmann, *Leipzig*, 127–226.
7. Bußmann-Strelow, *Kommunale Politik*, 69–130.
8. Th. Küster, 'Private Fürsorge und kommunale Wohlfahrtspolitik in Westfalen 1918–1929. Münster und Bielefeld im Vergleich', in Wollasch (ed.), *Wohlfahrtspflege in der Region.*

9. These were Hermann Luppe and Hermann Heimerich from Nuremberg, and Karl Flesch from Frankfurt. For the Städtetag see H. Beckstein, *Städtische Interessenpolitik. Organisation und Politik der Städtetage in Bayern, Preußen und dem Deutschen Reich 1896–1923*, Düsseldorf 1991.

10. Michael Ruck, 'Der Wohnungsbau – Schnittpunkt von Sozial- und Wirtschaftspolitik', in Werner Abelshauser (ed.), *Die Weimarer Republik als Wohlfahrtsstaat*, Wiesbaden, Stuttgart 1987, 91–123.

11. Sachße and Tennstedt, *Geschichte der Armenfürsorge in Deutschland*, vol. 3: *Der Wohfahrtsstaat im Nationalsozialismus*, Stuttgart 1992, 18–34.

12. H. U. Thamer, 'Carl Friedrich Goerdeler 1884–1945', in R. Groß and G. Wiemers (eds.), *Sächsische Lebensbilder*, vol. 4, Stuttgart 1999, 97–118.

AXEL SCHILDT

Urban Reconstruction and Urban Development in Germany after 1945

I

Hermann Göring, the head of the Luftwaffe in the Third Reich, boasted at the beginning of the war that no enemy aeroplane would ever be able to drop a bomb on a German city. The people facing the smoking ruins of their cities at the end of the war must have found this empty promise a bitter memory – about 2 million tons of bombs dropped by the British and US Air Forces had hit their targets. Many cities were attacked repeatedly: Berlin 29 times, Braunschweig 21 times, Ludwigshafen and Mannheim 19 times each, Kiel, Cologne and Frankfurt am Main 18 times each and Hamburg and Munich 16 times each.[1] In many large cities, such as Cologne, Essen, Frankfurt, Kiel, Bremen or Dresden, more than one third of all flats were destroyed. In Hamburg and Berlin approximately half of the housing stock was lost.[2] Schools and hospitals were almost equally damaged. Three quarters of all bombs dropped in the war on German cities were dropped in the last ten months of the war. Destroyed bridges, bomb craters and piles of debris in the streets caused a complete standstill of passenger and goods transportation. The amount of debris in the German Reich was estimated at approximately 400 million cubic metres – an unimaginable figure.[3] The only buildings receiving relatively little damage were the industrial plants, many of which had been moved underground or to less bomb-prone regions in central Germany.

As a result of this destruction most cities had far fewer inhabitants in 1945 than before the war. Those who had been evacuated returned quickly and even the allied authorities' restrictions on returning to the cities could not deter them. Streams of refugees from the Soviet-occupied zone and expellees from areas in Eastern Europe once belonging to Germany flowed into the western part of Germany as well. Nearly 10 million people migrated to the Federal Republic of Germany between the end of the war and 1950, the country's population rising by 24 per cent between 1939 and 1950;[4] most new citizens settled first in rural areas but then moved to urban centres in the 1950s.[5]

Five years after the end of the war the populations of most large German cities had not reached their 1939 levels.[6] Still, the shortage of housing had grown more acute, the cause of which was not only war destruction and the flow of refugees. Almost nothing new was built until the currency reform in 1948 and the founding of the two German states in 1949. In the cities, attention was given to clearing away the huge masses of debris with the aim of enabling traffic flow on major streets. The salvagers attempted to sort out bricks that could be used in reconstructing the cities. In some places women participated in this difficult task – the term 'debris woman' is still evocative of the period directly after the war. However technical equipment was in fact soon put to use in clearing the ruins. In some places piles of debris formed small hills, which were eventually covered by grass and became new landmarks.

In contrast to the debris-clearing projects, almost nothing was done directly after the war to further housing construction. Until 1947 more damaged flats were lost than could be saved by makeshift repairs. Dampness was often the cause of loss because, for example, windows could not be replaced.[7] Thus the housing situation was still catastrophic even in 1950.[8] As a rule each person was allowed 4–6 square metres of living space. Children counted as half a person. According to statistics three households were to share two flats. Most households did not have their own kitchen. Many did not even live in normal buildings but rather in sheds, bunkers, cellars below ruins and in other emergency accommodation. Especially unpopular among the urban population were the Nissen huts in the British occupied zone. They were named after Officer Nissen, who had designed them a few years earlier for the use of troops in India. The corrugated steel barracks rested on concrete foundations, had a floor area of $55m^2$ and were meant to house two families or twenty single persons. Their greatest problem was heating. In the cold winters following the war, temperatures inside the huts could drop far below freezing point.[9]

II

In the light of the extreme housing shortage, housing issues were central to the discussion of urban reconstruction. Although reconstruction did not really get underway until a few years after the war, it began *before* the end of the war. The important turning point for urban planning in Germany was thus not the end of the war, but the bombing which had already produced grave effects on the cities by 1942/3. This period of time between the first planning measures and the actual start of reconstruction was from 1942/3 to 1949/50. It can be characterized as 'Dreams in the Midst of Debris',[10] dreamt by urban planners and housing experts. Joseph Goebbels noted in his diary on 27 September 1944: 'The Führer is convinced that although the enemy terror from the air is awful at the moment, especially for our medieval towns, it also holds a positive element in that it opens up these cities for modern transportation.'[11] This cynical optimism dominated the thinking of architects, urban planners and housing experts as well.

They greeted the bombs as a great opportunity. Finally the stage was set for a radical new development of the cities. The greatest irritation to planners were the densely populated workers' housing areas built before the First World War in a phase of heavy urbanization. In most cities they formed a ring around the inner core. They were notorious neighbourhoods of dark 'tenement barracks', which were traditionally held responsible for social misery and left-wing political radicalism. Even before the First World War, calls were made for their refurbishment. Not even during the Nazi regime, though, were the financial resources made available for this undertaking. As a result of the bombardments during the Second World War, planners, in their own opinion, were finally offered a real chance to plan healthy cities according to modern concepts, which could also accommodate increasing traffic.[12]

The guiding vision for planning at that time was that of the 'orderly structured, low-density city' – a vision that remained unchallenged from the 1930s through to the 1960s. This consensus was strengthened by the fact that many planners of this generation continued practising after the war. The profession was only minimally affected by de-nazification measures.[13] As is pointed out by recent research, planning for urban reconstruction was in part influenced by the experience of planning Germanized cities in occupied Poland.[14] It is also worth noting that certain terminology used in the reconstruction discussion was a continuation of the biological vocabulary of the Third

Reich. So-called 'organic urban design',[15] which had also found followers among the modern architects of the 1920s (for example Hans Scharoun), continually emphasized the analogy between city functions and the human body, for example transportation and the human cardiovascular system.

However, the ideas of the planning elite in the Third Reich which found their way into post-war planning were not fundamentally different from ideas about urban design in other European countries.[16] The 'Hamburg Generalbebauungsplan 1944' for instance looked similar to the 'Greater London plan' of Abercrombie.[17] Even architects who had left Germany worked basically according to similar urban planning concepts held by their colleagues who had remained in the Third Reich. Two examples of this are Walter Gropius who, through commissions by the US government, gained much influence after the war, and Erwin Anton Gutkind in the British zone. This tendency could also be seen in the travelling exhibitions of American and British architects in 1947 and 1948, attended by a wide range of people.[18] The allied plans at first stemmed from the idea of spreading the German population evenly across the country, in order to lower the population of the cities, but this episode was short-lived.[19] It is a myth that modern-thinking urban planners were generally expelled from the country in 1933 and only received a fresh chance in 1945. Architectural differences of opinion and political attitudes towards the Nazi regime did not necessarily coincide. The co-authorship of a post-war standard planning work, *The Orderly Structured, Low-Density City* by Johannes Göderitz and Roland Rainer, published in 1957, illustrates this.[20] The Social Democrat Johannes Göderitz was required in 1933 to give up his position as the official head of urban development in Braunschweig; Roland Rainer was known in 1944 to have subscribed to biology-based ideology.[21] The third author, Hubert Hoffmann, had witnessed the debate surrounding the 'Charter of Athens' as a 29-year-old in 1933.[22] The co-operation between these urban planners was strange but typical of the post-war period.

'Structuring the city' was aimed – in the tradition of the Congrès International d'Architecture Moderne and other forums of the post-war era – at separating urban functions. Employment, housing and transport routes were to be located apart from each other. The residential neighbourhood was to contain several thousand inhabitants and the necessary infrastructure – schools, shopping and recreation. In the Third Reich this type of planning was linked to the organizational unit – 'local groups' of the Nazi Party ('The local group as neighbourhood unit'). But at the core was the neighbourhood unit concept brought over from England. For this reason it was not difficult in 1945 to place a church or school where the main party headquarters had been planned as the centre of the neighbourhood.[23]

Lowering the density of the city was the second component of the model. This meant the diffusing of particularly dense neighbourhoods into a sort of urban landscape with enough green space. In place of five- or six-storey tenement buildings, single-family houses and two- to three-storey buildings were to dominate. The need for protection from air raids was actually used as an argument for this urban form and this continued until well into the 1950s. If the cities were dissolved into urban landscapes, they would no longer be targets for enemy air fleets. The danger of bombs from the air was seen generally as a problem of the 'technological age' that needed to be dealt with.[24]

The hail of bombs during the war appeared to have completely destroyed many cities. Plans were considered to replace whole cities on new sites and reforest the deserts of ruins. One example is the idea of rebuilding Munich on the banks of Lake Starnberg. But such initial utopian plans did not consider the reality of the second, underground city: gas and water pipes, electricity and telephone lines, canalization, underground trains, etc. A modern city could not simply be replaced. And in the light of widespread poverty, the most frugal of solutions had to be given priority. Thus the utopian plans disappeared quickly into the desk drawers of their creators. Within the existing city structure, planners were not completely uninhibited in their designs despite the war damage. First of all, the course of city streets could not simply be changed. Secondly, although the combination of high explosive bombs and fire bombs used during the war had razed many buildings to their foundations it was usually less expensive to rebuild the ruins than to build anew. And keeping costs low was the prime goal. For this reason careful reconstruction of individual buildings was only considered for a few cities, for example Freudenstadt in the Black Forest. In general, preservation of the historic city centres was limited to a few small islands of restored buildings.[25] Planning the reconstruction involved a compromise between urban modernization and contending with existing urban design – a combination of reconstruction and new construction which is difficult to classify.[26] The few radical concepts conceived, such as that of Marcel Lods for Mainz in the French occupied zone, or the 'collective plan' by Hans Scharoun for Berlin, were met with rejection especially by the public. The city silhouette received special priority because it was meant to give the citizens a sense of belonging. For this reason church towers were repaired at substantial cost.

The debris heaps in the streets were thus by no means a *tabula rasa*. The urban planner Alfons Leitl concluded as early as 1954 in an essay on the *Mistakes and Teachings of the Reconstruction of Cities*: '[T]his debris held hidden beneath it an unidentifiable number of confusing ownership rights and interests, not least those of feelings and moods, the existence and depth of which no one had recognized.'[27] Looking back, nearly all those responsible stressed repeatedly – sometimes bitterly – the great animosity of much of the urban population towards planning measures affecting city structures that had evolved naturally. They blamed, first, the negative experiences in the Third Reich and then the radical expropriations in East Germany. The atmosphere at the beginning of the Cold War was consequently not conducive to modern urban planning measures. Above all, no fundamental reform of land laws came about.

Because of the bitter poverty even optimists predicted a very long period of reconstruction. It was estimated that only by about 1980 could the pre-war housing levels be achieved.[28] And already at that time experts had identified a significant lack of flats. The prognosis of a very long reconstruction period was even based on a flat size of 40–50m^2 for a four- to five-member family in mass public housing.[29] These plans for subsequent urban mass housing development could fall back on wartime rationalization and standardization solutions. But flat sizes had to be smaller now than in the standards for social housing drawn up according to the 'Führer's Decree' in 1940 because these standards were based on the assumption of a German 'final victory'.[30] With regard to floor plans the discussion of the post-war years was in the tradition of the inter-war period with its mention of 'housing for those of little means'.[31] The 'flat for minimum subsistence' had, even before the war, been the topic of the international architectural conference CIAM 1929. And propaganda for conscientious, rational use of the little space available followed a tradition reaching back to the turn of the century.

Planning during the post-war years found its place in the first housing construction law in the Federal Republic of Germany in 1950 – the Magna Carta of mass housing construction. Both the governing party and the social democratic opposition agreed to this law. It had the aim of creating, as cheaply as possible, 1.8 million publicly financed flats in six years. Housing construction in the following years far exceeded this goal.[32]

III

In the course of the ensuing construction boom, heated ideological discussions did not flare up again among the so-called modernists of New Building and local conservation traditionalists, as they had in the era before 1933 (key term: 'cultural bolshevism'). Instead the yearning for harmony commanded both sides of the debate and a common platform was sought. At most, one could say that the previous members of the New Building movement had a slight advantage at the start. The Werkbund, dominated by this movement, issued an appeal in which the vision of an 'orderly structured, low-density city' was stated to be the consensus and renowned architects from both camps signed it.[33]

Seldom did large public discussions erupt during this time. One such discussion was prompted by the question as to whether the 'vertical Garden City' made up of residential high-rise blocks should define the reconstruction or whether the idea of an 'urban landscape' should be followed. What prompted the discussion was the construction of a large housing estate in Hamburg in 1946.[34] Twelve huge, long, narrow residential high-rise blocks, 12–13 storeys tall, were planned to house British officers because Hamburg was to become the capital of the British occupied zone. This plan, the Hamburg Project, was given up when the decision was made to form a common British–American zone in 1947. At the time only the foundations had been prepared for the new high-rise blocks. A long battle followed in Hamburg and in all of Germany as to whether the buildings should continue to be built or not. To many opponents of the project it did not seem normal to house humans in such large buildings. Because of the great distance to the ground it was speculated, for instance, that the number of children would decrease and biological death would follow. Fritz Schumacher, head urban planner of Hamburg until 1933, even suggested designing the complete reconstruction of the city in the form of one- to two-storey housing as an urban landscape.[35] Advocates pointed out the spacious green areas and park-like landscape made possible in the city by building high-rise blocks. During the debate, which lasted until the mid-1950s, both factions presented themselves as conquerors of the tight urban density of imperial times who simply offered two alternatives to the same end. The Grindel high-rise blocks in Hamburg were eventually built. The architectural debate was not as crucial to this decision as were the underlying economic factors. The fact that the project had already been started made high-rise blocks the allegedly less expensive solution.

Urban mass housing in the Federal Republic of the 1950s did not represent a particularly wide variety of styles. In the north, flat roofs were most common; in the south gables were dominant. These differences were not critical, though. More important were the similarities in the structuring of the housing estates. As a rule, free-standing two- to three-storey linear buildings were preferred – as opposed to constructing a continuous string of buildings along the outer edge of a block, as was common in the reform housing settlements of the 1920s. The postulate 'light, air and sun' appeared to have finally been achieved. Architectural historians today characterize this period of reconstruction as the 'second' or 'moderately modern' phase. With regard to the historical development of style a gradual shift towards modern designs is apparent. This shift actually caused astonishment among advocates of modern architecture, as can be deduced from reports in professional journals.[36] Indeed – to be exact – it was not the rationalistic mainstream of 1920s modernism which experienced a renaissance but a so-called organic modernism. The best of these buildings – for representative or commercial uses – originated in the early 1950s when the demand for frugality nurtured an aesthetic of simplicity. They are characterized by a combination of glass and steel and the attempt to create an appearance of lightness.[37] 'Swinging' was 'the feeling of the new era' as stated concisely by the urban planner Rudolf Hillebrecht.[38] The conclusion, and result, of this phase was the grand exhibition of the West Berlin INTERBAU 1957;[39] otherwise, it was noted in the second half of the 1950s, public buildings and the buildings of private companies again appeared heavier and clumsier than at the beginning of the decade.

IV

The rapid, never correctly predicted development of car travel played a powerful role in influencing modern designs. In the early 1950s pre-war levels had already been surpassed. As an example, in Hamburg there were approximately 80,000 cars in 1938. In 1954 the number had grown to 120,000 and in 1968 to 430,000.[40] This rapid increase took place in all West German cities.[41] The 'transportation affliction' of large cities was one of the greatest problems of the reconstruction period. In the more recent history of urban planning it is generally believed that the experts planned ruthlessly wide streets to meet their own demands for modernism. In fact they were a step behind the vast wave of mass motorization. A critique by American planners who had travelled to Germany in the 1950s stated:

> Americans travelling in Germany will return home with the impression that German urban planners have no clue as to what the automobile will do to them. Even though the German version of this bacillus, the Volkswagen, is smaller than the American Ford, its numbers are increasing at an amazing rate and will soon achieve the dimension of an epidemic.[42]

Because the old streets were extremely narrow many cities were forced, by law, to close the inner city to lorries. In the mid-1950s the first multi-storey car parks were built and the first parking meters set up in the city centres. But these types of measures had little effect on the problem.[43] 'Super-Highways' without intersections were considered and in some cities were built, usually with negative impacts on social cohesion in the affected neighbourhoods. Building wide thoroughfares did represent a tradition of planning since the turn of the century. However, in comparison with to the plans for symmetrical streets and squares in the Third Reich, the dynamic, swinging concrete ribbons of the 1950s were seen as appropriate to the *Zeitgeist*. The flowing space of urban landscape was to offer the car driver a pleasant experience.

The 'car-city', and thus the strict separation of pedestrians and drivers, became the new vision of planners.[44] The six- to eight-lane Ost–West-Straße in Hamburg is an example which tore apart historic neighbourhoods.[45] The new wide thoroughfare was related to what proved to be one of the largest so-called 'demolition' urban renewal projects in Germany in the 1950s. Not only were bomb-damaged neighbourhoods demolished, but also those that had remained unscathed in the war were torn down. In their place the Neu-Altona neighbourhood was developed, which today is a shabby-looking high-rise area, with flats that are reached by outer walkways on each level.[46] In the 1970s this type of radical urban renewal, which erased existing urban structures, was termed by young social historians the 'second destruction'. At the time of its conception, however, it was heralded by professionals as a sign of dawning modern times.

V

The acceptance of modern building in the West was strengthened during the Cold War by bitter opposition to it in Eastern Germany. In the years following the war East Germany had experienced a short innovative phase of modern planning. But during late Stalinism in the late 1940s and early 1950s the national building tradition was extolled and the modernism of the 1920s' New Building movement was explicitly rejected. Architectural style proved to be one aspect in the battle against the Federal Republic as a mere creation of US imperialism. GDR propaganda for unification of the country – against the 'anti-national wedge-drivers' in Bonn – contained similar arguments used before 1933 by right-wing conservatives against the Bauhaus. Modern buildings such as the Grindel high-rise blocks were judged by Walter Ulbricht and other GDR politicians to be decadent and 'cosmopolitan'. 'Formalism' was the central negative term used for the modernism of the Federal Republic.

Urban development in the GDR can be divided into two general phases. The first was dominated by the previously mentioned adherence to national tradition and also to the socialist realism of the Soviet Union. The transfer of all land into state holdings gave the GDR better conditions than West Germany for rebuilding the cities without the impediment of private interests. But urban planning around 1950 was oriented towards traditionalist ideas and was not yet driven by visions of a socialist state. On 27 July 1950 the government of the GDR passed sixteen 'General Rules for Urban Development' which were meant to do justice to the 'national consciousness of the people'.[47] This programme was understood to be a counter-model to the 'Charter of Athens' of 1933. The idea of an urban landscape or garden city was clearly rejected and the development of multi-storey buildings was emphasized as opposed to lower buildings mainly for economic reasons. Beyond this, the similarities outweighed the differences with regard to the functional structuring of the city. In the East, though, the urban centre was emphasized as the 'decisive core' and as the 'political centre for the life of the citizens'. This emphasis took the form of large-scale streets and squares for military parades on special occasions such as 1 May, the 'battle day of the working class'. High East German building standards emphasized meticulous craftsmanship which led, owing to the lack of financial resources available, to very few neighbourhoods, let alone towns, being built in the early 1950s. Thus, few examples can be found with which to analyze the programmatic planning ideals of the time. One example is Stalinstadt, which began construction in 1951 and was later renamed Eisenhüttenstadt. The 30,000 inhabitants, mostly workers in the iron-processing combine, acquired a city reminiscent of a historic baroque town. A large square formed the centre and a wide avenue connected the town to the industrial plant. Residential buildings were arranged along the edge of the blocks with spacious courtyards in the middle for the residents. The East German press proudly reported that none of the housing blocks was the same as another and that the most 'magnificent building' was the day nursery.

The most important and frequently described urban planning project of the GDR is the Stalinallee in East Berlin with its decorative neo-classical buildings. Large, relatively luxurious flats, roomy staircases, stores and restaurants on the ground floor, and even terraces on the roofs were created to demonstrate superiority over the West German state. Very low rents for these town-centre flats made them affordable even for working-class families. Such flats were centrally managed, though, and priority was given, as a rule, to deserving loyal party members. The huge construction site along Stalinallee received highest priority to the detriment of other projects in the GDR. And yet it was the initial site of the workers' protests on 17 June 1953, which could only be restrained by Soviet tanks.

The second phase of urban development in the GDR – a radical shift – lasted from the mid-1950s until the end of the 1960s.[48] It is characterized mainly by the industrialization of the building process. Prefabrication and standardization and above all the use of large concrete slabs were important developments. The architect was made superfluous by the engineer. While assembly-type construction constituted approximately 12 per cent of building in 1958 it had increased to 74 per cent by 1963. The monotonous concrete slab buildings built in the 1960s, 1970s and 1980s continue to dominate the appearance of many areas in the former GDR. In some cases these areas were not only neighbourhoods but whole towns, which had been built overnight near industrial complexes. One example is Hoyerswerda, whose construction began in 1964 with a population of approximately 100,000. The largest of these satellite towns is Berlin-Marzahn, which was begun in 1977 and has a population of approximately 150,000.[49] While the GDR tried desperately to keep up with the rate of new construction in West Germany, it left older buildings to decay.[50] In 1958 the average age of residential buildings in the GDR was sixty-three years and in the Federal Republic it was forty-five years. This was a time bomb for the national economy. Until 1961 the emigration of approximately 3 million people from the GDR relieved some of the pressure, but after that it was necessary to make a great effort to construct enough housing. The most powerful man of the GDR at the time, Walter Ulbricht, set the tempo by stating that the GDR would surpass the Federal

Republic in housing construction. Erich Honecker, too, placed housing as his top social policy priority in the early 1970s. Beginning in the 1970s, over 100,000 flats a year were built in the GDR. Ambitious programmes fell short of their central goals, although they were declared to have been achieved from the 1970s onwards with the help of statistical manipulation. East Germany never achieved the same average level of supply and standard of housing as the Federal Republic. Public discontent with the housing problem remained one of the major factors that led to social crisis during the East German regime.

VI

While in the GDR mass housing schemes in the cities first began in the 1960s and increased in the 1970s, West Germany made this advance in the 1950s. The quantitative results of reconstruction in West Germany are impressive. Over 5 million flats were built in the decade from 1950 to 1959. And just as many were built in the following decade. Only in the 1970s did the number of newly built flats decrease substantially.

Over a third of all inhabitants of the Federal Republic of Germany have, since the early 1960s, lived in flats built after the Second World War. In the cities, where reconstruction was concentrated, this rate is even higher. The German expellees from Eastern Europe as well as the stream of refugees from the GDR, which lasted until the building of the Berlin Wall in 1961, contributed to the fact that the temporary barrack camps never really disappeared in some places. But no refugee ghettos were formed nor did any social crisis materialize as politicians and social scientists of the early 1950s had feared.

In the years of reconstruction the average size of flats being built increased steadily, from 55m^2 in 1953 to 70m^2 in 1960. And the number of people who wanted to buy their own home increased as well. This was shown by numerous demographic surveys. The purchase of homes was encouraged by law. The second Housing Law of the Federal Republic of Germany of 1956 mentions explicitly the value of home ownership; a broad spectrum of the population was to be encouraged to identify themselves with the land in order to lead a 'healthy family life' and to have numerous offspring.[51] This last point remained an unfulfilled ideological postulate of the Christian-Democratic Adenauer government, but the desire for better housing conditions was certainly a central issue to the citizens.[52]

Meeting the personal demands for more and more space, if possible a private house, was soon no longer feasible in the city. The pressure of rapidly growing central business districts on adjacent residential areas caused a major increase in the cost of building land. This in turn led to the consideration of the development of the periphery. Processes of suburbanization mark the wave of urban development that has continued strongly since the 1950s. The so-called dormitory cities evolved and expanded to areas up to a one-hour drive or train journey to the city centre. The growth of West German cities has since ended. The population actually even began to decrease slowly because much of the new housing was not located within the city boundaries.[53] An era of a new form of urbanization began and with it the spread of a new lifestyle which found its place quickly in the new neighbourhoods of single-family homes and rented flats. This development paralleled the shift towards a new level of consumerism, the shortening of working hours – the 'long weekend' (Saturday and Sunday) was achieved – and the beginning of the age of television. In 1960 a quarter of all households owned a television, a decade later three quarters did so. The new lifestyle is also illustrated statistically by the number of commuters. In 1950 18 per cent of all employees were commuters; in 1961 the rate had risen to 31 per cent.[54] A job in the city, a house in a green suburb and a car to bridge the space between: this combination represented the trend from the mid-1950s onwards.[55] To this day it still continues to create financial problems for the cities because taxes are collected according to where a person lives and not where he or she is employed.

VII

Around 1960, at the end of the reconstruction period, the visionary model of an 'orderly structured, low-density city' was for the first time truly called into question. Studies of daily life in the new neighbourhoods had found that, contrary to all hopes, no strong sense of neighbourliness had developed.[56] In fact the exact opposite was true: the radical renewal projects in old working-class areas had destroyed social structures. The 'inhospitableness of the cities',[57] which were no longer real cities, was deemed the result of post-war planning. Discussions revolved around the loss of urbanism and the disappearance of big city culture. The dominant feeling among urban development experts was that one should start again from the beginning.[58] And again, as with the appearance of the vision of an 'orderly structured, low-density city', this phenomenon was not exclusive to Germany but could be found internationally.[59]

The growth of major cities into amorphous forms that sprawled into urban regions was seen as the reason for a radically new definition of planning. Instead of the biological-organic metaphors, hard sociological empiricism and the comprehension of the city as a network of economic structures soon defined the discussion.[60] The eleventh general meeting of the German Congress of Municipal Authorities, a committee made up of members from all municipalities in the Federal Republic of Germany, met in 1960 under the banner 'Renewing Our Cities'. In his opening speech the Augsburg head urban planner, Walter Schmidt, asked, 'Does it not seem at the moment that one is striving to destroy the city as something to be experienced as a whole with the senses? Should in the end merely a central, abstract functional system made up of an agglomeration of partly rural, partly small-town suburban settlements remain?'[61] Unfettered use of land, sprawl, urban flight, environmental degradation and forced mobility of commuters, it was argued by many, had driven the original concerns of functionalism *ad absurdum*. The grand new planning idea of the 1960s, which would spur numerous programmes, was 'community through density' or 'urbanizing the large cities'.[62] This was the era of planning large-scale housing estates made up predominantly of high-rise blocks for thousands of inhabitants. The flats were generally quite spacious and contained modern kitchens and bathrooms, central heating, etc. But such housing estates, which still exist in nearly all large cities, are mainly located on the periphery where transportation to the city is difficult. They also offer very limited possibilities for communication. Many of the first tenants, primarily white-collar and skilled workers, left the estates. And because of the relatively high rents, poorer members of the population who were receiving state housing benefits moved in.[63] In the 1980s these large-scale housing estates were criticized as being soulless ghetto architecture by a public who also complained about city centres deserted in the evening. Desolate city centres and ugly anonymous large housing schemes were considered the bitter signature of modernism. The protection of old buildings has since become more highly valued. The remaining neighbourhoods of buildings from the late nineteenth century were rediscovered as comfortable urbane residential areas. And the amendments to the federal urban development law in 1976 reflected this shift. For the first time the goal of renewing old buildings was given the same status as building new ones.[64] Interestingly, the GDR experienced these same trends but with a certain delay and slight modification, at least in theory.

VIII

To conclude: the destruction that remained after the war was enormous. It was so extensive that no one could predict the rapid reconstruction that followed. The planning of the reconstruction began not at the end of the war, but rather it followed the bombing that marked its turning point. It was seen as an opportunity to redesign the city radically according to modern ideas. When, at the end of the 1940s, reconstruction actually began, other problems dictated development. Priority was generally given to the cheapest solutions for reconstruction projects. In West Germany it meant finding a compromise between preserving urban structure and creating new developments. This compromise had to be made taking into consideration existing infrastructure amenities and ownership conditions. The fact that modern concepts prevailed in the 1950s was mainly the result of growing urban traffic problems.

In the GDR the reconstruction can be seen in two phases. In the first, the modernism of the West was renounced and conservative German building tradition and the Soviet visions of the 1930s and 1940s were revived. In fact this form of urban planning was quite conventional. A few prestigious projects in addition, such as Stalin-allee, were to prove the superiority of the GDR. The second phase of urban development in East Germany began in the mid-1950s and was marked by the very functionalism that had been so vehemently rejected. Constructing completely new neighbourhoods and towns and at the same time allowing existing buildings to disintegrate proved to be a central problem of the GDR.

The reconstruction era in the Federal Republic ended around 1960. The large cities, which had started to fill after the war, began to empty again. New settlement structures evolved. Suburbanization and commuters dominated the picture. For the first time critiques of the vision of an 'orderly structured, low-density city' could be heard and the loss of urbanity was lamented. In the 1960s and early 1970s the cities made a great effort to increase building within the city boundaries; the results were the previously mentioned very large-scale high-rise housing estates. In the GDR the increase in new construction after the war did not begin until this time. The ambitious goal of surpassing West Germany in housing supply could never be achieved.[65]

For about the past decade, opinions on the reconstruction of German cities have changed drastically. Although the loss of urbanism was bemoaned after the 1960s and the architecture of the post-war era was characterized as shabby, many buildings from the 1950s are now being considered worthy of historic preservation. The era of reconstruction has become history.

Notes

1. Bundesminister für Vertriebene, Flüchtlinge und Kriegsgeschädigte (ed.), *Dokumente deutscher Kriegsschäden. Evakuierte, Kriegssachgeschädigte, Währungsgeschädigte. Die geschichtliche und rechtliche Entwicklung*, vol. I, Bonn 1958, 32–46; for Göring's announcement see R. Cartier, Der Zweite Weltkrieg, 6th edn, Munich and Zurich 1982, 251.

2. Bundesminister für Vertriebene, Flüchtlinge und Kriegsgeschädigte (ed.), *Dokumente deutscher Kriegsschäden*, 51–3.

3. Ibid. 50–1.

4. *Statistisches Jahrbuch der Bundesrepublik Deutschland für das Jahr 1952*, Stuttgart 1953, 12.

5. S. Bethlehem, *Heimatvertreibung, DDR-Flucht, Gastarbeiterzuwanderung. Wanderungsströme und Wanderungspolitik in der Bundesrepublik Deutschland*, Stuttgart 1982, 48–80; cf. M. Frantzioch, *Die Vertriebenen. Hemmnisse, Antriebskräfte und Wege ihrer Integration in der Bundesrepublik Deutschland*, Berlin 1987, 99–117.

6. W. Harmssen, *Am Abend der Demontage. Sechs Jahre Reparationspolitik*, Bremen 1951, 145; cf. G. Schöning, 'Aufbau in zerstörten Städten. Eine quantitative Bilanz', *Bauamt und Gemeindebau* 26 (1953), 233–6.

7. Bundesminister für Vertriebene . . ., vol. IV/1, pp. 4–5; cf. G. Schulz, *Wiederaufbau in Deutschland. Die Wohnungspolitik in den Westzonen und der Bundesrepublik Deutschland 1945–1957*, Düsseldorf 1994, 134–59.

8. A. Schildt, '". . . für die breiten Schichten des Volkes". Zur Planung und Realisierung des "Sozialen Wohnungsbaus" in der Bundesrepublik Deutschland (1950–1960)', in H. Siegrist and B. Strath (eds.), *Wohnungsbau im internationalen Vergleich. Planung und gesellschaftliche Steuerung in den beiden deutschen Staaten und in Schweden 1945–1980*, Leipzig 1996, 26.

9. See U. Höhns, 'Wer einmal unter'm Blechdach saß. Nissenhütten in Deutschland', *Archithèse* 14, Heft 5 (1984), 29–32.

10. See W. Durth and N. Gutschow, *Träume in Trümmern. Planungen zum Wiederaufbau zerstörter Städte im Westen Deutschlands 1940–1950*, 2 vols, Braunschweig and Wiesbaden 1988.

11. Hitler, quoted by *Die Tagebücher von Joseph Goebbels. Im Auftrag des Instituts für Zeitgeschichte hg. von E. Fröhlich. Teil II: Diktate 1941–1945*, vol. 11. Bearbeitet von D. M. Schneider, Munich etc. 1995, 576.

12. One example: H. Dörr, 'Bomben brechen die "Haufen" Stadt', *Raumforschung und Raumordnung* 6 (1941), 269–73.

13. See W. Durth, *Deutsche Architekten. Biographische Verflechtungen 1900–1970*, Braunschweig and Wiesbaden 1986, 252–72.

14. Cf. the documentations by R.-D. Müller, *Hitlers Ostkrieg und die deutsche Siedlungspolitik: Die Zusammenarbeit von Wehrmacht, Wirtschaft und SS*, Frankfurt am Main 1991; M. Rössler and S. Schleiermacher (eds.), Der "Generalplan Ost". Hauptlinien der nationalsozialistischen Planungs- und Vernichtungspolitik, Berlin 1993; C. Madajczyk *et al.* (eds.), *Vom Generalplan Ost zum Generalsiedlungsplan. Dokumente*, Munich etc. 1994.

15. See H. B. Reichow, *Organische Stadtbaukunst. Von der Großstadt zur Stadtlandschaft*, Braunschweig 1948.

16. See J. M. Diefendorf (ed.), *Rebuilding Europe's Bombed Cities*, London 1990.

17. See D. Schubert, *Stadterneuerung in London und Hamburg. Eine Stadtbaugeschichte zwischen Modernisierung und Disziplinierung*, Braunschweig and Wiesbaden 1996, 365–8.

18. See F. Fischer, 'German Reconstruction as an International Activity' in Diefendorf (ed.), *Rebuilding Europe's Bombed Cities*.

19. For the German town planning policy of the USA, the UK, France, and the Soviet Union see Durth and Gutschow, *Träume in Trümmern*, vol. 1, pp. 119–40.

20. See J. Göderitz, R. Rainer, and H. Hoffmann, *Die gegliederte und aufgelockerte Stadt*, Tübingen 1957; cf. G. Köhler and B. Schäfers, 'Leitbilder der Stadtentwicklung in der Bundesrepublik Deutschland', *aus politik und zeitgeschichte*, B 46–7 (1986), 29–39; Durth and Gutschow, *Träume in Trümmern*, vol. 1, pp. 161–233.

21. See K. von Beyme, *Der Wiederaufbau. Architektur und Städtebaupolitik in beiden deutschen Staaten*, Munich and Zurich 1987, 53.

22. See H. Hoffmann, 'Die "Charta von Athen"', *Stadtbauwelt*, Heft 3 (1985), 104–12.

23. See E. Pahl-Weber, 'Die Ortsgruppe als Siedlungszelle', in M. Bose et al., '. . . Ein neues Hamburg entsteht . . .' Planen und Bauen von 1933–1945, Hamburg 1986.

24. See A. Schildt, 'Die Atombombe und der Wiederaufbau. Luftschutz, Stadtplanungskonzepte und Wohnungsbau 1950–1956', *1999. Zeitschrift für Sozialgeschichte des 20. und 21. Jahrhunderts* 2, Heft 4 (1987), 52–67.

25. See J. Paul, 'Der Wiederaufbau der historischen Städte in Deutschland nach dem Zweiten Weltkrieg', in C. Meckseper and H. Siebenmorgen (eds.), *Die alte Stadt: Denkmal oder Lebensraum?* Göttingen 1985.

26. A. Schildt and A. Sywottek (eds.), *Massenwohnung und Eigenheim. Wohnungsbau und Wohnen in der Großstadt seit dem Ersten Weltkrieg*, Frankfurt and New York 1988, 26; cf. Winfried Nerdinger, 'Wiederaufbau oder Neubau?', in *Aufbauzeit. Planen und Bauen. München 1945–1950*, Munich: Ausstellungskatalog Münchner Stadtmuseum; an overestimated account of the conservative tradition by J. Petsch and W. Petsch, *Bundesrepublik eine neue Heimat? Städtebau und Architektur nach '45*, Berlin (West) 1983.

27. A. Leitl, 'Irrtümer und Lehren des Wiederaufbaus der Städte', in J. Moras and H. Paeschke (eds.), *Deutscher Geist zwischen Gestern und Morgen*, Stuttgart 1954, 141.

28. A. Schildt, 'Vom Wiederaufbau zur "neuen Wohnungsnot". Entwicklungen und Probleme im Wohnungsbau seit 1945', *Gegenwartskunde* 38 (1989), 463.

29. See K. Erdmannsdorffer, 'Zum Problem der künftigen Kleinwohnung', *Der Baumeister* 44, Heft 4 (1947), 101–11.

30. See G. Fehl and T. Harlander (eds.), *Hitlers Sozialer Wohnungsbau 1940–1945. Wohnungspolitik, Baugestaltung und Siedlungsplanung*, Hamburg 1986.

31. See D. Häring, *Zur Geschichte und Wirkung staatlicher Interventionen im Wohnungssektor. Gesellschaftliche und sozialpolitische Aspekte der Wohnungspolitik in Deutschland*, Hamburg 1974, 63–8.

32. See Schildt, '". . . für die breiten Schichten des Volkes"', 31–7; the most sensitive regional and local study of housing policy is by G. Wagner, *Sozialstaat gegen Wohnungsnot. Wohnraumbewirtschaftung und Sozialer Wohnungsbau im Bund und in Nordrhein-Westfalen 1950–1970*, Paderborn 1995.

33. For an overview of the urban development debate see A. von Saldern, *Häuserleben. Zur Geschichte städtischen Arbeiterwohnens vom Kaiserreich bis heute*, Bonn 1995, 259–65.

34. See A. Schildt, *Die Grindelhochhäuser. Eine Sozialgeschichte der ersten deutschen Wohnhochhausanlage*, Hamburg 1988.

35. See N. Gutschow, 'Fritz Schumacher. Vordenker für den Wiederaufbau zerstörter Städte in Norddeutschland', *Stadtbauwelt* 84 (1986), 346–9.

36. Cf. the documentation by U. Conrads et al. (eds.), *Die Bauhaus-Debatte 1953. Dokumente einer verdrängten Kontroverse*, Braunschweig and Wiesbaden 1994.

37. Numerous examples in W. Durth and N. Gutschow, *Architektur und Städtebau der fünfziger Jahre*, Bonn 1987; *Architektur und Städtebau der fünfziger Jahre. Ergebnisse der Fachtagung in Hannover 1990*, Bonn 1990.

38. See W. Durth, 'Vom Sieg der Zahlen über die Bilder', *Stadtbauwelt*, Heft 48 (1985), 362–8.

39. See D. Hanauske, *'Bauen, bauen, bauen . . .!' Die Wohnungspolitik in Berlin (West) 1945–1961*, Berlin 1995, 715–44.

40. See T. Südbeck, *Motorisierung, Verkehrsentwicklung und Verkehrspolitik in der Bundesrepublik Deutschland der 1950er Jahre. Umrisse der allgemeinen Entwicklung und zwei Beispiele: Hamburg und das Emsland*, Stuttgart 1994.

41. For the first summary of damage after the war see W. Harmssen, *Reparationen, Sozialprodukt, Lebensstandard. Versuch einer Wirtschaftsbilanz*, Bremen 1947, Anlage VIII.

42. See H. Wandersleb (ed.), *Neuer Wohnbau*, vol. 1: *Bauplanung*, Ravensburg 1952, 129.

43. See A. Schildt, 'Vom Wohlstandsbarometer zum Belastungsfaktor – Autovision und Autoängste in der westdeutschen Presse von den 50er bis zu den 70er Jahren', in H.-L. Dienel and H. Trischler (eds.), *Geschichte der Zukunft des Verkehrs. Verkehrskonzepte von der Frühen Neuzeit bis zum 21. Jahrhundert*, Frankfurt and New York 1997, 298–9.

44. See H. B. Reichow, *Die autogerechte Stadt. Ein Weg aus dem Verkehrschaos*, Ravensburg 1959.

45. See M. Wawoczny, *Der Schnitt durch die Stadt. Planungs- und Baugeschichte der Hamburger Ost-West-Straße von 1911 bis heute*, Hamburg 1996, 44–76.

46. See C. Timm, '". . . Die Kraft des freien Westens". Neu-Altona – Wiederaufbau als Stadtsanierung' in Schildt and Sywottek (eds.), *Massenwohnung und Eigenheim*.

47. Printed by K. von Beyme et al. (eds.), *Neue Städte aus Ruinen. Deutscher Städtebau der Nachkriegszeit*, Munich 1992, 30–1; cf. L. Bolz, *Von deutschem Bauen*, East-Berlin 1951.

48. Cf. F. Werner, *Stadt, Städtebau, Architektur in der DDR. Aspekte der Stadtgeographie, Stadtplanung und Forschungspolitik*, Erlangen 1981; T. Topfstedt, *Städtebau in der DDR 1955–1971*, Leipzig 1988; T. Hoscislawski, *Bauen zwischen Macht und Ohnmacht. Architektur und Städtebau in der DDR*, Berlin 1991; A. Schätzke, *Zwischen Bauhaus und Stalinallee. Architekturdiskussion im östlichen Deutschland*, Braunschweig and Wiesbaden 1991.

49. For information on urban development in the GDR cf. Hoscislawski, *Bauen zwischen Macht und Ohnmacht*; Siegfried Grundmann, *Die Stadt. Gedanken über Geschichte und Funktion*, East-Berlin 1984, 258–60; B. Hunger, 'Städtebau, gesellschaftliche Entwicklung und Stadtforschung in der DDR', *Archiv für Kommunalwissenschaften* 29 (1991), 9–49.

50. Cf. M. Hoffmann, *Wohnungspolitik in der DDR – das Leistungs- und Interessenproblem*, Düsseldorf 1972; A. Schildt, 'Wohnungspolitik', in H. G. Hockerts (ed.), *Drei Wege deutscher Sozialstaatlichkeit. NS-Diktatur, Bundesrepublik und DDR im Vergleich*, Munich 1998.

51. See G. Schulz, 'Eigenheimpolitik und Eigenheimförderung im ersten Jahrzehnt nach dem Zweiten Weltkrieg', in Schildt and Sywottek (eds.), *Massenwohnung und Eigenheim*.

52. Cf. Neue Heimat (ed.), *'So möchte ich wohnen!' Ergebnisse einer Wohnungswirtschaftlichen Befragung der Bevölkerung in 11 deutschen Städten*,

Hamburg 1955, 16; GAGFAH (Gemeinnützige Aktien-Gesellschaft für Angestellten-Heimstätten) (ed.), *Wie wollen wir wohnen? Eine zweite Wohnungsumfrage in Berlin, durchgeführt vom Landesverband Berlin der Deutschen Angestellten-Gewerkschaft*, Berlin 1955, 15–18.

53.   See O. Boustedt, 'Die Stadtregionen in der Bundesrepublik Deutschland', in *Stadtregionen in der Bundesrepublik Deutschland. Raum und Bevölkerung 1: Forschungsberichte des Arbeitskreises "Städtische Regionalprobleme" im Ausschuß "Raum und Bevölkerung" der Akademie für Raumforschung und Landesplanung*, Bremen 1960; cf. N. J. Lenort, Entwicklungsplanung in Stadtregionen, Cologne and Opladen 1961, 110–26.

54.   *Wirtschaft und Statistik*, N.F. (1952), 65–7; *Wirtschaft und Statistik*, N.F. (1964), 216.

55.   Cf. W. Polster and K. Voy, 'Eigenheim und Automobil – Die Zentren der Lebensweise' in Voy, Polster and C. Thomasberger (eds.), *Gesellschaftliche Transformationsprozesse und materielle Lebensweise. Beiträge zur Wirtschafts- und Gesellschaftsgeschichte der Bundesrepublik Deutschland (1949–1989)*, vol. 2, Marburg 1991; A. Schildt, 'Freizeit, Konsum und Häuslichkeit in der "Wiederaufbau"-Gesellschaft. Zur Modernisierung von Lebensstilen in der Bundesrepublik Deutschland in den 1950er Jahren' in H. Siegrist, H. Kaelble and J. Kocka (eds.), *Europäische Konsumgeschichte. Zur Gesellschafts- und Kulturgeschichte des Konsums (18. bis 20. Jahrhundert)*, Frankfurt and New York 1997.

56.   Cf. H. Klages, *Der Nachbarschaftsgedanke und die nachbarliche Wirklichkeit in der Großstadt*, Cologne and Opladen 1958; H. Oswald, *Die überschätzte Stadt. Ein Beitrag der Gemeindesoziologie zum Städtebau*. Olten and Freiburg im Breisgau 1966; H. Hollmann, 'Nachbarschaft', in Akademie für Raumforschung und Landesplanung (ed.), *Handwörterbuch der Raumforschung und Raumordnung*, Hanover 1966; B. Hamm, *Betrifft: Nachbarschaft. Verständigung über Inhalt und Gebrauch eines vieldeutigen Begriffs*, Düsseldorf 1973; for information on modern communication networks, which also evolved as a result of the expanse of mass media, see von Saldern, *Häuserleben*, 293–301.

57.   See A. Mitscherlich, *Die Unwirtlichkeit unserer Städte. Anstiftung zum Unfrieden*, Frankfurt 1965; cf., among others, H. P. Bahrdt, *'Humaner Städtebau'. Überlegungen zur Wohnungspolitik und Stadtplanung für eine nahe Zukunft*, Hamburg 1968.

58.   See H. Kampffmeyer, F. Spengelin and W. J. Siedler, '"Zu Beginn der 60er Jahre hatten wir das Gefühl: Jetzt müssen wir von Grund auf neu anfangen"', *Stadtbauwelt*, Heft 88 (1985), 326–37.

59.   See G. Albers, 'Das Stadtplanungsrecht im 20. Jahrhundert als Niederschlag der Wandlungen im Planungsverständnis', *Stadtbauwelt*, Heft 65 (1980), 485–90.

60.   See Durth, 'Vom Sieg der Zahlen über die Bilder'.

61.   *Erneuerung unserer Städte. Vorträge, Aussprachen und Ergebnisse der 11. Hauptversammlung des Deutschen Städtetages. Augsburg, 1.–3. Juni 1960*, Stuttgart 1960, 37.

62. H. P. Bahrdt, *Die moderne Großstadt. Soziologische Überlegungen zum Städtebau*, Reinbek 1961, 108.

63. Cf. K. Heil, 'Neue Wohnquartiere am Stadtrand', in W. Pehnt (ed.), *Die Stadt in der Bundesrepublik Deutschland. Lebensbedingungen – Aufgaben – Planung*, Stuttgart 1974; U. Herlyn, *Wohnen im Hochhaus. Eine empirisch-soziologische Untersuchung in ausgewählten Hochhäusern der Städte München, Stuttgart, Hamburg und Wolfsburg*, Stuttgart 1970; U. Herlyn (ed.), *Großstadtstrukturen und ungleiche Lebensbedingungen in der Bundesrepublik: Verteilung und Nutzung sozialer Infrastruktur*, Frankfurt and New York 1980; U. Herlyn, A. von Saldern and W. Tessin (eds.), *Neubausiedlungen der 20er und 60er Jahre. Ein historisch-soziologischer Vergleich*, Frankfurt and New York 1987.

64. Von Beyme, *Der Wiederaufbau*, 140.

65. See von Saldern, *Häuserleben*. 323–6.

STEFAN ZAPPE

Three Cities, Three City Models – Urban Development: Perspectives for the Twenty-First Century

The structure of a city is the organizational pattern of its areas and spaces. The basis for the structure is the geographical situation (*genius loci*). This and the city pattern, made of streets and blocks, determine the picture of a city.

This essay is based on the conceptual differentiation between the centre and periphery of cities. The centre is a three-dimensional construction. Living, working and service functions lie on top of each other in separate layers. The centre expands vertically. Centres comprise the inner city, including road networks as well as centres for shopping, services and leisure. Everything that is not a centre is periphery. In the periphery these same functions lie side by side. The periphery expands horizontally. Typically, peripheries are areas with detached houses, industry and road networks as well as places that remain undesignated.

The introduction of this essay refers to two cities on this theoretical basis. The model for a centre city is New York and the model for a peripheral city is Los Angeles. New York is a three-dimensional space; Los Angeles is an area. City pattern, city structure and the picture of the city will be described. At the end of the twentieth century we are looking back to the American era of urban development. The modern age of urban development began with the proclamation of the Charter of Athens.* Today the mere desire for a new city no longer

---

* A proclamation concerning the shaping of metropolitan areas. It demanded the separation of working and living environments.

determines urban development. Rather it is economic and social factors that influence the city pattern, intellectual and physical content. Often there is little space for creativity. Therefore the city models also describe the American era of European urban development. It is a fundamental way of looking at things, which makes the current urban contexts accessible. The American era of urban development is a global model.

The main part of this essay deals with the specific German situation, with the focus on changes in Berlin since 9 November 1989. Twelve years ago the centre of Berlin was still periphery because of the city's division. Since reunification, the concepts of centre and periphery have been turned upside down. The city had been characterized by the geopolitical situation of the Cold War. Now, in a phase of radical change the missing pieces of the city jigsaw puzzle are being put together again. The global urban model becomes apparent in the structures of the New Berlin.

The division of a city into centre and periphery is a way to approach the conceptual determination of city and metropolis. The intellectual and physical state of the city will be described and at the same time left to one's personal judgement. The contemplation of a collage made of three metropolises gives a picture of the state of the city at the end of the twentieth century.

New York

New York is synonymous with Manhattan. Manhattan's *genius loci* (the natural conditions of a place) is unique. Manhattan is a city centre without man-made boundaries. The boundaries are the Hudson River and the East River. The experience of a dense city centre is enhanced by the surrounding expanse of water.

New York shows that splendour and myth are based on quite simple conditions. The regular pattern of blocks and streets, laid out on an east–west axis; a big central open area – Central Park – and a skyline which increases the sense of distance, when seen from the opposite coast.

The only special feature in the city pattern of Manhattan is a diagonal that cuts across the pattern of blocks. This peculiarity is enough to give splendour to the place and create its myth. This feature is Broadway. Manhattan develops vertically. Buildings rise like needles from the pattern of blocks and become part of Manhattan's skyline.

There is no single dominant, symbolic building. In Manhattan even the Twin Towers or the Empire State Building only have a special position in relation to the whole cityscape.* The notable quality of New York is that all the buildings and skyscrapers are connected and relate to each other on the basis of the city pattern. Manhattan has the distinctive qualities of space and spatial connections. It is the diversity of its components in the unity of the skyline. From a distance Manhattan takes on a nearly human scale; as if the concrete is personified – like figures on a stage.[1] The image of New York is therefore physical and tangible.

We must go back a few decades and to the outskirts of New York to understand the origin of the tremendously fast development of this city. Only a few decades separate Manhattan's important boom years from the mature silhouette of the 1920s skyline, the inspiration for the metropolitan vision in the film *Metropolis*.[2] These early years were so 'crazy' that people overestimated the possibilities of construction technique. They wanted to take the sky by storm, building tall structures with fantastic designs. And these high buildings were to be temples of entertainment. They weren't conceived for Manhattan

Figure 1   Metropolis 1925/6, directed by Fritz Lang, Poster for premier in France: Boris Bilinsky, 1927 SMPK, Kunstbibliothek

* This article was written in 1998 and cannot therefore take into account the terrorist attacks on the Twin Towers on 11 September 2001. After this date the significance of buildings as symbols has changed dramatically but this is not the subject here.

but for Coney Island; Coney Island, the embodiment of a 'crazy' town, fed by the city inhabitants' craving for the 'good life'. Coney Island is a spit of land in New York's Lower Bay and precursor of every Disney World and theme park. Rem Koolhaas is one of the most significant contemporary architects and thinkers on urban development programmes. His considerations and analyses of metropolitan processes are impressive and form the basis of his own urban development designs. He writes: 'Coney's continuing fertility is a breeding ground for revolutionary architectural prototypes.'[3] The impact of fantastical designs for Coney Island was the first step towards the prototypes of skyscrapers. This was a necessary precursor of the city projects that continued to be dreamt up for Manhattan's soil. Only the construction technique together with the approximately simultaneous invention of concrete and, later on, reinforced concrete, put the skyscraper on the road to success.

Figure 2   'Globe Tower, second version, with exploded exterieur. *From the top: roof gardens, layer of theatres; revolving restaurant; ballrooms;* chambres separées; *Africa, one of the continent/circuses; lobbies; entrances; etc. Special gravity elevator connects interior with underground metropolitan arteries.' (Illustration and text Rem Koolhaas, 'Delirious New York')*

In its overall appearance Manhattan has maintained the fantastic element of the dreams and visions of this early period. The more rational architecture of later skyscrapers responds to other laws, governing the utilization of office and living space. However, sometimes there are still reminders of the bygone dream, as for example in the embellishment at the top of the Chrysler Building.

Manhattan is a centre city.

Los Angeles

In Los Angeles the horizontal dominates. The wide, flat landscape, the boundless expanses, canyon after canyon separating the extended plains of the desert region.

The city organism is kept alive by its water supply. Artificial irrigation cultivates an enormous urban landscape.

David Hockney's picture *mulholland drive the road to studio* is like a plan for an artificial city. He divides the city into areas, recalling the structure of his pictures. Hockney doesn't think in three-dimensional

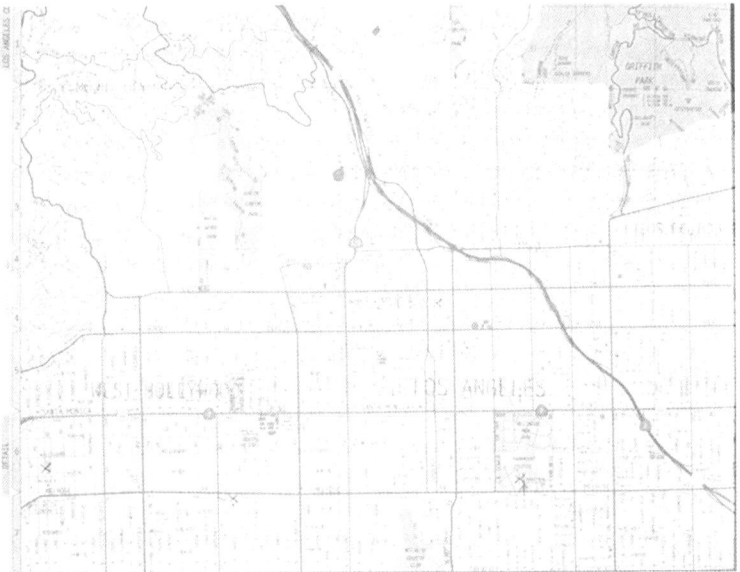

Figure 3   Extract from map of Los Angeles

spaces when he looks at the landscape. He explains this as follows. 'I go back to the old Chinese ideas: that landscape surrounds us and we move in it. Therefore perspective is rejected because it assumes one's absence.'[4] Hockney's way of looking at things is multi-directional; he is in the middle of the event 'urban landscape'. Space and perspective don't exist in his model. Instead the colours of his pictures describe the climate, vegetation, streets and buildings with an incredible intensity. At the top of the picture is the plain of L.A. County with its city pattern, which is broken up by the edges of the mountain ranges. It is not unlike New York's city pattern, only slightly more irregular because of its specific topography. Here the pattern organizes the geographical area, but not the spaces of the town. The remaining part of the picture describes further areas: hillsides, fields, tennis courts, swimming pools, streets. The picture *mulholland drive* is like part of a Los Angeles' street map. The picture's landscape corresponds to the reality of the city.

Los Angeles expands more and more every day and reclaims new pieces of land from the desert. And this process always occurs according to the same principle: first the street pattern, then the invisible

Figure 4   'San Fernando California', Joe Deal, Los Angeles 1978

artificial irrigation mains laid in the desert sand; houses are built
and, before the house is even finished, the garden is already in place.
This is the substance of the American dream. The American town
also means the dream of the American landscape in front of one's
own house. The expanse of the landscape extends in front of the
slightly elevated veranda.

In a lecture on utopian symbioses Julius Posener describes the idea
of garden cities of the nineteenth century. He quotes Ebenezer Howard,
the founder of Letchworth, the first garden city, situated on the outskirts of London: 'Howard criticizes the growth of cities coming with
the simultaneous erosion of the countryside. He desired to reconcile
city and countryside.'[5] His answer is the idea of a garden city in the
face of the slums of England's industrialized nineteenth-century
towns. The illustration of a map entitled 'Los Angeles varied flora'[6]
shows rare plants – not from some botanical garden or national park,
but migrants in the city landscape of Los Angeles. Nature is conquering
the fallow land and the empty spaces left by mankind. This is much
easier to achieve in Los Angeles than in New York. 'Los Angeles can
be a world garden, some growing equivalent of a world city.'[7]

Is Los Angeles the garden city of the twenty-first century?

Los Angeles, however, is the 'fear of the disappearing'[8] as Günther
Kunert, a contemporary German author, entitles his essay concerning
a farewell to the city of yesterday. The microcosm of the individual's
personal fate – the house, the garden, the car in front of the door –
has to remain without a defined place, being a repetition of millions
of other individual fates. This is perhaps the price one has to pay for
a city without a spatial sense. There are no spatial connections in
Los Angeles. But what determines our picture of Los Angeles, if it is
so difficult to form an idea about it? 'The city of the present is a
machine that changes us radically.'[9] The transformational machine
for Los Angeles is the Hollywood film industry. This, and not reality,
determines our idea of the city. And the world of film fills the vacuum
of this flat, boundless city without space.

Los Angeles is driven onwards by another quality: the fantastic.
The fantastic is the ability to bring about urban change in a way that
makes it possible to interchange places and pictures. Los Angeles
allows for the projection of countless artificial ideas, dreams, fantastic
worlds which are also produced in Hollywood's dream factories. The
sombre world of the *film noir*, of the chain-smoking Philip Marlow in
the figure of Humphrey Bogart who fights in the dark jungle of the
cities against shady characters; the fascination of the urban terror

in *Blade Runner*;[10] the nightmare of the future in *Terminator* and the total psychosis of a society in David Lynch's film *Lost Highway*, and also the endless soap operas with their pretence of reality.

We can experience the fantastic element of Los Angeles' design on the screen. It replaces the fascination of reality, for example a skyline of New York. The fantastic elements of Los Angeles are the pictures of a city that doesn't exist.

Los Angeles is a peripheral city.

Berlin

As far as Berlin is concerned concepts such as centre and periphery lose clarity and are even interchangeable. This leads to misunderstanding. Berlin's old centre was periphery before the coming down of the Wall and after this it was suddenly meant to become the centre again. Today only a few places in Berlin's cityscape are unambiguous.

Two introductory quotations:

Berlin's centre is condemned to always becoming and never to be.[11]

A city is built over a fairly long period. A city can't be conjured up out of thin air. The development of Berlin was suspended and after the collapse of the Wall it suddenly turned into speculative exaggeration. In the hectic rush of events, one has to reflect carefully on both the intellectual and the physical dispute. However, city is intellectual as well as physical. Both belong together as 'civitas' and 'urbs'. What is now happening in Berlin is 'urbs' for the sake of exploitation. What is happening at the Potsdamer Platz is, if at all, only alive in the technical ritual that takes place there.[12]

Berlin's History before 9 November 1989

In the Middle Ages Berlin consisted of two insignificant villages, Berlin and Kölln, which grew together. With the rise of Prussia and the House of Hohenzollern, Berlin developed into an important capital. The building of Hohenzollern Castle at the western edge of the old town was not an expression of sympathy with the medieval town, but rather a demonstration of the interest, which was significant, in a strategic expansion of the town. This interest influenced Berlin's development in a westerly direction from then on. The succeeding

Figure 5   Berlin's first significant expansion called 'Friedrichstadt', about 1800

Prussian kings ordered their citizens to settle to the west of the castle. The baroque and the classical-style Berlin, which shaped the plan of the city, were built in a strict pattern of blocks and streets. The expansion was called 'Friedrichstadt' and is one of Berlin's most important city expansions. After its foundation, the Second German Empire was under Prussia's command and Berlin became the capital. The emperors remained where the kings and the Elector already resided, but the representatives of the people moved westwards to the outskirts in front of the city gate, the Brandenburg Gate. There the building housing the parliament of the German Empire, the Reichstag, was built. While the powers of the emperor declined, the Reichstag became more powerful. Even the representatives of the state during the era of the Second German Empire felt drawn to the outskirts of the city. It was much more pleasant to reside in the vicinity of the Tiergarten.

After the First World War the Republic was proclaimed. The Weimar Republic governed from the Reichstag up to the decisive turning point brought about by the Third Reich. The parliament was deprived of its power and the Reichstag became insignificant. The dictatorship wanted to change the city completely. The east–west axis straight through the city, the vertebral column of bygone powers, wasn't sufficient for the effective staging of the dictator's power, despite its structural changes.

Hitler intended to build along a north–south axis, which was planned to be five times wider than the existing east–west axis. However, this plan had no relation to the established centre of Berlin. The National Socialists had already begun to demolish the city but the Second World War interfered with all their plans for the complete rebuilding of the city. Wartime bombing reduced entire city quarters to rubble. The Nazi dictatorship disappeared and with it a third of the city. The topography of Berlin was changed by the heaps of rubble (today sometimes used as ski slopes) and the demolition went on. The old city wasn't loved in the 1950s and 1960s, when everything had to be new and modern. However, the city was already split as an expression of the world systems' conflict. The administrative centre of the GDR was based in the eastern centre. West Berlin established itself around the popular Kurfürstendamm, the entertainment boulevard of the 'roaring twenties'.

The young GDR returned to the roots of the old city and set about destroying the last remaining vestiges after the war. The old centre had almost completely disappeared. Large areas for public rallies were planned once again. The Wall divided the city into two. Berlin's topography was definitively turned upside down. The baroque and the classical-style centre, the Friedrichstadt, became the periphery, lying isolated and lifeless right at the border. On the border of West Berlin, the Potsdamer Platz became a no man's land, and yet also an attraction for tourists, who stood on the lookout platforms of the wooden towers. The consequences of the Cold War could be seen here. The Reichstag, situated in the western periphery with its back to the Wall had, if anything, only a symbolic significance, empty of real meaning.

Berlin after 9 November 1989

The Wall has disappeared and suddenly the old centre is once again very close at hand. There was immediate affection for the

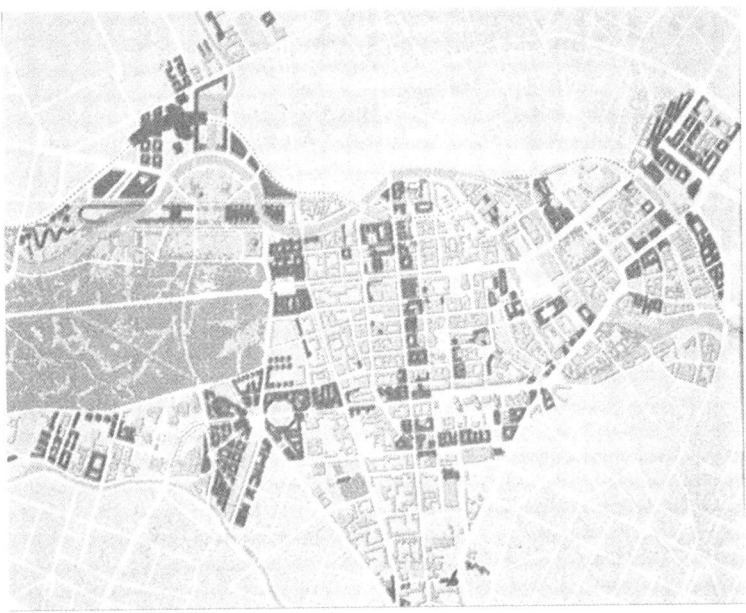

*Figure 6   The Tiergarten, the Friedrichstadt, Berlin East-city, the dark areas are
reserved for projects after 9.11.89*

royal-imperial Friedrichstadt. It is reckoned to be the middle of the
city. But Friedrichstadt has never been the middle; the middle of the
city, if there was any at all, was the old part of Berlin, which disappeared
during the war and the post-war period. Today these areas are semi-
deserted, unloved witnesses of the lost part of both German states.
The eastern centre around the Alexanderplatz and the Marx-Engels-
Forum provides no inspiration when considering the city's future. If
you emerge from the underground station Stadtmitte, you realize very
quickly that you are only somewhere in the centre, but not at its heart.
Berlin has never had a defined, physical focal point. Berlin possesses,
if at all, a centre with main foci that have shifted continuously throughout the course of its history. After the collapse of the Wall Berlin's centre
became a maltreated city body made up of the remains of bygone
times. Soon after the 'change' politics and business were looking for
their own middle in the city centre. Today the shapes of the business
centre 'Potsdamer Platz' and the political centre 'Reichstag' area become
more clearly defined every day.

The Claims on the City (The New Economic and Political Centre of the City)

The Potsdamer Platz was the densest traffic junction of the world in the 1920s. Following the Second World War, a subterranean city survived, made up of underground shafts and bombed-out air raid shelters. Above ground nothing remained apart from a large excavated strip of land. The boundary of this strip of land, the Wall, disappeared very quickly. Because the myth of a central area is still perceptible after reunification, Potsdamer Platz has become one of the most sought-after places in Berlin. Here the first decisions were taken; political decisions under heavy economic pressure. The big multinationals and the powerful forces of commerce and industry made their centre at Postdamer Platz. A fascination with the places of reunification was clearly more important to them than Berlin's old city history on the other side of the Wall.

There was only a short time for the experimental planning of Potsdamer Platz, with no room for fantasy. Nevertheless some planner or other dreamt up a New York skyline, a silhouette, with the Tiergarten lying at its feet. But the place is unsuitable for skyscrapers. The Tiergarten is not Central Park, nor does it have a complete city boundary.

Figure 7   Proposal of Hans Kollhoff, architect, Berlin

Nevertheless the concept is worth consideration. The concentration and dense stacking up of floors with offices and a few flats in sky-scrapers on the Potsdamer Platz would facilitate the development of a real city landscape. In this way open spaces could be created in the city, for possible leisure and recreational use, even if those in Berlin might simply be used for barbecues on long summer evenings in the middle of the city, which are very popular with the Turkish immigrant population. Or to have open spaces for experiments, for example the 'Tempodrom' in the Tiergarten, a place for music that became very popular. Now it has to give way to government buildings. An element of urban variety is going to be lost here. Unusual city landscapes were traditional in Berlin before the coming down of the Wall. At the time when the Wall was erected, railway lines were cut and stations disappeared into nowhere. Urban playgrounds for discovery and spontaneous urban life arose here, fascinating many, not just students of architecture.

What is now being created around the Potsdamer Platz is a compromise. The old ground plan, the eaves of buildings at a height of 22 metres and a few high-rise blocks at particularly important points

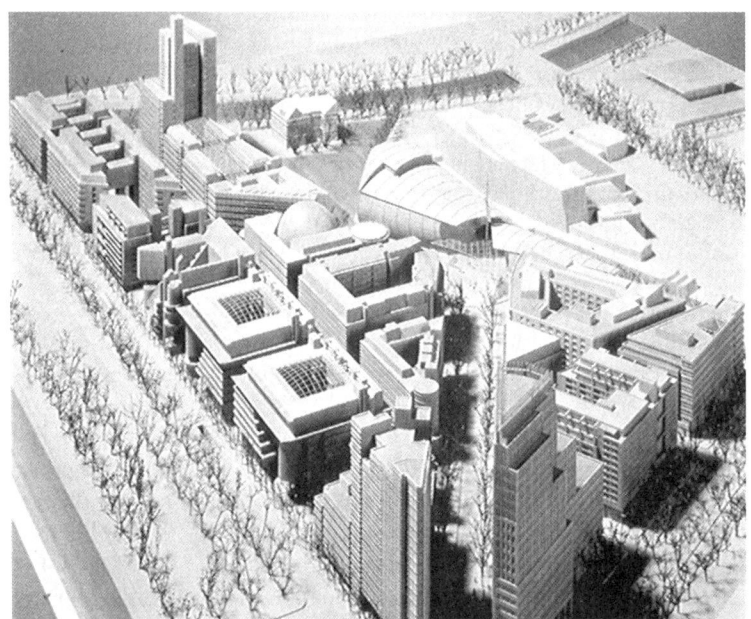

Figure 8   Masterplan Renzo Piano architect, Genoa

for urban development, are the structural frame. The works at the Potsdamer Platz already show these preconditions and one looks at the rising city structure with mixed feelings. This city structure seems to wear a suit that is turned out on the short side. One feels that this city quarter is going to exploit every square inch to the utmost. Streets will turn into ravines. The quarter will have few links to the adjoining districts. This place was intended for the reconciliation of the new with the lost city of the legendary Potsdamer Platz. People wanted to connect old and new. Here the wide sphere of a new Berlin could have emerged in a more varied and diverse way. But to achieve this would have required a more intense 'intellectual and physical dispute'.[13] The crazy, the fantastic elements of ideas could have given a background inspiration. One can only hope that this area will not be used only as a commercial site. One will be able to judge this better after completion.[14]

The establishment of business and commerce in this area was followed by the desire of the politicians to find a place for themselves in the middle of the new capital. The Reichstag building will again be the political focal point of the united Federal Republic of Germany. The centre of political power will therefore once again be situated outside the old centre. It will be completed by the representative power of the Federal President, who will reside even more westwards at the northern boundary of the Tiergarten Park around the Bellevue Castle.

> Berlin's shape, which is moving more and more towards the west, is perhaps an expression of the turn towards the west of Germany. Like the eastern Prussian countries from Silesia to the region of East Prussia, which disappeared in the smoke of history, history has led to Berlin, showing on a small scale what happened in Germany on a larger scale.[15]

This quotation shows that there is hardly any other city in the world that has been so much influenced by geopolitical developments as Berlin.

Another observation concerns the distribution of the ministerial headquarters in the city. Nearly all the ministries of the Federal Republic will move to Berlin. The idea is to establish these throughout the city using existing buildings, renovating and enlarging them. This idea rightly receives attention. But the government buildings of the GDR are little favoured by the political decision-makers. The Foreign Ministry of the GDR, situated at the Schloßplatz, has already been demolished. There will be no ministry around Alexanderplatz, the former eastern centre of the city. The ministries will be distributed in Friedrichstadt and National Socialist large-scale buildings are preferred to socialist government buildings. In particular the fortress of the former Aviation Ministry of the Third Reich, the seat of Hermann Göring, will now become the headquarters of the Finance Ministry and will enhance the idea of an inflexible government apparatus counting the money of the nation. The aura and the spirit of a building are underestimated. (There is simply bad as well as good architecture.)

Summary

The centuries-old orientation towards the west continues after the opening of the Wall. Friedrichstadt isn't Berlin's focal point but just one part of the city centre. However, the emphasis for the new building in Berlin is here. There is a risk that the eastern part of the centre with the dominating buildings of the lost GDR will degenerate into a peripheral location. Berlin stays true to its principles. What once was the centre can soon become periphery and vice versa. History shows this. Today Berlin-Alexanderplatz is, like Potsdamer Platz, the myth of a lost place. But Potsdamer Platz was a dead spot in the ostensible peace of the Cold War. Alexanderplatz in comparison gave GDR society a lively sense of identity for about forty years. These people still live there.

Possibilities

If we are looking for a vision we only have to look at Berlin. Europe's completion began fifty years ago in this city. The signal for a really peaceful Euro-Atlantic world is best heard if Berlin sends it as loudly and clearly as possible. Berlin can thus stimulate the fantasy of those who want to replace the miracles of the past.[16]

I should now like to move from the larger to the smaller context, and to try to describe a special but complicated place in the scenery of this city and to assess its chances. We go back to a specific part of the city, which was already mentioned at the beginning of the historic retrospective. It is the former seat of the Prussian kings. Today it is called 'Schloßplatz'. Here the intellectual and physical westerly orientation of the city began as described in the urban development of Berlin.

In the period after 1989–90 this location wasn't on the list of places which those in power would have considered an attractive situation in the united city. The castle of Hohenzollern, castle of the Prussian kings and emperors, when seen from a westerly direction, stood at the first bend of the east–west axis. The castle has disappeared. Today the spot is occupied by the Palast der Republik, a building unused and

Figure 9   The Schloßplatz before the world wars with Altes Museum, Berliner Dom and Berliner Schloß

Figure 10   The Schloßplatz today with the imitation of the old castle. The Foreign Office of the former GDR has already been demolished

contaminated with asbestos. Until a few years ago the former Volks-kammer (the People's Chamber), East Germany's parliament, sat here. Besides its historical significance the peculiarity of this place is its geographical situation. It lies on an island, called 'Museumsinsel'. The northern part of the Museumsinsel is a unique landscape of urban culture, a kind of cultural Acropolis with many important museums. While each building is different from the others, together they present a cohesive whole.

They remind us of the powerful unity created by an ensemble of build-ings which also characterizes the city scene of New York, even if in a different physical dimension.

Today the Schloßplatz is an asphalt car park. The square, which is sometimes used as a fairground or Christmas market without reference to its surroundings, radiates a deep emptiness. Discussions about the fate of the area lead nowhere. Opinions range from the conservative friends of the castle, coming from the western part of the city, who promote the demolition of the Palast der Republik and a half-hearted reconstruction, to a political party which fights for the preservation of the Palast der Republik. Its supporters come from the eastern part of Berlin. The argument is not about function but only about appearance.

Even the government's move to Berlin cannot give any sense of meaning to the area in terms of its function. Only the ministry for town planning and construction will move into the neighbouring building of the former Council of State, once Erich Honecker's seat. Perhaps we should be grateful that after reunification there were no claims for the Schloßplatz. But time is not being used to develop new ideas. Discussions and planning are anaemic. Apart from a small initiative by a local newspaper, there has been no big public forum, a debate of fantasy and the fantastic, of any kind whatsoever. And to answer John Kornblum: in such an important part of the city, which could unite east and west, nothing is happening that could recreate the miracles of the past. We don't find the vision of a city with a clear and distinctive statement here. Coney Island appeared to Rem Koolhaas as 'a breeding ground for revolutionary architectural prototypes' during Manhattan's boom years and so one would like to say: 'The Museumsinsel, the breeding ground for revolutionary architectural prototypes.' After all, the period after Germany's reunification is nothing else but new boom years!

The physical debate about the place follows on from the intel-lectual. After all, city structure, city pattern and the geography of the place are independent factors.

Berlin's centre possesses glamour and an aura where the fine compositions of urban development of the eighteenth and nineteenth centuries have created a unique city structure. The model is the classical-style urban expansion, the 'Bürgerstadt', the civil servants' town. It is the pattern of a few axial baroque orientations towards important points in the city.

The Museumsinsel is characterized by its particular geographical situation. The island and river lie in a prehistoric valley formed in the Ice Age on the flatland of the North German Plain. Therefore an area of conflict emerges between city and location (*genius loci*), between geometrical city pattern and the organic course of the Spree's riverbed. In the works of the great Berlin master builder Karl Friedrich Schinkel this area of conflict is an important element of the structural composition of its buildings (Altes Museum, Bauakademie . . .).

The northern part of the Museumsinsel is a real Treasure Island. It has been previously described as an Acropolis of arts and antiquity. The Bode Museum, the famous Pergamon Museum, the Neues Museum, the Alte Nationalgalerie, the elevated buildings whose shapes are reminiscent of the Parthenon on the Acropolis and Karl Friedrich Schinkel's Altes Museum as already mentioned. The Lustgarten in front of the Altes Museum and the Berliner Dom (Cathedral) to the east add to the ensemble opposite the Schloßplatz. Now the unique ensemble of buildings is complete and the Altes Museum is the starting point of this demonstration of diversity of urban spaces.

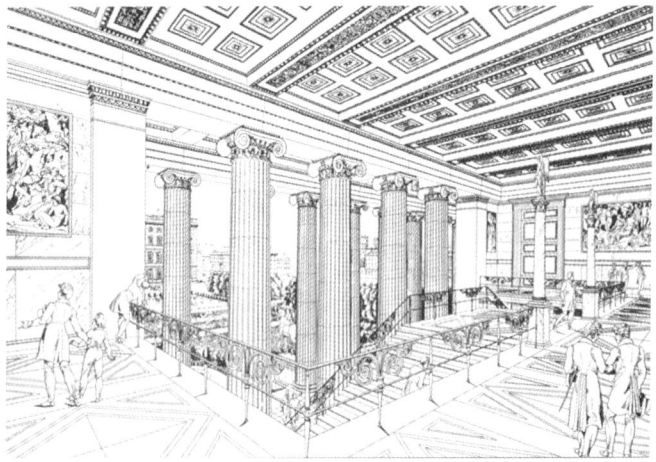

Figure 11   Altes Museum with a view to Berliner Schloß and Schloßplatz

'The structure's effect is so strong that it is even noticeable for those who see the museum from the air. Indeed the effect of pure architecture, not comparable to anything in its surroundings, is extremely gratifying, seen from an aeroplane. It is a real pleasure to look at the museum.'[17] The special feature of this building is its straight structure and its connection to the Lustgarten and Schloßplatz. The experience is of moving in external space with visual connections to the city while already being in the building. Only in the halls and small rooms do you find yourself really inside the building. The vestibule is an urban space of transition, mediating between the inside and the events in front of the building. This three-dimensional experience is a premonition of the twentieth century architecture with its buildings made of steel, glass and concrete. These buildings have broadened architecture by adding the concept of transparency.

But this experience needs a counterpart on the other side of the Lustgarten where the castle was situated. Today, as already noted, there is only empty space. Unlike the castle, the front of the Palast der Republik turns away from the front of the Altes Museum. The ensemble of the Museumsinsel would require this place to be its continuation. If the city structure of the Potsdamer Platz has got a 'too close-fitting suit', the Museumsinsel in its actual state is 'partly undressed'. It has a shirt but no trousers. Here a building element is missing. And the most difficult of all questions is this: what could happen here? There are still many possibilities for the development of fantastical ideas.

Consider a suggestion from the previously mentioned initiative by a Berlin daily newspaper. It represents an attempt to express and to outline fantastical ideas for the Schloßplatz. Buildings shaped as letters, apparently positioned freely in relation to each other. Here again is the principle of unity in the variety of the elements. The Altes Museum has a complex counter part again. Something quite unlike a castle, but rather a self-confident ensemble of buildings, a modern attitude towards the city. In conclusion, I refer again to Berlin's east–west axis. This is a connecting line between the eastern and the western part of the city, the Tiergarten and Frankfurter Allee. We could investigate how a distinctive orientation towards the west, which can also be seen from the political point of view, seems to become established in the city scene. Wouldn't the effect of Berlin acting as a symbol for an orientation towards the east, both in the city scene and on a political level, be at least just as important, as John Kornblum described?

I suggest therefore the creation of a centre of Eastern Europe's cultures for the Schloßplatz. The architect Benedict Tonon called his

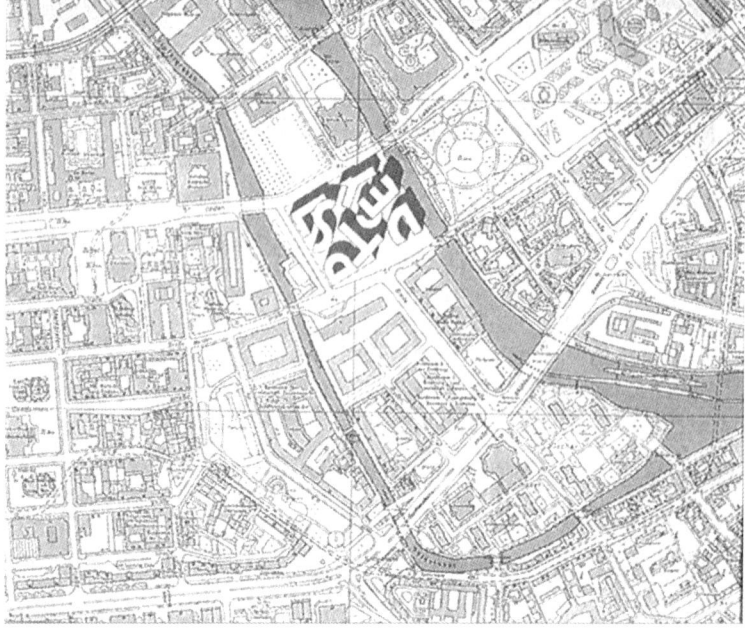

Figure 12   Proposal Benedict Tonon architect, Berlin

building idea 'the magic play of letters'. In the magic play of thoughts
are the secrets of the stories and myths of cultures, which are unknown
to us. Virtual trips into other cultural areas are staged by means of
the letters. From Finland to Armenia, from Poland to Mongolia . . .
remember the imaginative world of the continents in the Globe Tower
on Coney Island. The walkways in the buildings should, as in a myster-
ious labyrinth, lead us to unknown treasures. The walkways and spaces
in the building can be so varied that we can go on the discovery trips
again and again. The miracles of the past have been described. John
Kornblum has based his vision of Berlin upon the miracles of the
past. But Berlin was also the symbol of Europe's division. The iron
separation of world systems had been physically present in Berlin for
decades, embodied by the Wall. This has now come down and the
vision of Europe's completion has to be implanted into the body and
the spirit of the city. But which model will be based on the physical
and intellectual signals of a European Berlin? What will the concept
of the city's unity and variety of its urban appearance, inhabitants

and institutions look like in the end? A last glance at New York. We look at the city and the homogeneous basis of the city design and at the same time its heterogeneous ensemble of building elements and its multi-ethnic population. All this together forms the unity within the variety of this metropolis. New York is the headquarters of the UN. The UN is our established world peoples' community. The homogeneity of its chosen political structure is represented by the heterogeneity of the world's peoples. The structure of the institution is like the structure of the city. And these signals of a 'civitas' and an 'urbs' are being sent every day to the world.

Acknowledgement

I thank Gudrun de Novellis for the translation of this transcript.

Notes

1. *Filmarchitektur*, exhibition catalogue DAM, Munich and New York 1996.
2. ibid. 1.
3. Rem Koolhaas, *Delirious New York*, New York 1994, 72.
4. David Hockney, quoted in a review in *Tagesspiegel*, Berlin, December 1997.
5. Julius Posener, *'Vorlesungen zur Geschichte der Neuen Architektur'*, *'Utopische Gemeinschaften: Fourier, Godin, Buckingham, Howard'* lecture, Zeitschrift ARCH +, ARCH + Verlag Aachen, August 1983, 20.
6. Charles Jencks, *Heteropolis, Los Angeles, Riots and Strange Beauty of Hetero Architecture*, London and Berlin 1993, 130.
7. Ibid. 6.
8. Günther Kunert 'Angst vor dem Verschwinden', *Zeit*, no.47, 19.11.1993.
9. Ibid. 8.
10. *Filmarchitektur*, 1.
11. Karl Scheffler, *Berlin ein Stadtschicksal*, reprint of the original edition, 1910, Berlin 1989, 219.
12. Hardt Walter Hämer in an interview with the *Tagesspiegel*, Berlin, 10.4.97.
13. Ibid. 12.

14. V. M. Lampugnani and R. Schneider, *Ein Stück Großstadt als Experiment, Planungen am Potsdamer Platz in Berlin*, Stuttgart 1994.

15. Wolf Jobst Siedler, 'Die Westverschiebung Berlins', *Tagesspiegel*, Berlin, 25.1.98.

16. John C. Kornblum, American ambassador, quoted in *Tagesspiegel*, Berlin, 27.1.1998.

17. Posener, *Konstruktion und Baukörper in Schinkels Architektur*, lecture, 46.

Notes on Contributors

FRANZ-JOSEF BRÜGGEMEIER is Professor of Social and Economic History at the University of Freiburg. His publications include: with Th. Rommelspacher, *Blauer Himmel über der Ruhr. Geschichte der Umwelt im Ruhrgebiet, 1840–1990*, Essen 1992; *Das unendliche Meer der Lüfte. Luftverschmutzung, Industrialisierung und Risikodebatten im19. Jahrhundert*, Essen 1996; *Tschernobyl, 26. April 1986. Die ökologische Herausforderung*, München 1998.

FRIEDRICH LENGER is Professor of Medieval and Modern History at the University of Giessen. He is currently at Georgetown University. His publications include: *Zwischen Kleinbürgertum und Proletariat. Studien zur Sozialgeschichte der Düsseldorfer Handwerker 1816–1878*, Göttingen 1986; *Sozialgeschichte der deutschen Handwerker seit 1800*, Frankfurt am Main 1988; *Werner Sombart (1863–1941): Eine Biographie*, München 1994; *Industrielle Revolution und Nationalstaatsgründung: Deutsche Geschichte 1849–1871*, Stuttgart 2002.

GISELA METTELE is a Postdoctoral Fellow of the Volkswagen Foundation, Hanover. Her publications include: *Bürgertum in Köln 1775–1870. Gemeinsinn und freie Association*, München 1998.

AXEL SCHILDT is Deputy Director of the Forschungsstelle für Zeitgeschichte in Hamburg and Adjunct Professor of Modern History at the University of Hamburg. His publications include: *Moderne Zeiten. Freizeit, Massenmedien und Zeitgeist in der Bundesrepublik der 50er Jahre*, Hamburg 1995; *Konservatismus in Deutschland. Von den Anfängen im 18. Jahrhundert bis heute*, München 1998; *Ankunft im Westen. Ein Essay zur Erfolgsgeschichte der Bundesrepublik*, Frankfurt am Main 1999; with Karl C. Lammers, Detlef Siegfried (eds.), *Dynamische Zeiten. Die 60er Jahre in den beiden deutschen Gesellschaften*, Hamburg 2000.

SYLVIA SCHRAUT is Adjunct Professor of Modern and Contemporary History at the University of Mannheim. Her publications include: *Sozialer Wandel im Industrialisierungsprozeß, Esslingen 1800–1870*, Esslingen 1989; *Flüchtlingsaufnahme in Württemberg-Baden, 1945–1949. Amerikanische Besatzungsziele und demokratischer Wiederaufbau im Konflikt*, München 1995.

KLAUS TENFELDE is Director of the Institut für soziale Bewegungen and Chairman of the Stiftung Bibliothek des Ruhrgebiets, Ruhr-Universität Bochum. His publications include: *Sozialgeschichte der Bergarbeiterschaft an der*

Ruhr im 19. Jahrhundert, 2nd edn, Bonn 1981; *Proletarische Provinz. Radikalisierung und Widerstand in Penzberg/Oberbayern 1900–1945*, 2nd edn, München 1982; with Gerhard A. Ritter, *Arbeiter im deutschen Kaiserreich 1871–1914*, Bonn 1992; (ed.), *Sozialgeschichte des Bergbaus im 19. und 20. Jahrhundert*, München 1992; (ed.), *Wege zur Geschichte des Bürgertums*, Göttingen 1994.

HANS-ULRICH THAMER is Professor of Modern and Contemporary History at the University of Münster. His publications include: *Revolution und Reaktion in der französischen Sozialkritik des 18. Jahrhunderts*, Frankfurt am Main 1973; with Wolfang Wippermann, *Faschistische und neofaschistische Bewegungen in Europa. Probleme empirischer Faschischmusforschung*, Darmstadt 1977; *Verführung und Gewalt. Deutschland 1933–1945*, Berlin 1986; with R. Schlögel (eds.), *Zwischen Loyalität und Resistenz. Soziale Konflikte und politische Repression während der NS-Zeit in Westfalen*, Münster 1996; (ed.), *Kunst und Bürgertum*, Köln/Weimar/Wien, 2001.

STEFAN ZAPPE is an architect who runs his own office in Berlin. He also teaches at the Technical University of Berlin, mainly on solar and other energy-saving building concepts.